Inside Box 1663

Inside Box 1663

by
Eleanor Jette

Los Alamos Historical Society
Los Alamos, New Mexico
Second Edition
Second Printing
2012

Library of Congress Cataloging-in-Publication Data

Jette, Eleanor, 1907-1964.
  Inside box 1663 / by Eleanor Jette. -- 2nd ed.
      p. cm.
  Includes index.
  ISBN-13: 978-0-941232-02-9 (pbk.)
  ISBN-10: 0-941232-02-6 (pbk.)
1. Atomic bomb--History. 2. Jette, Eleanor, 1907-1964. 3. Nuclear energy--Research--
New Mexico--Los Alamos--History. 4. Wives--United States--Biography. I. Title.
  QC773.3.U5J47 2007
  355.8'251190978958--dc22
  [B]
                              2007022927

Cover Art and Design: Margaret Rice Jette

Photo Coordination: Betty Lilienthal
Photos Courtesy of:
Jack Aeby
A.W. Betts
The Jette Family
N. H. Krikorian
Los Alamos Historical Society
Los Alamos Scientific Laboratory
Raemer E. Schreiber
Edward F. Wortmann

Composition: Veenis Graphics

Los Alamos Historical Society
P.O. Box 43
Los Alamos, New Mexico 87544

www.losalamoshistory.org

Printed in Canada

To my friends

whose love and patient understanding

supported my belief that

this story must be told

Contents

Acknowledgments

I should like to acknowledge the kind assistance of Bill McNulty and the staff of the *Santa Fe New Mexican*, as well as the invaluable help given by the staffs of the University of California and Atomic Energy Commission's record section.

My special thanks go to friends who opened their personal files and their minds for my perusal: Harriet Holloway, Rebecca Bradford, Ruth Haley, Marge Schreiber, and the men who are mentioned specifically in the book.

Friends who appear in the story as well as friends who do not have helped to make the experiences related here into adventures in enthusiastic living. Perhaps some of you will notice slight changes in context. I hope you will forgive me. The changes were made in the interest of continuity and security.

Betty Love Kyriacopulos, who acted as my secretary, was generous with her help and encouragement. Once the work was started, she kept me on the job and criticized and collected my wandering tenses. She served beyond the call of duty, and I cannot thank her enough.

I had a "Board of Senior Responsible Reviewers" who read and sat in judgment. Their helpful comments and accurate criticism were of inestimable value. Thank you, one and all.

E. B. J.

Introduction

Many stories have been written about Los Alamos—"Home of the Atom Bomb," "First Bastion of the Nation's Defense," "Birthplace of the New Era," and on and on. I, too, am going to write about Los Alamos. It was my home for more than five years.

The *Smyth Report* states, "There was no laboratory, no library, no shop, no adequate power plant. The sole means of approach was a winding mountain road. That the handicaps of the site were overcome to a considerable degree is a tribute to the unstinting efforts of the scientific and military personnel." Sciencewise, I believe every word of that statement. Otherwise—well, that's what I want to talk about.

This is my story only in so far as I happen to be the participating observer. It is the story of the lives of men and women who lived and worked in grim secrecy to hasten the end of the war. It is the story of those who shared the bitter post-war struggle to hold this establishment together and rebuild its prestige in the face of seemingly insurmountable obstacles. We were all part of it whether we served in the laboratories or in the homes.

Eric Jette

1

In 1943, I lived in Croton-on-Hudson, New York, with my husband Eric and my son Bill, who was almost ten years old. At that time I had no idea there was a Box 1663 in the Santa Fe post office, nor that I would disappear into it, lose my identity, and emerge from it at the end of 1945 an entirely different person.

Eric was then a professor of metallurgy at Columbia University's School of Mines. He described himself as a classical, physical chemist gone wrong. He meant that he took a Ph.D. in physical chemistry and later, when he went abroad as a Scandinavian-American Scholar, became interested in metallurgy and made it his career.

After Pearl Harbor, most of the students in the School of Mines disappeared. A unit of the Chemical Warfare Service (CWS) moved into the School of Mines and took charge of Eric and his laboratory. By early October 1943, I knew that the problem assigned to the unit was either solved or no longer important, and Eric was aching for a war job where he could be of real service.

I didn't have much time to worry about how Eric was going to find another war job. I was busy with family matters: trying to keep track of Bill and trying to keep the local defense office staffed.

I came downstairs one evening after I had tucked Bill into bed and found Eric sprawled out in his big chair smoking his churchwarden pipe. He is a tall man, and he looked as self-satisfied as our cat, Johno, when he caught a mole and laid it at my feet.

"How'd you like to live in the Southwest?" he greeted me, holding a match to his pipe. (He smoked thousands of board feet of lumber.)

I dropped abruptly into a chair, a trick of Bill's that annoyed me excessively.

"Where in the Southwest?" I was born and raised in Colorado, and I loved the vividly-colored, arid Southwest even more than my native state. I recalled, however, there were a number of places in that vast area that were unfit for human habitation, notably the smelter sites. I thought of one lonely manager's wife who broke out her husband's fifty-year-old Scotch to celebrate my one-day visit.

"I don't know. Gus came to see me today." (Gus was an old friend, A. B. Kinzel of Union Carbide Company.) "He's a consultant for a big, super-secret project run by the army engineers. They have a laboratory some place in the Southwest. The whole thing is absolutely hush-hush. Cyril Smith is in charge of the metallurgical work out there. Gus wanted to know if I'd be interested in another war job. He said Cyril would be in New York in a couple of weeks, and if I was interested, he would tell me more about the job."

"Why didn't Gus tell you where the laboratory was located?"

"Security. It's absolutely imperative that this project doesn't become generally known. They hope the work they're doing will end the war. Gus said the laboratory was in an isolated spot."

"Well, I'm all for ending the war, and if the laboratory is in an isolated spot, I'll bet I can find it. To run a laboratory, you have to have power and water," I announced oratorically while I dug the maps out of the bookcase. I flipped one of them open and laid my finger on a spot just south of Hoover Dam. It was completely isolated, and the dam would provide plenty of power and water.

Eric looked dubious. "I don't think it's as isolated as that. I somehow or other got the impression it was in north-central New Mexico."

"But Eric, there is no *water* there, at least not enough to generate power!"

When I was a child my mother used to take my brother, Preston, and me to visit an aunt and uncle who had a ranch in northern New Mexico. I knew that overgrazed land where it took eighty acres to support a cow. Land gripped by drought for most of the year, but where, when the rainy season came, the clouds literally burst and vomited tons of rain on one location in a single hour. There was no grass to absorb those deluges. The water washed away the topsoil and eroded the substratum into fantastic shapes as it raced for the arroyos where the roiling, stinking run-off devoured everything in its path.

I knew the great prehistoric Indian cities of the Southwest, where archaeologists proved by tree ring studies that they were abandoned during the twenty-three-year drought at the end of the thirteenth century. I expressed the opinion it would be sheer madness to build an important installation in the Southwest unless it was near a dam.

Eric agreed with me. "But," he reminded me, "don't forget the army engineers are running this show. They've been building dams and waterways for a long time. I'll bet they have ways to get water and power if they've built a laboratory in northern New Mexico."

"I piously hope so," I retorted. "Let's take another look at the map."

We finally decided that the laboratory might lie within the confines of Bandelier National Monument. Frijoles Canyon, a part of the monument we once visited, had a small but permanent stream of water.

We spent the rest of the evening speculating about the job; Eric's last words before we turned the lights out were, "Don't mention this job to anyone."

"You know I won't talk about it, but please, Sir, may I ask the cats if they'd like to move?" Eric's chuckle was reassuring.

Eric's report of his interview with Cyril Smith was cryptic.

"I'm very much interested in this job, darling. When Gus makes his November trip out there, I'm going with him."

Eric's association with the Chemical Warfare Service had taught me it would be useless to question him about the nature of the job he was about to inspect, but I could, and did, ask where it was located.

"I don't know yet. Gus's office will make all the arrangements."

"That's a big help. What if I have to get in touch with you when you're gone?"

"They'll know how to reach me. You're perfectly capable of taking care of anything that might come up here. There is a war on, you know."

"I'm well aware of it." I reminded myself I was lucky to be able to accompany my husband wherever he went.

"Let's make a list of the things you want to know about living conditions," Eric suggested.

We made the list. It contained all the questions a woman about to be uprooted would ask: how are the schools? is there a hospital? And on and on.

Eric left on the ninth of November. I accompanied him to the midtown terminal, tried to force some dinner down my throat in the terminal restaurant, and watched him disappear through the doors to the limousine entrance. I stood in the middle of the lobby, overwhelmed with a sense of grief.

Where was Eric going? What was he going to do, and how would it affect our lives? How would a move affect Bill? Would this dreadful war never end?

Where was my brother, Preston? He was a doctor devoted to bringing new lives into the world. What was he doing in the South Pacific? I knew he was in Australia for a while because he sent me a bracelet made of Australian coins, and his letters reported the progress of a young kangeroo with a broken leg. They adopted the youngster and put his leg in a cast. When the cast was taken off the leg, Preston reported proudly that the break was perfectly healed. Then there was silence, and we received a notice of a new APO number. Bill got some sketches of "Unkey" reclining in a hammock under a palm tree, so I concluded that Preston was still behind the battle lines. How long he'd remain there, I couldn't guess.

After the bloody battle for Guadalcanal, our fighting forces literally inched their way forward. Less than three hundred and fifty miles of savagely contested territory was earned in the South Pacific. Almost four thousand miles of water, guarded by fortified islands, had to be secured before the island fortress of Japan could be assaulted. News photos of bodies sprawled on strange beaches rose before my eyes.

I took a firm grip on my imagination and went into a telephone booth where I called my good friend, Jean Mason, in Croton.

"Jean, will you meet me at the station? I just can't bear to go home alone."

When I got to the Harmon Station, Jean was waiting for me at the top of the stairs. She had a chicken sandwich in one hand and a flask in the other. She looked like a ministering angel.

While Eric was away, I continued my various activities.

Whenever I had spare time, I sorted linens and clothing in anticipation of our almost-certain move. When Bill questioned my activities, I told him we were going to spend Christmas with my family in Denver. He was delighted with the prospect. I dreaded the day he learned the truth.

History was written with the speed of lightning in November 1943. The Russians recaptured Kiev and drove relentlessly toward the perimeter of Hitler's Europe. The campaign in Italy was admittedly off schedule. There was bitter fighting for each cold, wet hill. Roosevelt, Churchill, and Chiang Kai-shek conferred in Cairo and decided to press the Japanese war. The Marines secured a toehold on Bougainville and landed on Makin and Tarawa. There were more pictures of bodies sprawled on beaches.

Eric came home just before Thanksgiving. When we were alone, he said, "We were almost right about the location of the place. Actually, some of the detached sections of Bandelier monument are inside the fences. The place is called Los Alamos; it used to be a boys' school."

"I never heard of it."

"It's about halfway between Frijoles Canyon and the Puye Cliffs. The setting is similar to Puye. That whole section in there is known as the Pajarito Plateau. The Jemez Mountains rise from the plateau. They are all that's left of a prehistoric volcano, but even so they're pretty good-sized mountains; the highest ones are almost 11,000 feet. The plateau was built up from the volcanic eruptions. The ash was compressed and hardened into tuff—a soft porous rock. Thousands of years of erosion cut deep canyons into it; most of the people there refer to Los Alamos as a mesa, but it really isn't, it's a *potrero*, a tongue of land. The altitude is 7,200 feet, and there's a magnificent view of the Sangre de Cristos. You'll love the country."

"You are going to take the job?"

"Yes, we'll leave just as soon as I can get things straightened up at the university. It shouldn't take long to get my clearance after my stint with the CWS. If you want to work, you can; most of the women do."

"I don't know whether I want to work. We have to get there

first. I don't know how Bill is going to react to this move, and I'm hideously tired." I *was* tired. Eric's mother passed away after a long illness just before he left for the West, and I commuted to New York regularly to help care for her during the last weeks. I did all the driving for the family, and a twenty-five hundred mile trip was ahead of me.

"There aren't any telephones in the apartments," Eric said. He knew I'd like that item; our telephone rang incessantly.

"The commissary is well stocked, and you'll like their prices," he continued. "I visited the school and talked to Bill's teacher. The fifth and sixth grades are in the same room, but I don't think you have to worry about it. I think she can handle any situation. Her husband is the school principal, and they're both professional educators. Some women from the nearby pueblos and villages come up every day to do housework. There's a regular maid service set-up; of course, the women who work and have small children have top priority for maid service.

"I picked an apartment for us while I was there. There are two sets of apartment buildings in addition to the school buildings, and our apartment is in the set that was finished just before I got there. Those apartments aren't nearly as well built as the first lot, but their setting is much nicer. Our apartment has a wonderful view out to the north. We have a fireplace, and the wood lot is right outside the front door. The back doors open onto service roads. There's only one drawback to the apartment I picked, it has five rooms; with one child we should be in a four-room place."

"I'm not worried about taking care of a five-room apartment, but if the laboratory grows, won't we have to move?"

"No, indeed. The laboratory is a small operation. At first they thought they could do this job with sixty to eighty physicists and a few chemists and engineers. They've upped that figure to five hundred, and it probably won't go beyond it. There's a pond, called Ashley Pond, in honor of the man who founded the school. It lends charm to the place. The work in the laboratory is carried on in a tranquil, academic atmosphere. The people in the housing office assured me we wouldn't be disturbed."

"Humph, did you get it in writing?"

"Don't be silly."

"Do they use the pond for drinking water?"

"No, it's used for recreation. It's also a reserve supply in case of fire. The army engineers have built dams in Guaje Canyon, about seven miles north of Los Alamos. The water is piped into town."

"I suppose there is plenty of water, if that's the case."

"Last winter was dry. One woman said the *Bulletin*—it's a mimeographed sheet issued by the laboratory three times a week—carried hints of ways to save water. As she put it, 'Half a glass of water a day, keeps halitosis away.'"

We talked far into the night. Eric said the former school faculty houses were the only homes in town with bathtubs. People referred to them as Bathtub Row. They weren't allowed to mention Los Alamos by name, so they called it "the Hill." There were two large ex-school buildings, the Big House and Fuller Lodge. The school boys had slept on the porches at the Big House. Their classrooms and study hall were inside the building. Army administration converted the classrooms into offices and the study hall into a combination library-recreation room.

Fuller Lodge was only a few years old. There was a large dining room and kitchen on the first floor. There were rooms for visitors on the second floor. The school infirmary used to be on the third floor, but the rooms up there were now occupied by bachelors. Eric stayed at Fuller Lodge when he was at Los Alamos. He said it was really a lovely building.

"It's fun to go to Fuller for Sunday dinner. The gals wear ski pants, blue jeans—"

"BLUE JEANS!" I was horrified. "I wouldn't be caught dead in the things!" I donned wool undies and flannel slacks the winter before to combat fuel rationing, but blue jeans? Uh-uh.

"You'll have to buy a ski suit. The women said skirts were impossible in bad weather."

All the buildings except the original school buildings were built by the army engineers, and they do all the maintenance work. The buildings and apartment houses were frame and clapboard construction. The engineers were building a new road up the hill.

"It should be finished when we get there," Eric said. "MPs guard the gates and patrol fences. When they're on duty they wear battle helmets. A troop of mounted MPs patrols the town fence and remote parts of the site.

"The University of California runs the laboratory. There are a lot of University of California men there. One of their bright young physicists, J. Robert Oppenheimer, is the director of the laboratory. Nobody out there has a last name, and everyone calls him Oppie. Oppie and the technical staff call the shots when it comes to the work in the Tech Area." He paused thoughtfully. "I gathered there's some friction between the scientific staff and the boys in Washington. It's probably because of that."

"If you ask me, I think it's a good thing not to have an important job snarled up with army red tape," I said, recalling Eric's struggles with red tape in the CWS. "Well, I'm about ready to go to bed," I added, stretching. "Guess I'd better resign my job in the defense office right away."

"You can't resign your job at the defense office until just before we're ready to leave. Nobody's supposed to know we're moving except the people who actually move us and those who attend to our other business. We can't tell our friends I'm leaving the university. We can't even tell Bill we're going to move. Children his age are considered to be very poor security risks. Our families will have to know that we're moving, but we can't tell them where we're going. They're really clamping down on security. There's already been too much talk about the place. They're even going to censor the mail."

"Well, I don't mind the mail being censored, and I've already told Bill we are going to spend Christmas in Denver, but I'm certainly not going to leave Croton without saying goodbye to Jean and her family. I'm not leaving without saying goodbye to Dobby, either. (Dobby was the chief of police in Croton.) He's such a dear, and he's been wonderful to me!"

"I guess you're right. I'd hate to leave without saying goodbye to them. We ought to say goodbye to the Snells, too. They're the best neighbors we ever had. We don't have to tell any of them where we're going. We'll spend Christmas in Denver. I have business at the Manhattan District installations in Chicago and Ames, Iowa. I thought you'd like to spend Christmas in Denver. You won't see your folks again until the end of the war."

Eric took some papers out of his briefcase. "You'll want to read these carefully tomorrow; put them in the desk tonight."

Among the papers was a document stamped RESTRICTED in large red letters (see appendix, part 1). I opened it. It began:

THIS IS A RESTRICTED DOCUMENT
Within the meaning of the Espionage Act,—

"It's a brochure about the Los Alamos project," Eric said. "It will give you a good idea of the set-up."

The next two weeks were busy. I sorted, packed, and made arrangements for the things we couldn't take with us, including the piano. I was overjoyed when Eric told me there was no music teacher on the Hill. After three years of piano lessons Bill played well, but when he practiced he beat out the most exquisitely ear-splitting medley of sour notes ever to assault a maternal ear. Every morning for the last three years I'd risen from my bed resolved not to scream at him *that* day.

I visited the ration board. The clerk took a surreptitious look at the letter I had from the authorities at Los Alamos and put it in a locked file. She gave me enough gas coupons to take us to California and back. Bill's teacher agreed to furnish the papers necessary to transfer him to destination X.

Eric persuaded his assistant at Columbia, Frank Schnettler, to take a job at Los Alamos. When he told me about it, he said, "You know, this secrecy makes me feel like a fool at times. Frank likes to hunt. When I told him he could hunt wild turkeys if he took the job I was offering him, he said, 'That laboratory must be in north-central New Mexico. It's one of the few places in the United States where there are wild turkeys!'"

We arranged to have our furniture moved by lift van. I didn't know what a lift van was. The mover explained. A lift van was a large box. Each piece of furniture was wrapped separately and packed into the box just as china was packed in a barrel. After the box was packed, it was hauled to the railroad yard and hoisted onto a freight car. When the box reached its destination, it was hoisted from the freight car onto a lowboy and delivered right to the house. There was nothing to it, they assured us. It sounded like a fine idea, and Eric arranged to have the Schnettler's furniture travel with ours.

I called our real estate agent, the man through whom we'd rented and bought our house. He came to see me. He assured me he would see that the house was kept in good repair and rented as soon as possible. I walked to his car with him when our business was finished.

"I'll keep an eye on your garden, too," he said as we paused at the entrance through the hedge.

I looked back at my garden, asleep in the pale winter sun, and was seized by a premonition I'd never see it bloom again.

The next day, when I was in the defense office, Dobby came in with tears in his eyes. "I hear you're leaving us, little lady."

"Oh, Dobby, where did you hear that?"

"A man came to see me. He said Eric was leaving Columbia to take an important war job. He was checking up on you."

"I hope you gave me a good character."

"You know I did. We're going to miss you."

I thought it strange that anyone was checking up on me. When I told Eric about it, he said, "That's odd. I suppose they're trying to find out what kind of a person you are. They're scared to death of gossip. A reporter from the *Cleveland Plain Dealer* took his vacation in Santa Fe last summer. He apparently heard some gossip or maybe picked up the piece in the local paper about the strange sight of Indian women and world-famous scientists going back and forth between Santa Fe and Los Alamos in GI buses. Anyway, he went to investigate. He got as far as the first gate and was peeved when the guards wouldn't let him go through it. He went back to Cleveland and published an article speculating about what went on beyond the gate. The *Plain Dealer* published a cartoon of the gate along with the article. It pictured the guards in their battle helmets and decorated them with bulldog faces. Quite understandably, the security boys hit the ceiling. They landed hard on both the *Santa Fe New Mexican* and the *Plain Dealer*."

The first of December fell on Thursday. The weather turned bitterly cold. Eric's sister and her six-year-old son spent the week with us. With Eric's consent, I wrote to my brother and gave him the Box 1663 address. It took a long time for mail to reach the South Pacific.

I wrote my resignation from the defense office and gave it to Dobby. He was to turn it in the morning we left. In it I wrote, "We are leaving Croton to make our home in the southwestern United States." Dobby assumed my responsibilities in the defense office. He told people I was sick in bed. I let the phone ring unanswered. Bill thought it queer that people were asking how his poor, dear mother was, when I was tearing around the house like a tornado.

Everyone in the CWS knew Eric was leaving. Alan Leerburger, a young captain with connections on Broadway, called to ask what show I wanted to see for a going-away present. *Oklahoma!* had just opened, and it was my first choice. Alan conjured up three choice seats for it. We had dinner in a small French restaurant, one of my favorites, and I had an evening I could put in my pocket for the "duration" and treasure for the rest of my life.

We said our goodbyes quietly. Jean was intrigued when we explained that we couldn't tell her where we were going. When we bade her mother and aunt goodbye, her aunt said, "I won't let you off to goodness-knows-where for the duration unless you give us the recipe for your raisin-sour cream pie. This war might last for years!"

The Snells promised to keep an eye on the house, and Ethel asked what we were going to do with our cats.

"We'll be glad to keep both of them for you," she said, "but we especially want you to let us have Johno. There hasn't been a mole in the garden since he was old enough to catch one."

Eric and I sorted books, those to go into storage, those to go with our furniture, and those to go into Eric's office. Eric told me no technical books or journals were allowed in the homes at Los Alamos. I thought the prohibition strange, and it deprived me of one of my sources of amusement.

I, too, was technically educated. My education was coated with rust, but I loved to play mathematical games. I hated to see my math books go into storage. I was somewhat surprised when Eric selected a small volume of mine. He put it with the books he intended to ship to his office.

Once, during my academic career, I had a couple of unused hours. To fill them, I took a course on the theory of probability. It had a high-sounding name but a very practical application. It enabled me to figure the odds on certain combinations of cards coming up in card games like bridge and poker. It was also useful to figure odds on horse races. The book Eric selected was the text for the course.

"Why do you want that? Are the army engineers running a bookie joint?"

"I'm going to be up against long odds. This book may help me figure them."

Eric's sister and her child left on Saturday. Monday, after Bill went to school, the packers came. When Bill came home from school, everything except our beds and the things we were to take with us was wrapped or packed, ready to go into the lift van the next morning.

I was in the kitchen when Bill got home. He handed me a sealed envelope.

"The teacher said to give you this." He glanced into the dining room. "Say, what goes on here?"

He stalked past me and went through every room in the house. I followed him with my heart in my boots. Finally, he said, "This seems to be quite a lot of stuff to take on a vacation."

"It is, dear. We didn't tell you we might live in Denver because we weren't sure about it until the last minute."

The next morning, the lift van arrived. There was no chance of keeping it secret. It was huge, and we lived on a main street. Everybody in town drove by to see our furniture packed into the van. Dobby called about noon. He said there was a rumor going around town that Eric Jette had a wonderful job in California, and he was encouraging it. I will never understand why anything west of the Mississippi River automatically becomes California to the uninitiated.

After the furniture left, we packed the things we needed into the car. Then we gathered up our cat Mikey and our son Bill, both of whom we'd kept under close surveillance all day, and left home early in the evening. It was December 7, 1943.

Mikey developed a psychosis immediately. She buried her head under the steamer rug on the back seat and refused to budge unless I moved her forcibly.

Bill had a wonderful time. He was out of school, and there were no music lessons. He was on his way to Denver, where he had lots of relatives to spoil him. Every time he mentioned Denver I shuddered.

Eric and I were both bone tired when we left Croton. I hadn't driven much since the beginning of the war, and I ached with weariness when we reached Chicago. The temperature was four below zero.

Our old friends John and Lib Miles were in Chicago. John was a DuPont man. Just before I left Croton, I read a short paragraph in the paper. It said DuPont was building a war production plant at Hanford, Washington. The Miles were going to leave the Manhattan District installation in Chicago and go to Hanford when the plant was finished.

I split the shoulder of my ancient seal coat driving from Croton to Chicago, and I wasn't going to part with it in the bitter cold weather. The first thing I did was hunt up a five-and-ten to buy a tube of glue. I hastened to the Miles' apartment, where I glued the skins firmly to the lining. Lib and I visited while Bill went off with the two Miles boys to explore Chicago.

Eric came from the Chicago laboratory with John, who enveloped me in a bearlike hug that almost broke my ribs.

"Gad, it's good to see you again! Where are you going?"

"I can't tell you."

Eric grinned. Lib hooted.

"What do you mean, you can't tell me?"

"I can't tell you."

"Now you're getting a dose of your own medicine. That's what you tell me every time I ask a question," Lib taunted.

John wasn't to be sidetracked. "Let's see your gas coupons," he demanded.

Eric nodded. I took the coupons out of my purse.

John's eyes bugged. "My God, Ellie, you're going to Y! If you go there, you can't leave until the end of the war!"

"It must be the place our moving men told me about," Lib said. "One of them said, 'People sure go funny places these days. I just delivered a load of furniture to a godforsaken place on top of a mountain.'"

A couple of evenings later I sat in the living room of our hotel suite, drowsily listening to Eric and a friend discuss academic matters. Specifically, they deplored the lack of well-trained inorganic chemists. I woke up with a jolt when our friend mentioned the chemistry of uranium and thorium. Both elements were radioactive. Mathematics was my first love, but my background included many hours of both chemistry and physics. I tried frantically to remember if work on either uranium or thorium was mentioned in any of the journals I'd seen before I left Croton. I didn't recall any references. I looked up. Eric was watching me intently.

I mentioned the conversation when the lights were out. "This evening's conversation was illuminating."

Eric muttered something about some people talk too much. Then he said, "I have complete confidence in your discretion."

I drifted off to sleep trying to fit the small bits of knowledge I'd garnered into places in a large puzzle. The DuPont plant in Washington and the laboratory in New Mexico were both part of the Manhattan District. I tried, without success, to remember the properties of uranium and thorium. Eric was a metallurgist. He hadn't been asked to join the laboratory staff because his background was chemistry. It wasn't nearly as soporific as counting sheep.

The temperature at Ames, Iowa, was fifteen degrees below zero instead of four. Our stop there was notable for two reasons: the car congealed and Eric came down with the flu. He burned with fever and shook with chills all the way to Denver. When we got there, he crawled gratefully into bed. I laced him up with aspirin and a good, hefty hot toddy before I went to cope with my family.

My family was always articulate, but on this occasion they outdid themselves. My father and the two aunties were indignant when I refused to reveal our destination. The great light dawned on Bill—we were not going to stay in Denver. He expressed loud doubts of his parents' sanity. My cousin came calling and flung out of the house angrily, demanding to know if I thought they were a bunch of Nazi spies. Mikey slunk around the house like a lost soul.

The next day was better. The junior auntie did personnel work for the Mountain States Telephone Company, and Dad was at the office. Eric and I smoothed the feathers of the senior auntie. We convinced her we weren't keeping our ultimate destination secret just to bedevil the family. Mikey began to show signs of normality, but Bill was unreconciled to his fate. "I wanna go home, M-a-ah!" was his constant plaint.

I picked my father up at his office in the evening. He took a new tack. "I am your father, you can tell me anything."

"Look, Dad, I'll bet you didn't heckle Preston this way when he stopped here on his way to his port of embarkation."

"Of course not, he was traveling under orders."

"So are we, and I want no more questions. If you don't stop asking them, I'm going to pull up right now, and you can walk the rest of the way."

When we reached the house, Bill, who realized he had reinforcement in the person of my dad, started to moan again. My parent seized the opportunity to emphasize the great injustice I was doing my child. Just then, the junior auntie came home from the office. She hopped into the melee with her hat on.

"Let her alone. She can't tell you where she's going. If she did, Eric would be in serious trouble."

"What do you know about it?"

"We ran telephone lines into the place. My brain wasn't functioning last night, honey," she apologized to me.

She produced the desired effect on everyone except Bill. Aside from his complaints, the rest of our stay in Denver was uneventful. We picked up an item in the December 13th issue of *Time* magazine that brightened Eric's Christmas. It noted that Niels Bohr, who received the Nobel Prize for his work on the atom, had been spirited out of Denmark and was safe in England.

When Eric was studying abroad, he spent several months in the Bohr Institute. He spoke of the great man with affection and respect. Eric told me about Bohr's personal kindliness, his superb absent-mindedness in all mundane matters, and the ever-present possibility that he would get himself mislaid or run down. In fact, Eric almost ran him down once himself when Bohr popped up unexpectedly in front of his bicycle.

When the Nazis overran Denmark, Eric worried greatly for fear he had fallen into their hands. The news that he was safe in England was one of the best Christmas presents Eric could have been given.

We planned to leave Denver on New Year's day, but there was a heavy blizzard which extended south into New Mexico. We put chains on the car and started south the following morning. Mikey buried her head under the blanket, Bill protested, and driving was wicked. We stopped at Raton that night. The next day we slithered and slipped on roads coated with glare ice as we crept toward Santa Fe. Bill was sunk in miserable silence. We disclosed our destination to him as soon as we left Raton.

It was four o'clock in the afternoon when we pulled up in front of the U.S. Corps of Engineers Office at 109 East Palace Avenue, Santa Fe. Dorothy McKibbin presided there. She phoned ahead to make certain we were expected at Los Alamos and then issued the three passes necessary for us to enter the sacred portals of Site Y.

"We have our cat with us," I said. "Won't she need a pass, too?"

Dorothy laughed. "No, but I never know what they are going to dream up next."

Dorothy was an extremely attractive woman. She radiated assurance, and I needed it badly. I was distinctly the worse for wear. She took a map out of her desk and penciled the route to Los Alamos. We were to travel 15 miles north on U.S. 64 to a place called Pojoaque, where we would turn left on a dirt road. We would travel approximately 10 miles on the dirt road and cross the Rio Grande at a place called Otowi. Shortly thereafter, the dirt road would join the new hard-surfaced road which was completed after Eric's November visit to the laboratory. I read the mileage, and the car hummed perkily. The warm New Mexico sun had melted the ice during the day, and the road was clear. The speedometer burned 14.9 miles.

Eric said excitedly, "Look, there's the sign."

I saw the sign. It said POJOAQUE. There was no indication of human habitation. I stopped the car beside the sign. The ground was

Eleanor Jette and Dorothy McKibbin

snow covered. A pair of muddy tire tracks led off to the west.

"Are you sure this is our turnoff?"

"Certainly I'm sure. Look, there it is!" He pointed again.

I looked. An umbrella of black smoke hung over one of the potreros of the Pajarito Plateau. Bill looked, too.

"Oh, MAH, *please*, let's go home!"

I turned my head to glare at him. "I don't want to hear another word from you. Our home, till the end of the war, is there!" I waved my arm.

"Provided," I said silently, "I can get the car through the so-called road." My eye fell on the cat. "Ellie, my girl," I continued silently to myself, "you should have made this trip with your head under a blanket, too, but you should have had it examined before you put it there." I started the car and eased it into the muck.

The New Mexico adobe mud was two inches of grease under the

wheels. We wallowed and swayed. Every few hundred yards Eric got out to wipe the slush we churned up off the windshield. Several years later we topped a small rise. There was a sharp little slope and a sharp right turn onto a one-lane bridge. If we missed the turn, we landed in the muddy Rio Grande.

We slid gracefully down the grade at five miles per hour. I warped the wheels, slammed on the brakes, and we lit neatly on the bridge. I paused to recover. Eric looked back. There was a scar on one of the uprights.

"Look, someone hit it," he observed.

"I never did approve of reckless driving," I laughed shakily.

Eric pointed out Edith Warner's house on the west bank of the river. She and her Indian helper, Tilano, served meals by appointment to people from Los Alamos. Eric had a meal there when he visited in November. I was looking forward to meeting Miss Warner and sampling her excellent cooking.

After we crossed the bridge, the road was uphill and dry. It wasn't long before we were on the new, hard-surfaced road. The long, low rays of the winter sun were in my eyes as we climbed, but even so, the new road looked like the road to heaven. I could see the abandoned school road snaking up the side of the potrero in its narrow, serpentine path. I gave silent thanks that we didn't have to finish our journey on IT!

We stopped at the first guard house about half an hour after we crossed the Rio Grande. It stood just east of the fence, which was a seven-foot chain link affair with three strands of barbed wire at the top of it. It was liberally festooned with signs which read:

U.S. Government Property
DANGER! *PELIGRO!*
Keep Out

The MPs in battle helmets who manned the guardhouse were a formidable-looking bunch of young men. They inspected our passes and recorded their numbers. "No wonder the cartoon in the *Plain Dealer* portrayed them with bulldog faces," I thought.

fter we left the gate, the road wound through thickets of piñon and juniper for a couple of miles. The sun sank behind the Jemez Mountains. The umbrella of black smoke ahead marked the town site. As we approached it, the thickets gave way to an open field. Green construction workers' huts stood disconsolately on the right. There was a barracks area on the left. The whole scene was as raw as a new scar.

Eric talked cheerfully. "They heat with New Mexico soft coal."

"So I see." The fresh snow was covered with soot.

We halted in front of the town gate. The MPs inspected our passes, and we entered.

"We have to go to the housing office to get the keys to the apartment. It's up by the water tower, but where's the tower? The place has changed in the last six weeks."

~~ *Apartment T-185*

It was after 5:30 when we reached apartment T-185, our home for the next two years. The apartment buildings looked like hell. The green barracks-type structures sat jauntily in a sea of mud. The back porches were lined with garbage cans. When we pulled up in the back of our own building, the car sighed and sank hub-deep in the tundra.

"We made it."

"We certainly did, and a good job, too." Eric gave my arm an affectionate pat.

"Hand Mikey to me, Bill," I instructed, "and put your galoshes on before you get out of the car." I climbed out wearily, clutching the cat, and waded to the steps. When I reached the top step, a woman's voice called, "Hi!"

She popped her head out the door of the other second floor apartment. "Oh, I beg your pardon! I thought you were my husband. You must be the new neighbors. We're the Haleys, Ruth, Jano, and the children. If you need anything, yell." She disappeared.

Eric opened the door and escorted me into my new home.

"Isn't it nice?" he asked proudly. He indicated the view.

There was a beautiful view of the mountains to the north, but I didn't see it. I saw soot-covered walls, ceilings, and floors. "No wonder the brochure suggested cleaning materials should be available."

Four GI cots and three GI bureaus stocked with bedding were in the middle of the living room. Some straight-backed chairs and a table made of two-by-fours and sheet rock were in the dinette. The table looked like a workbench, cast off because it was too flimsy.

I dropped Mikey with a thud and wandered through the house. There was no linoleum on the bathroom floor. The fixtures were filthy. "What madness possessed me to leave my lovely home and come to this place?" I wondered. I stifled an impulse to cry.

"They were supposed to clean this place before we arrived," Eric said.

A young couple came bursting in; they were laughing and rosy with cold. Eric introduced them as Cyril's secretary and her fiancé. The girl said she made a dinner reservation for us at Fuller Lodge.

Eric looked at his watch.

Fuller Lodge

"They serve promptly at six. We'll have to hurry, or we won't have anything to eat."

"It's only a quarter of six. You can go down to the car and get out the bag with the whiskey in it. I need a drink, and I'll take it neat."

Fuller Lodge *was* a lovely building. The interior surfaces of great logs used for the construction of the building were waxed to a warm honey color. In the dining room, massive, hand-hewn vigas supported the cathedral ceiling. Wrought-iron chandeliers hung from the vigas. A fireplace, built of varicolored tuff stone, dominated the south end of the room. The five-foot logs ablaze on the hearth cast a warm glow over the scene. French doors were used instead of windows along the east wall of the dining room. They opened out onto a patio and overlooked the Sangre de Cristo Mountains, the range the early Spanish explorers named because they were bathed each evening in the blood-red color of reflected sunset. You reached the balconies that ran around the other two sides of the room by a stairway in the entrance foyer. Guest rooms opened off the balconies, and there was a closed stairway to the third floor.

As soon as we sat down, I discovered the chairs and tables were relics of the Los Alamos Ranch School. The chairs had ladder-backs *and* seats, but they did nothing to diminish my enjoyment of our meal. George Kistiakowsky sat at our table that night. The talk was of trivialities. George and Eric knew each other in pre-Los Alamos days, but I hadn't met him before. Later, I asked Eric to identify him. "He's the top of the heap in the field of explosives," he said.

Frank and Margaret Schnettler came in before we finished our meal. They came west by train. They were expecting their first child in mid-January and wanted to be settled before the important event took place. We were almost finished with our meal when Cyril Smith came puffing into the dining room. He was tall and spoke with a British accent.

"Colloquium meets at seven o'clock, Eric," he announced. "You should come."

"Okay, I'll be along right away."

I was thunderstruck. We had to clean up the mess in the apartment. The darn place apparently ran on bells—dinner at six, colloquium at seven. What happened at eight?

Cyril Smith rushed away. I later discovered he was addicted to tearing up and down the sides of mountains. Such intelligence would have done me no good at the moment, save to give me hope he might slip and break his neck. I opened my mouth.

"Of all the brass! If you think for a single minute you're going off and leave Bill and me alone to cope with the mess in the apartment—"

Frank interrupted. "I've got to go to colloquium, too. Why don't you two go home with Margaret? You can keep each other company. Colloquium is always over by nine. Eric can pick you up at our place."

It seemed like a reasonable suggestion. We went home with Margaret Schnettler and spent a pleasant two hours. Since it was Monday, she had a copy of the current *Bulletin*; it was issued Mondays, Wednesdays, and Fridays. I perused it with considerable interest. It carried an intimidating banner line:

THIS BULLETIN IS PUBLISHED FOR THE SITE—
KEEP IT HERE!

There were a few notices of meetings, women's club, etc. The housing office announced that the number of Indian women coming to the Hill to do housework had been augmented, and a couple of army edicts began *YOU WILL*. There was a tag line at the bottom of the page:

REPORT LEAKY FAUCETS IMMEDIATELY!

The *Bulletin* didn't look like a very promising source of news.
"Almost everybody takes the *New York Times*," Margaret said.
"There are a few Santa Fe papers in the PX but not nearly enough to go around."

Frank walked home with us after colloquium. Cyril and some of the other men from CM Division were waiting for us at the apartment. CM meant chemistry and metallurgy. Joe Kennedy, brilliant and ebullient, was the division leader. Cyril was associate division leader in charge of metallurgy. Eric was a group leader and acting associate division leader if Cyril was absent.

The men fell to work with a will. They unpacked the car and set up Bill's cot so I could settle him for the night. They moved the few bits of furniture into place. They unpacked my box of "Useful Odds and Ends," scrubbed the fixtures, and swept the floor. One of the men brought his "borrowing basket" with him. Every family in residence kept a basket with towels, dishes, silver, soap, and such to tide new arrivals over until their own supplies arrived.

Cyril stayed after the others left. I felt a lot happier about Cyril then than I did at dinnertime. We brewed nightcaps.

"I know you're tired," he said, "but I have to warn you about the furnace. These apartments are built of green wood, it's filled with pitch, and there aren't any fire escapes."

"You mean we'll be trapped if the house catches fire?" Eric asked.

Cyril nodded. "The furnaces in these buildings were designed to heat sixteen apartments of this size; there's constant danger they might overheat and start a fire."

"Couldn't we get down the stairs?" I inquired.

"No. The furnace room is under both the front and back stairs. The people in the downstairs apartments might get out through the windows."

"What a jolly prospect," I thought. "The people downstairs might get out the windows if they don't suffocate. We'll have our choice of broken bones or being broiled."

Cyril was talking to Eric. "The provisional engineers maintain the furnaces. It's probable nine out of ten of them never saw a furnace in civilian life, and the firemen are a real problem. Many of them speak no English or very broken English. Some of them stoke with such abandon there's real danger the house will catch fire. Others sleep beside their furnaces while the occupants of the apartment freeze."

"Can't anything be done about the overheating?"

"Oh, yes. The engineers are venting the furnaces to the outdoors. They haven't reached this building yet. Don't close the hot air ducts until they do. If you get too hot, open the windows."

Eric and I looked at each other when Cyril left.

"When we go to Santa Fe, we're going to buy fifty feet of good strong rope. We'll anchor it to something sturdy in the corner of Bill's room."

Eric said, "Amen."

We learned more about the furnaces early the next morning. A mighty strangling sound rent the air. Soot and coal gas poured into our bedroom. I heard our downstairs neighbors muttering. There was no sound-proofing between the floors. "Woe to the man who cusses his wife and beats his children. The whole town will know it," I whispered.

We had no more sleep that night. Eventually we dragged ourselves out of bed. We roused Bill, who could sleep through anything, and repaired to Fuller Lodge for breakfast. Ralph Carlisle Smith, a captain in the Corps of Engineers, preceded us. Smitty was a bachelor and lived at Fuller Lodge. He introduced himself and asked us to join him. The conversation turned to our arrival, and we told him about our trip from Denver.

"Nobody comes to Los Alamos without complications," he said. "I came last summer. I had orders to travel in civilian clothes and not to identify myself with the army in any way. I was to get off the train in Lamy, go to the best hotel, and lay low until I was contacted by Colonel Ashbridge. He's the CO here. I got off in Lamy, took a look at the place, and knew somebody'd goofed. I went up to Santa Fe and holed up at La Fonda. Ashbridge found me without any trouble. Do you folks know Lamy?"

We laughed. We knew Lamy: a station, a diner, a few run-down houses, and an occasional goat wandering the streets. There used to be a Harvey House there, but it was torn down a few years before all of us came to Los Alamos.

"The first contingent of Wacs to arrive here were all girls who'd applied for overseas service," Smitty said. "When they got to Lamy in January of '43, they were ordered off the train, loaded into GI buses with covered windows, and hauled to the Hill. They were absolutely burned to the ground, and still are, for that matter."

Harriet Peterson arrived in her crisp white uniform. Smitty introduced us, and she joined us.

"Petey here was one of the first three nurses on the Hill," he explained. "Ma Roberts and Sara Dawson were the others. "

"How interesting!" I exclaimed.

Petey chuckled. "It was interesting in more ways than one. The first aid room was set up with a triple-A priority, but it didn't mean a thing. We found some supplies left over from the ranch school in a trunk on the third floor of Fuller. They were all we had for a long time. We used ranch school mercurochrome and iodine for everything. When the hospital was finished, but not furnished, our first patient arrived. He had yellow jaundice. Sara had to uncrate a bed and set it up for him."

"It sounds a trifle primitive."

"It was. The kitchen wasn't finished for quite a while. All the trays were prepared here in Fuller. Ma was the tray courier, but no matter how she hurried, the food was always cold. We only had one small decrepit sterilizer. When the kitchen was finished we used the oven for a dry sterilizer. All the linen we used for deliveries and surgery was treated in the kitchen oven."

I decided the peculiarities at Los Alamos were not confined to the security measures mentioned in the brochure.

"How did you happen to come to Los Alamos, Petey?" I asked.

"I worked with Dr. Nolan in St. Louis before he was in the army. He's really an Ob-Gyn. He takes care of all the deliveries as well as the surgery. His baby, Linda, was the first baby born on the Hill."

"You mean born inside Box 1663, don't you?" Smitty corrected. Even Bill laughed.

I told Smitty we needed linoleum in the apartment bathroom and asked who took care of such matters. He gave me the name of a WAC lieutenant and told me where to find her.

"You'd better drive around a bit and get yourself oriented, Eleanor," Eric suggested. "I'll meet you here for lunch."

"I will," I promised. "I've got to take Bill to school first."

I felt that the sooner Bill was deposited among his contemporaries, the better it would be for both of us. I knew that one more day of his complaints would finish me; I'd doubtless bop him.

Bill and I finished our breakfast after the others left and wandered schoolward. The school was a nice-looking building. Bill viewed it with distaste. We entered. I was briskly in the lead. I inquired for the fifth grade and was directed. We entered the room and approached the woman at the desk.

"Mrs. Cook, I'm Mrs. Jette, and this is my son Bill. We arrived yesterday. I produced the paper Bill's former teacher provided.

"I'm sorry, Mrs. Jette, I'm not Mrs. Cook. Dr. and Mrs. Cook left the Hill during the Christmas holidays. I'm substituting until they can find a regular teacher."

I stifled a gasp. Johnny Miles was wrong. People did leave Los Alamos.

"I'm Mrs.—." In my confusion I didn't catch her name. "I'm sure Bill will be happy in Los Alamos. My children love it."

Bill made a sound. A strangled "Ugh."

"Oh, I'm sure he'll be happy!" I cast him to his fate and fled.

I returned to the apartment to air Mikey. The night before, she refused to leave the apartment until I accompanied her. I sat down on the living room cot to consider the plight of the fifth and sixth grades. Mikey jumped into my lap and purred. Then she jumped to the floor and mewed to go out. I opened the door for her. She sat down inside the open door and wailed loudly.

"What's the matter with you?" I inquired.

She wailed louder. I hastily grabbed my jacket and went down the front steps. She followed me, bounced out into the snow, and picked her way gingerly for a few feet before digging her hole. When she finished, she rushed back and up the steps, as though all the hounds of hell were in pursuit

"Good Lord, if this goes on, it's going to be worse than walking a dog. Maybe I should have left her with Ethel." I decided to interview the WAC lieutenant about the linoleum.

I hunted her down and told her my problem. She was downright rude. She implied that the scientific staff were nothing but a bunch of prima donnas. The army provided them with luxurious quarters, but they were constantly making impossible demands, such as the one I made. She made it clear she thought I was in quarters far superior to any I previously occupied, and said flatly, "If you want linoleum on the bathroom floor, you'll have to buy it and have it laid."

"I most certainly will buy linoleum and have it laid," I sizzled with rage. I simmered while I drove around.

There was a small pond south of Fuller Lodge. I was sure it was the one Eric described. A few buildings were clustered around it. I identified the hospital, a small green structure, and the commissary, a slightly larger, yellowish building. There were a couple of buildings on the south side of the pond opposite the Tech Area. They were built of tuff, so they were originally school buildings. Closer investigation disclosed that one of them was an ice house, and the other was an eating place. I was told that it was called the Tech PX. It served sandwiches and snacks at odd hours and was open until 10 P.M. My informant pointed out the regular PX at the corner of the field in front of Fuller Lodge.

The regular PX was an ex-school building, too. It was built of logs. I investigated it. It didn't seem to be very well stocked. I asked for a scrubbing brush.

"I'm sorry," the Wac behind the counter said, "we've ordered them, but they haven't come in yet. We're not supposed to exist, so our orders frequently aren't filled. Could you use a nail brush?"

I thought it was going to be quite a chore to scrub the soot off the walls with a nail brush, but I bought it anyway. I realized I hadn't eaten a meal I'd cooked myself for almost a month. I decided to stock up at the commissary so I could cook dinner that night.

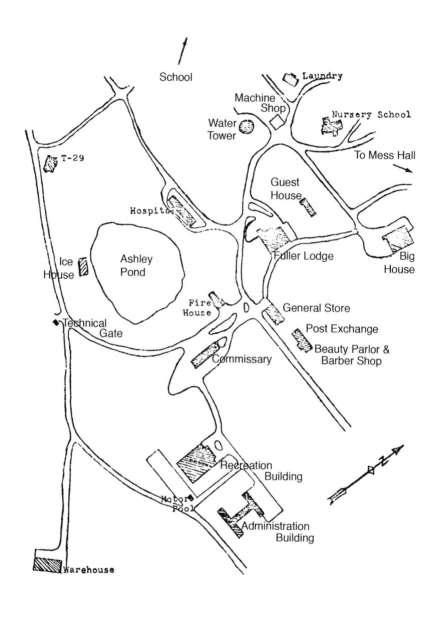

School

Laundry

Machine
Shop

Nursery School

Water
Tower

T-29

To Mess Hall

Hospital

Guest
House

Ice
House

Ashley
Pond

Fuller Lodge

Big
House

Fire
House

General Store

Technical
Gate

Post Exchange

Commissary

Beauty Parlor &
Barber Shop

Recreation
Building

Motor
Pool

Administration
Building

Warehouse

Early Map of the Hill

The Commissary

There weren't any grocery carts in the commissary, just clumsy metal baskets. I loaded several of them and lugged them to the checking counter. I reflected that the baskets must be a part of the luxurious living provided by the army for the scientific staff. The commissary was very well stocked, and the prices were delightfully low. Several other women were shopping. We introduced ourselves and visited, leaning on the vegetable counter. I learned three important things.

First, there were sources of news other than the *Bulletin* and the *New York Times*. There were two "grapevines"—the regular "grape" and the "foreign-born grape." News from the latter source was apt to be hotter and more authentic.

Second, everyone at Los Alamos had to be a United States citizen except the members of the British Mission, some of whom were already in residence. Our foreign-born citizens were students of the American Bill of Rights, intrepid fighters when it was necessary to battle with the army.

Third, the WAC lieutenant I encountered earlier pursued the

>~~~ *The Trading Post*

Washington line. Our General, the HIGHER AUTHORITY who ruled our lives from distant Washington, was an advocate of the simple life. He attended a little red school house when he was a boy. Any nickel spent outside the laboratory was going to scream blue bloody murder before it was spent. (The general was Leslie Groves.)

I was fresh from the "Outer World." My new friends knew it the moment I walked in the door—I was wearing a dress and stockings. They were eager for news. Where did I get my stockings? Was it possible to buy them any place but the black market?

I spent the balance of the morning in the commissary and arrived at Fuller Lodge a few minutes early. Bill joined me.

"How did school go, son?"

"Awful. Those sixth grade kids make such a racket you can't hear yourself think. The teacher can't do a thing with them. Ma, do we have to stay here?"

"Yes, we do."

"I don't see why you and I can't go back to Croton. Dad could come back at the end of the war."

"Oh, shush, the end of the war is a long time off. They're beginning to serve in the dining room. Suppose you go in and start your lunch." I wandered into a small sitting room off the foyer. Eric joined me shortly. His face was glowing.

"Eleanor, come out here," he propelled me into the foyer. "There is someone I want you to meet." He led me to a genial-looking, white-haired man seated on the sofa.

"Dr. Bohr, may I present my wife?"

"Shuuush!" the great man put his finger to his lips. His eyes twinkled. He exuded good humor. "I am now Nicholas Baker— Uncle Nick." He chuckled and indicated a young man standing near the end of the sofa. "This is my son, Jimmy Baker."

"You were a baby when I saw you last," Eric said to Jimmy. Turning back to Bohr, he added, "I never thought I'd see you here, Sir."

"You almost didn't. I can't tell you about it. There are too many people around, and besides, I was unconscious."

I assumed Jimmy was traveling with his absent-minded parent to take care of him and said so. Jimmy confirmed my guess. We visited with the Bakers for a few minutes before we went in for our lunch. Mrs. Baker was also safe and in good health. Eric told me later that Jimmy's real name was Aage Bohr and that he was a promising young physicist.

After lunch, I drove back to the apartment to unload my groceries. The apartment was stifling. I tried to open a window, but the windows were painted shut. I finally succeeded in opening the window of our unused bedroom. I laid down on the living room cot to ruminate. Mikey curled up on my stomach, purring.

"Uranium and thorium were radioactive. There weren't enough well-trained inorganic chemists. We had dinner with the top of the high explosives heap last night. Today I met the man who won the Nobel Prize for his work on atomic structures. What was the Manhattan District? The laboratories at Chicago, Ames, and Los Alamos were part of it. So was the war production plant DuPont was building in Washington. What were the long odds Eric mentioned when he selected my little math book?

"Stop fussing about it," I told myself, "You have your job cut out for you. Bill's going to be a handful. You weighed out in Denver at less than a hundred and five. You'd better get some meat on your bones or you'll be a pushover for the first bug you meet."

I wondered why I had to use our ration books to buy food in an army commissary. My throat felt sore. I decided I had Eric's flu bug.

The back door opened, and a feminine voice called, "Anybody home?"

"Come in," I croaked.

It was Alice Smith, Cyril's wife. She was tall, brisk, and blessedly down-to-earth. "What's the matter with you?"

"Oh, Eric caught the flu in Ames. I think I have his bug."

"Nonsense, you're just suffering from the shock of arrival. I'm going to have a tea party for you on Thursday."

"You'd better not plan a party until we find out whether I have the flu."

"You don't, and I'm going right ahead with the party."

Alice told me she taught history in the high school. She was a history teacher by profession. When I spoke of my concern over the departure of the fifth and sixth grade teacher, she shook her head.

"I'm afraid those grades are going to be in trouble. The school board isn't allowed to hire teachers from the Outer World. The teachers have to be people who'd be at Los Alamos anyhow. One of our best teachers came with her daughter and son-in-law. Another good teacher is the wife of the man who runs the meat department in the commissary."

When she mentioned the commissary, I recalled our ration books.

"Why do we have to use our ration books in the commissary? When my brother was stationed in Virginia, his wife didn't have to use their ration books."

Alice snorted, "Our General doesn't believe in coddling civilians. Have you tried your Black Beauty yet?"

"My Black Beauty? I thought Black Beauty was a horse."

"Your stove. They're aptly named. They're just as balky as horses."

We chatted and discussed all sorts of minor problems that beset women newly arrived at Los Alamos. Alice's visit was worth ten shots in the arm. I was a new person when she left.

The apartment was getting cold, so I went to close the window. I pulled the pegs to release it; they came out in my hands. The window stayed open, and my efforts to dislodge it were in vain. I dropped the pegs on the floor and closed the door when I left the room.

"It's a good thing I couldn't get the living room window open," I reflected. I went to the back door and looked out. Bill was coming down the road with two boys about his own age.

"Who are your pals?" I asked when he came into the house

"Oh, they're two of the guys in the sixth grade. They live across the street from us. Ma, you aren't going to do that to me, are you?"

"Do what to you? What are you talking about?"

"Have a baby. They said," he nodded to the other side of the street, "we were going to have a baby because we lived in a five-room apartment."

"We were assigned a five-room apartment because there weren't any four-room apartments available." I said. "Wait, don't take your coat off. I'll get my jacket, and we'll go take a look at the skating pond. As soon as the furniture arrives we'll have our skates."

The skating pond was down in Los Alamos Canyon where the hot midday sun didn't reach it. The pond was small, but the ice was in excellent condition. (When our skates arrived we unpacked them immediately, but when we returned to the pond, the army engineers were there before us. They were cutting the ice to store for use in the PX!)

When we returned to the apartment, I fired up my Black Beauty and got it going without incident. Bill retired with a funny book. Eric came home about 6:00. He looked tired.

"How did it go?" I asked.

"Grumph." He handed me a small tan booklet. I opened it:

RESTRICTED
THIS IS NOT TO BE TAKEN FROM THE SITE
CENSORSHIP REGULATIONS

"How fascinating!"

"It is. You'd better study it carefully or G2 will get you. What happened to you today?"

I told him about Bill's departed teacher, my interview with the WAC lieutenant, and the other events of the day. He promised he'd phone for a carpenter to fix the windows the first thing in the morning. Then he said, "We're going over to the Smiths' this evening."

"I'm not going out and leave Bill alone in this firetrap."

"There aren't any sitters here. At least one family in the apartment house is at home when you want to go out. You tell them where you're going and how to reach you. Everyone does it."

He retired to the living room to stretch out on the cot. He studied the nailholes in the ceiling while he pondered the problems ahead of him, behind an impenetrable wall of silence.

Years later, he told me he was projecting a study of the metallurgy of the man-made element plutonium, using "stand-in" materials such as uranium, lanthanum, and cerium. Plutonium itself was available only in minute amounts. Enough plutonium was produced in the cyclotron at Berkeley to study its chemistry by microscopic methods. Construction of the DuPont plant at Hanford, Washington, was begun on the basis of those studies. Before the work at Berkeley was finished, some microscopic metal beads, supposedly plutonium, were produced in the Chicago laboratory. No one was really sure it was metal. Anyway, microscopic amounts of plutonium were not enough for a full-scale attack on the preparation of the metal and the study of its metallurgy.

If I'd known all that at the end of our first twenty-four hours at Los Alamos, I'd have known why Eric took my little math book with him. I'd probably have been in the living room helping him count the nails. As it was, I roused him from his reverie long enough to swallow some dinner. He returned to it while I cleaned up the kitchen and settled Bill for the night. I went next door and knocked.

"Come in," Ruth called cheerfully. She was sewing. Jano was reading. He was a debonair redhead with a sporty red beard. The Haleys looked comfortably settled; they had lamps, easy chairs, and things.

"I hate to intrude on you, but we've been asked to go to the Cyril Smiths' tonight. Are you folks going to be at home?"

"Indeed we are. We'll be glad to keep an eye on your son. It certainly is nice to have next door neighbors at last.

"If the place catches fire, I'll toss the kids into nice soft snow banks," Jano promised cheerfully.

3

he evening at the Smiths was an unqualified success. We met Jean and Bob Bacher, Betty and Clare Balke, Dot and Al Seybolt, and others who were to be our friends. No titles were used when introductions were made. After the introductions were over we were simply Eleanor and Eric; it was a welcome change after the formality of university life. My orientation course, begun by Smitty that morning and carried on by others during the day, continued in bits and snatches of conversation.

The men, who worked six days a week, were allowed one day a month to do their shopping. Everyone shopped in Santa Fe, which was full of men from G2; you could always spot them because they wore snap-brim hats—straw in the summer, felt in the winter. G2 men followed Hill people around town to see that they didn't speak to anyone on the street.

People from Los Alamos were supposed to cut their own parents if they met them on the street. G2 saw to it that they didn't mail any letter surreptitiously and tailed them into La Cantina (La Fonda's bar). It made sure they didn't divulge any classified information or gather in groups of more than four people when they bent their elbows.

The censorship regulations were panned. The monitored phone calls were a nuisance. You'd tell Papa, or Uncle Joe, that you went on a picnic last Sunday. He'd ask where you went and the monitor would cut the connection to caution your answer. Frequently, you were never able to get your connection again.

Oppie, in addition to his duties as director of the laboratory, was co-administrator of the town with the commanding officer. The situation was a mistake; Oppie was much too busy to be bothered about town administration. One man told a story to illustrate the point.

47

In the fall, Oppie attended an international conference. The names Churchill and Roosevelt sparkled through his report to the Los Alamos scientific staff. The conference discussed portentous matters. It was agreed that the British should send a scientific mission to Los Alamos. Oppie gave a glowing report of a notable meeting. When he concluded, he asked the routine question, "Is there any further business to be discussed by this body?"

A small accented voice was raised in the back of the room.

"Please, Mr. Director, when do we have a shoemaker on this Hill?"

Our new friends deplored the fact we came to Los Alamos via Pojoaque. They said the Española approach was twenty miles longer but much better. All the trucks used it. The bridge at Otowi was too narrow and low for them.

The three-day laundry service mentioned in the brochure was a thing of the past.

"Don't send Pappy's shirts to the laundry," Dot cautioned. "I sent some of Al's shirts six weeks ago and don't have them back yet."

In addition to the foregoing, I learned that Los Alamos was administered by a lieutenant colonel, a major or so, a few captains, and assorted junior officers, all from the reserve. The only honest-to-goodness, regular officer was the security officer. Quite understandably, he was unpopular.

It was an instructive evening with the Smiths!

For the next two weeks I hovered precariously on the verge of apoplexy. The milk tasted like sagebrush. I was positive the eggs came from the hundred thousand cases reportedly rotting in storage during the early fall. I did the family washing—*including* pappy's shirts—and when I brought the wash home from the community laundry, a woman from the next house had preempted the clothes line. Alan Ayres came up from the apartment below to apologize for hitting our car; he was only trying to steer his own car out of the muck.

I continued to walk Mikey. Bill's complaints about the school were loud and many. Eric communicated with the ceiling nails. He brought two letters to me. Both were stamped, "Opened by the Army Examiner."

The first letter was from my brother, Preston. It was a model of restraint. He couldn't imagine what took Eric to New Mexico, but "good luck in the new venture." Little did he know how much Eric needed luck. The second letter was from Jean. It was forwarded from Denver. She wrote, "I'll bet you're going to the war production plant DuPont's building in Washington."

"That tears it," I said when I read the letter. "Security will be on my neck."

"I don't see how you could get into any trouble over that letter" Eric said. "The plant isn't even finished."

"Nonetheless, I'd better send some censorship cards to our loving friends and relatives before they put us in real hot water."

I spent a whole morning getting six censorship cards. The office was understaffed. It was overcrowded with women and their small children. The latter stepped on my toes and lacerated my shins while their mothers gossiped. The Wacs trying to cope with the situation were needlessly abrupt.

After I got the cards, I inquired about converting my temporary pass into a permanent one. I was told the pass system was about to be changed. "You will bring your pass into this office for renewal every two weeks until the change is made." The army's YOU WILL never failed to raise my hackles.

I was apprehensive about Jean's letter and wondered what happened to people who received such letters. The carpenter came to fix the window. He had apple-red cheeks and twinkly blue eyes. He said, "I've been with the army engineers for twenty years, and they're a fine outfit."

I said I had the same impression *before* I arrived at Los Alamos.

Alice's party was fun, but in my four days at Los Alamos, I received so many impressions, so fast, that my facile memory for names deserted me. I connected a few faces with their owners' names. Sally Flanders, with her rosy cheeks and bangs, was easy. Martha Parsons wore a ski suit! I was attracted to her immediately. When Alice identified Martha as Capt. Deak Parsons' wife, I decided they were army people. Muriel Cuykendall was an M.D. One young woman had a lovely, flower-like complexion. I gathered she was a

Mrs. Gurney. I later discovered she was Gurney Ashbridge, wife of the commanding officer, Whitney Ashbridge. Conversation was light, but I managed to learn more about my new neighbors.

Muriel spent her spare time at the hospital. Orders for hospital supplies were always balled up. The hospital ordered a thousand dozen aspirin tablets and got a thousand gross instead. One woman said it was scarcely enough for all the headaches on the Hill.

The health of the troops on the Hill was the hospital's first responsibility, civilian health was second. All three full-time doctors were very good, and civilian medical care was free. The birthrate at Los Alamos was phenomenal. Our General wanted the CO to halt the flood of babies!

The two theaters on the Hill were known as Theater Number One and Theater Number Two. Both were equipped with wooden benches, but Number One, in the barracks area, had cushions on the seats. Both showed first-run movies for fifteen cents a head. Theater One showed movies every night in the week. Theater Two showed movies three nights a week. The other four nights it was used for community activities. The GIs had their Saturday night dances in Theater Two, and it was used as a chapel on Sunday mornings.

The priest and ministers, imported from Santa Fe, were early risers. They had to sweep out the cigarette butts and beer cans from the previous night's dances before they could address their congregations. When services were conducted, the congregations faced the back of the theater. The rectors faced the stage.

It was rumored that people from San Ildefonso Pueblo and the Pojoaque Valley hiked up the trails to the fifteen cent movies in Theater One. My tea party friends thought the town was fenced separately to keep the intruders out of it.

We had a fine time. When the party was over, I drove Muriel home.

"I hope your family has had typhoid shots," she said.

"No, we haven't had typhoid shots. Why should we?"

"Typhoid is endemic in the valley, and the water situation here isn't nearly so good as people think it is."

"Eric said the army built dams in Guaje Canyon, and the water is piped into town."

"That's right, but the dams don't have much storage capacity."

"What about the dam in Los Alamos Canyon? I saw it when I took Bill to inspect the skating rink."

"It was the water supply for the ranch school. I think our water supply is adequate for now, but we'll be in trouble if the town gets any larger. Trevor, my husband, says they need more personnel in the laboratory."

"I'm glad someone's husband can talk. Eric doesn't say anything. He comes home late, and I report my activities for the day. He snaps Bill's head off and lies down on the living room cot to count the nails in the ceiling. I hope he isn't going to do the strong, silent act indefinitely."

Muriel chuckled. "He'll relax when your furniture comes."

I had a lot of chit-chat for Eric that night.

During those first days, I tried to scrub my soot-covered walls with the nail brush I acquired at the PX. I worked all one day, almost took my arm off at the shoulder, and cleaned a circle about fourteen inches in diameter over the kitchen sink. It looked like the rising sun but was plenty good enough for me.

I built a sled for Bill. Either he, or his smaller cousin, broke a runner on his sled just before we left Croton. It couldn't be repaired, and not even the mail-order houses of Montgomery Ward and Sears Roebuck had sleds in those days. Eric's toolbox was shipped with the furniture. I searched out the carpenter who fixed the window, and he lent me the necessary tools. He said the needed materials were available at the salvage yard, where Sergeant Baker presided. I contacted the sergeant apprehensively; the WAC lieutenant was fresh in my mind. Sergeant Baker, however, was most helpful. Together we searched through mountainous piles of junked lumber to select the choicest items for the projected sled.

The finished product was sturdy. Every time I hit a nail I concentrated on something that riled me; I waxed the wooden runners with candle grease. The sled would never win a beauty contest, but Bill could do "belly flops" on it and it raised his morale.

I met dozens of people, both men and women. Some were thin; some were fat. Some were handsome; some were homely. Some were American-born citizens; some were naturalized citizens. A few members of the British Mission were already in residence. The roster of names sounded like a reading from *American Men of Science* and then some. A dazzling galaxy of scientific stars was gathered for a common effort. They hoped to end the slaughter with a weapon so diabolical it would preclude war forever.

In the Outer World, bombs rained on Berlin. The campaign in Italy was stalemated. The Red Tide swept forward in Russia. "Vinegar Joe" Stilwell scoffed at allegations that the Chinese troops were not good fighters. Merrill's Marauders and Wingate's Raiders harassed enemy supply lines in Burma. A retired American chief of staff cautioned that the war wasn't even started. He told us to wait until Germany and Japan started to fight on their own soil. The United States Marines fought for, and won, two airstrips on Cape Gloucester. They met heavy resistance. Casualty lists were grim reading. I wondered where Preston's hospital unit would see action.

The Schnettler's baby arrived about ten days after we did. On the evening of January 16th, Eric arrived home from the Tech Area beaming. Our furniture was in Santa Fe.

"Oh, goody." I hoped the furniture would reconcile Bill to his sojourn in New Mexico, cure the cat's nervous breakdown, and occasionally stimulate Eric into a little light conversation.

"Are they going to bring it up tomorrow?"

"Dear, you have just one thing in common with the army engineers."

"What is it?"

"They never heard of lift vans either. Even if they did know about lift vans, it wouldn't do us any good. There's no lowboy to haul our van up the hill, and there's no hoist in the Santa Fe freight yard!"

"What do we do now?"

"I've arranged everything." He was downright smug.

"You and Frank go to Santa Fe in the morning (the Schnettlers had no car). The furniture will be unpacked inside the freight car; you two sort it out. There'll be five army trucks to haul it up here. I'll take tomorrow afternoon off to receive it."

It sounded like a good plan.

Frank and I left early in the morning. We got to the first gate, and the young MP looked at my pass.

"I'm sorry, Ma'am, your pass expires today. You better get it renewed, or you won't be able to come home tonight."

We went to the pass office. Sometime later we departed for Santa Fe. I was flaming. We traveled via Pojoaque; the road was still frozen in the early morning. We spent the day in a frigid freight car, pausing only for lunch in a nearby Mexican restaurant. The temperature hovered near zero. Two truckloads of Schnettler furniture and two truckloads of Jette furniture were en route. The third Jette truckload was almost ready to leave when I sat on one of my coffee tables and broke its leg. It was the only piece of furniture damaged in the move. The van was finally empty, and we sloshed home, triumphant. I was visualizing Eric bossing the stevedores who were to unload the trucks.

When I dropped Frank in front of his apartment, there was no evidence that a furniture truck had preceded us. "I'll bet the drivers are drinking beer in Santa Fe," Frank said. "I'll go over to the hospital and pick up the baby's diapers. I can put them to soak before dinner." The new fathers washed their infant's undies; the hospital had no facilities for such activity.

When I reached our apartment, one truckload of our furniture was firmly mired down between the front entrance to the apartment and the woodlot. Eric, Jano, Alan, the GI driver, and every other man in the neighborhood were trying to shove pine boughs and pieces of wood under the wheels. Ruth Haley and Virginia Ayers were superintending the job and trying to keep assorted children out of the mess. I joined them. It didn't seem auspicious to ask who thought of unloading the truck at the front door.

Finally the GI said, "Look, why don't we leave this thing where it is? The ground will freeze tonight. I can drive it out in the morning."

Early the next morning the truck was moved to the back of the house where it could be maneuvered when the big thaw set in. There were no stevedores; they arrived after Eric had carried all the furniture from the first truck and half the stuff from the second truck up the stairs on his back—spraining it in the process. For the past two weeks he'd borne my beefs with a martyred air. After the moving venture, he repeated everything I had said and added a few choice new angles of his own.

The presence of the furniture didn't have the desired effect on Bill; he continued to brood over the implications of the extra bedroom. One of his pals across the street had a baby brother and was occasionally called from coasting to babysit. The lad enjoyed his babysitting duties, but Bill viewed the possibility of such an eventuality as a fate worse than death.

He spent long periods draped over the porch rail, watching the girls who were pushing baby carts or who were about to push them. After such baby-watching sessions, he habitually came indoors and inspected me from every angle to make sure I had no suspicious bulge. It was positively demoralizing.

Bill also developed the habit of shrieking MA! in a blood-curdling voice if he needed my attention for any small matter. It was the cry he'd used in the Outer World when he fell out of a tree or laid his scalp open. The cry always summoned me, post haste. I think it was his idea of a big joke. I warned him repeatedly, that, like the boy who cried WOLF!, he would shriek MA! once too often.

I was much concerned about his school work. The substitute teacher I met when I enrolled him in school retreated before the combined onslaught of fifth and sixth grades; another substitute was in her place. These women tried, but their teacher training was as rusty as my technical training. (All told, Bill had five different teachers, at seven different intervals, that term. Two of the hardier individuals returned to the fray for second rounds.)

The furniture ended my cat walking days; it cured Mikey's psychosis. The arrival of her favorite chair restored her self-confidence, and she became her bright, busy self. The arrival of Eric's favorite chair made a great difference in his ceiling scanning activities. He could now count the nails in comfort; the ceiling received his full attention.

The presence of my own possessions was some comfort to me, but I was bitterly lonely. I missed Eric's late day banter. I was indignant when a man from Eric's group stopped at the apartment one evening. He had an idea that wouldn't keep until morning. He and Eric let it be understood the space I occupied was more desirable than my company. Eric asked me to step out of the room for a while; I spent half an hour fuming in the bedroom. The atmosphere when we were alone was funereal enough, without such extracurricular activities.

A night or so later, Cyril Smith paid a call. I assumed he came to see Eric and rose to leave the room. I wasn't going to have Eric ask me to leave a second time.

"Don't leave, Eleanor. I stopped in to find out what you wanted to do."

"Do?" A great light dawned on me. Have Cyril and Eric cooked up a scheme to put me to work in the Tech Area? The man who went to see Dobby was working on my clearance. Eric knows I'm exhausted. I don't want to work in the Tech Area yet. I can't desert Bill when he's so disoriented.

I started to explain, "I don't want to—"

Cyril interrupted me; his expression was horrified. "That is not patriotic!!!"

My pent-up weariness, worry, loneliness, and resentment rose in a flood and deluged both of them. I discussed the events of the autumn and their effect on my well being. I expressed my opinion of living conditions in Los Alamos, particularly the fire hazards. I was sure the wives, who should be at home taking care of the children, were intimidated or encouraged to work because the penny-pinching Washington administration didn't want to build housing. I theorized that properly qualified teachers weren't hired for the same reason. I set forth my obligation to my child and finished with Eric.

"If he keeps looking at the ceiling, he's going to have a nervous breakdown. One of THOSE is enough for any family! Wild horses won't drag me into the DAMN Tech Area!!" My whole outburst was, of course, liberally punctuated with well-chosen expletives. A fulsome vocabulary is an unofficial part of engineering school curriculum.

Cyril fled. Eric was galvanized into conversational action. "Honest, darling, I didn't have any idea you were cleared to work in the Tech Area. I don't want you to work in the Tech Area. I've got enough troubles without coming home to a cold dinner. It's wonderful to come home to a cheerful fire and a good dinner. No woman who can cook like you do has any business working in the Tech Area. Look, your birthday is the 30th. I'll take my shopping day. We'll go to Santa Fe and have ourselves a time. We need a lot of things—rope, linoleum, a new shower head, and lots of things—let's make a list."

I saw Alice in the commissary the next day.

"Alice, will you tell Cyril I'm sorry I blew my stack last night?"

"He'll get over it. I told him you weren't ready to work yet. I wouldn't be working myself if my classes weren't finished before the children come home from school."

I paid calls on the way home. School was over when I reached the apartment.

Ruth Haley greeted me. "Come in, your son is here playing with Jana."

Ruth sparkled. She was a tawny blonde, a trifle shorter than I was but of approximately the same proportions. We later discovered we could wear the same clothes, which, since we moved in different circles, lent welcome variety to our wardrobes.

On that particular afternoon, I met nine-year-old Jana and five-year-old Mike. Bill said, "Hi, Ma." He and Jana continued their game.

"The grape says Eleanor Jette is NOT going to work in the Tech Area," Ruth said. Her eyes twinkled.

I laughed. News traveled fast in this isolated community.

"The grape is correct. I'm not going to work in the Tech Area."

"I'm glad you're not going to work. I work mornings; the children get home about ten minutes before I do, that's not bad—it's these occasional weekly vacations that worry me."

"Occasional weekly vacations? Why should the children have occasional weeks of vacation? Don't they have a summer vacation?" I was genuinely puzzled.

"Oh, the lugheads who planned the school system last summer thought it would encourage mothers of school age children to work if there was no long summer vacation. This school term lasts until August first. The youngsters are given an occasional week of vacation to make up for the rest of the summer vacation. Those weeks are never announced in advance so you can plan for them. Friday afternoons, the children bring home an announcement that they'll have a vacation the following week. If you work, as I do, you either lay off your job for the week or leave your children without supervision. It's a mess."

I recalled the statement in the brochure concerning nursery school care of infants of four months or more. I asked Ruth what had happened to the plan.

"It never came off, thank goodness. It's bad enough to have some mothers of nursery school-age children working. If the young ones have a sniffle and can't go to school, mothers just dump them on the neighbors if the maids don't show up. The maid service isn't particularly reliable."

We agreed it would be an excellent idea to have an adult present on the second floor of T-185 during vacation weeks. Another problem vexed me.

"There are some barracks out by the west gate; who are the unfortunate soldiers who occupy them?" I had passed the barracks several times and could see triple deck bunks from the road.

Ruth laughed. "Oh, those are the SEDs—Special Engineer Detachment. My boss is one of them, and they are packed into the barracks like sardines. In spite of the crush, they have a marvelous esprit de corps. They call themselves "The Soldiers Different." Every one of them is technically trained, but for various reasons they weren't deferred.

"Some of those boys were snatched off the draft boards and sent to various installations in the Manhattan District without the formality of basic training. I guess the army figures it's cheaper than hiring them as civilians. There aren't any privates. They're all corporals or sergeants. You should see them on parade."

I couldn't imagine any army parade in a place like Los Alamos.

Ruth reassured me. "Oh, yes, the military puts on a parade every so often to commemorate a national holiday or something. Timoshenko always leads the parade. After him comes Lieutenant Bush on his big, black horse, leading the mounted MPs who aren't on duty. The Wacs are next; they're the snappiest group in the lot.

After the Wacs come the provisional engineers and the MPs. The SEDs are at the end of the line, and then only the ones whose bosses haven't had them excused from the parade. They straggle along with a dejected air, every one of them is out of step with the guy next to him. It's quite a sight."

Ruth's vivid word picture amused me.

"Who's Timoshenko?"

"He really belongs to Sara Dawson. He's a Russian wolfhound. He ate up all her meat coupons, then deserted her to join the MPs, where the rations are unlimited. He's crazy about horses and likes to go along when the boys patrol the fences. In spite of that, Timmy keeps up his social contacts in town. If he honors you with a visit, you reciprocate with a handout."

I prepared to leave; it was time to get dinner.

"Is the current on yet? It went off when I started to vacuum after lunch."

Ruth snapped a light switch. The lamp lighted, and she shook her head.

"Lordy, those broken down diesels must be surplus from the first world war. Every time they need more power in the Tech Area, they turn off the town. All you have to do is get a maid to do the ironing, and a power failure is guaranteed." She walked to the door with me and waved a hand at her stove.

"How do you like your Black Beauty?"

"It's quite a contraption. I tried to make doughnuts the other day. I heated the grease to fry them, but when I dropped the doughnuts into it, it cooled off. The stove didn't throw enough heat to keep up the temperature. I had greasy doughnut dough all over the place. Since then, I've been using my hot plates and the electric oven."

"Keep your hand skillful with Black Beauty," Ruth cautioned. "She burns wood as well as oil. If the power fails, you leave the burner going and put some wood in the fire box to finish dinner."

"Life in the Outer World was never like this," I thought wryly, as I entered my own apartment.

January 30th dawned clear and cold. My pass didn't expire until the next day. Bill was Ruth's houseguest for the day.

"Don't worry about a thing, Chiquita," she said. "This is your birthday. Have a lovely time."

"Let's go to Santa Fe via Española today," Eric suggested.

"That's a wonderful idea." We were as excited as a pair of six-year-olds about to embark on their first train trip. We swung north at the bottom of the Hill road. The dirt road was frozen but looked to be in good condition. It wound uphill and around some curves before it leveled out. Deep ruts stretched northward. I stopped the car.

"Those ruts are too deep for us to drive in them."

"Do you suppose you could straddle them?"

"No one ever got ruled out for trying. Hang on."

I moved the car forward, astride the ruts. The ground on the side of the road was, for the most part, level. "We should have had Aunt Melinda's covered wagon for this trip," I observed. "If you don't mind, we'll take to the bushes."

"Atta girl."

The rest of the trip was without incident, except for a couple of fences and a few arroyos. Our first stop in Santa Fe was 109 East Palace Avenue. Dorothy McKibbin was the Los Alamos oracle. She knew where we could buy the things we needed and get the services we required. There was no dentist on the Hill. We both needed dental attention.

"Dr. Lord's office is in the Coronado Building. It's at the east end of this block on Palace Avenue. Tell him you're from the Hill."

"But we can't tell him we're from the Hill."

"Nonsense. The Lords have two sons in the service. Dee's a busy man, but he always makes time for Hill people."

We showed Dorothy our list of proposed purchases. She directed us to the hardware store. When we left her office, she said, "If you need anything in Santa Fe, Eleanor, and aren't able to come to town yourself, Eric can phone me. Don makes two daily trips to the Hill. He can bring whatever you want. You can send the checks back with him." Dear Dorothy.

We approached Dee Lord. He couldn't have been nicer. He took care of Eric's small emergency with dispatch and made an appointment for me. We went to the hardware store.

We went through our list—$90's worth. When we reached

"showerhead," the clerk said, "I have just the thing for you." She produced a hard plastic showerhead.

Eric examined it. "Will the plastic stand up against very hot water?"

"We've sold hundreds of those since Los Alamos started. From what I hear, they stand up against live steam. We haven't had a single complaint."

We exchanged glances and meekly added the showerhead to our purchases. "How did you know?" I whispered.

"You're wearing a hat."

I made a mental note to put my hats in cold storage.

The linoleum was poor grade, but an inoffensive pattern. We bought a can of Tiger Grip and a linoleum knife. We lunched on Shrimp Louisiane a la Conrad at La Fonda. It wasn't as good as the one I prepared with fresh shrimp in Croton, but Croton was a thousand years ago.

After lunch we wandered about hunting for a liquor store that would sell us some whiskey. It wasn't that the liquor stores didn't want to sell whiskey; most of them didn't have any. The allocations for liquor, as well as other commodities, were made on the basis of the pre-war population of Santa Fe and the wartime population at Bruns Hospital.

The Lost Almosts, as we occasionally wryly referred to ourselves, weren't part of the world of Santa Fe and Bruns Hospital; there were no allocations for us. We were all expert foragers.

When we took our first shopping trip, we wanted to repay in kind the hospitality showered on us during our first month. We could buy rum almost everywhere, but our friends preferred whiskey. We hunted until we found the newly-opened Washington Avenue Liquor Store, operated by Whit and Pat Whittington. We bought their entire stock of whiskey—four bottles. We also bought some rum, just in case we ran out of the favored beverage before we returned to town.

We locked our liquor supply in the car and strolled along San Francisco Street familiarizing ourselves with the stores. We stopped to look in a store window. I had the sensation I was watched and glanced over my shoulder. I poked Eric with my elbow.

"Look, the little man who isn't there."

He nodded. A young man with a snap-brim hat was studying the window of the store we just passed. We retreated to La Cantina for a drink before we started home.

The return trip was uneventful until we left Española and started south on the dirt road. The morning's frozen ruts were mud-pie consistency. After we crossed Santa Clara Creek, there was a slight upgrade. We got part way up it and slid back. We backed up and accelerated the car to gain momentum, but it was no use. Eric stepped out into the mud, wearing his going-to-town clothes, to put on the chains. A small crowd of Santa Clara Indians were gathered to watch our attempts to get up the hill. They gave a faint cheer when we crested the rise.

Buying linoleum and attaching it to the floor were two different matters. My carpenter friend didn't know anyone who laid linoleum. Sergeant Baker was also at a loss. The linoleum was going to be laid on the bathroom floor come hell or high water. I unrolled it in the spare bedroom to let it flatten out and borrowed some old Denver papers from Ruth to cut patterns around the bathroom fixtures.

I fastened the patterns to the linoleum and tried to cut around them, but it was too dull. The kitchen scissors worked much better. An attempted fitting disclosed the fact that there should be seams behind the toilet and water pipes. I cut them and laid the unglued linoleum on the floor. I struggled with the linoleum all that day. In the evening, we held a family council; the linoleum must be glued to the floor. Otherwise, it might slip or water might collect under it.

The next morning, I donned a pair of ancient slacks and a tattered shirt. I wrapped an old dishtowel over my hair and threw Mikey out the front door. Armed with the kitchen spatula, the Tiger Grip clutched firmly under my left arm, I slithered under the linoleum.

An hour later, I emerged, feet first. There was enough Tiger Grip under the linoleum to hold it firmly until eternity. I was soaked with perspiration and panting. I didn't dare lean against the wall to catch my breath. Had I done so, I'd have adhered to the wall until Eric came home from the Tech Area to chisel me off. Our linoleum was a sensation.

4

e were unable to buy two important items on the list we took to Santa Fe, a doormat and the rope for our proposed fire escape. I wrote to the senior auntie in Denver. Our need for a doormat was easy to explain without offending the censors, but I was sure they would object if I continued my letter: "Will you also send fifty feet of good stout rope? We live on the second floor of a firetrap built of green, pitch-filled lumber and clapboard. The stairs are over the furnace room where the fire would probably originate."

The Haleys were enthusiastic about the idea of an escape rope. Jano suggested we could buy it at Bond and Nohl in Española, a ranchers supply store. I went to Española early one morning and returned triumphant. We secured the rope firmly so it would be ready for action if we needed to get out the window. Two other things transpired to allay my fear that the apartment might become our funeral pyre.

The army engineers finished venting the apartment furnaces to the great outdoors. We could now close the ducts in the apartment. The outdoor vents expelled the excess hot air above the apartment coal boxes. It became a common sight, even on the coldest day, to see a woman sitting on the coal box of an apartment drying her hair.

To further ensure our safety, I waylaid our furnace man and greeted him in my shaky Castilian Spanish,

"Buenos dias, Señor. ¿Como esta usted?"

He was enchanted and inundated me with a flood of archaic Spanish, the language of the conquistadors. We became *muy simpatico*. He didn't realize he was putting too much coal on the fire and would correct the mistake immediately. He was a nice man. Like most Spanish Americans he had an inborn sense of courtesy. He knocked on my door at regular intervals to inquire as to the climate in the apartment. The danger of us going up in smoke receded.

I became aware of other matters, ones over which I had no control. The number of blasts on the fire siren indicated the location of a fire, whether it was in the town or Tech Area. One day the fire siren sounded while we were at lunch. Eric blanched and laid down his fork. He half rose from the table but sank back with a sigh of relief when the siren signaled a fire in the town.

In Chicago I began to suspect Eric was going to work with radioactive material at Los Alamos. The elaborate health checks the men in his group were subjected to confirmed my suspicion. I didn't know whether Eric's fear of fire in the Tech Area stemmed from the fact radioactive materials might contaminate the Tech Area and town or the fact that it might destroy irreplaceable equipment. Even in early 1944, an air of desperate urgency emanated from the Tech Area.

It was time for us to get New Mexico plates for the car.

"You'll have to have a New Mexico driver's license, too," Eric said.

"What's the matter with my New York license? It has two years to run."

"The personnel people want everyone to have New Mexico licenses. It won't hurt you to have two licenses. Here, I brought you an application. The personnel office will get the plates and driver's license for us."

Some days later, Eric came home bearing the license plates and my driver's license. I took one look at the license. We laughed until tears ran down our cheeks. My name was "44," my resident address was "Special List B," and my usual signature was "not required."

We examined the car registration. I was Number 268, and my resident address was Special List A. I had joined the secret society whose membership was closely guarded. Thus, I later became Number 9 for income tax purposes, and when the laundry service was resuscitated, I was Number 464. We were numbered for everything except our ration books, and the numbers were never the same. The ration board was not amenable to security's nebulous reasonings. Our official address was Box 1663, Santa Fe, and we had to get our ration books in Santa Fe; it was a pleasure to use our own

	STATE OF NEW MEXICO **444**

OPERATOR'S LICENSE No.

	FIRST NAME	MIDDLE OR MAIDEN NAME	LAST NAME
FULL NAME	Number 44		

	NUMBER	STREET
RESIDENT ADDRESS	Special List B	

CITY OR POST OFFICE	Santa Fe.

DATE OF BIRTH	SEX	COLOR OF EYES	HEIGHT	RESTRICTIONS
1/30/07	Fem	Blue	5'4" IN.	

WEIGHT	COMPLEXION	COLOR OF HAIR	OCCUPATION
110 LBS.	Med.	brown	Housewife

USUAL SIGNATURE   Not required

THIS LICENSE IS ISSUED IN ACCORDANCE WITH CHAPTER 110 OF THE SESSION LAWS OF 1937 AS AMENDED AND MUST BE IN IMMEDIATE POSSESSION OF LICENSEE WHEN OPERATING A MOTOR VEHICLE.

THIS LICENSE EXPIRES DEC. 31, 1944

J. O. GALLEGOS   DIRECTOR
COMMISSIONER OF REVENUE   DRIVER'S LICENSE DIVISION

Eleanor's New Mexico driver's license

names. We often wondered what would happen if, perchance, we drove into another state and were stopped for an infraction of the law. We'd doubtless land in the local pokey.

The winter wore on. There was lots of snow. Everyone was happy about the snowstorms; they would, we hoped, raise the level of the water table. Plenty of moisture lessened the ever-present threat of fire. The *Bulletin* continued to carry a tag line:

REPORT LEAKY FAUCETS IMMEDIATELY!

I turned on the cold water tap in the kitchen one morning and leapt for my life when it erupted with hissing steam and boiling water. When it simmered down, I approached it gingerly and turned it off. Later in the morning I moved in cautiously on the faucet's flank, where I was sure to be out of the line of fire. I turned it on and cold water flowed. It refused to budge when I tried to turn it off. I took the wrench out of Eric's toolbox and throttled it. I had no washers, and the valves for the water lines were in the furnace room which was locked to keep the apartment occupants from turning down the furnace controls. At lunch I asked Eric to report the jammed faucet as

65

soon as he went back to the Tech Area. No plumber arrived. Eric called repair service twice a day for the next six weeks; Ruth Haley called every morning. There was still no plumber. I carried cold water from the Haley kitchen, which was closer to our kitchen than our own bathroom.

I was thoroughly exasperated. The kitchen faucet was the last straw. The civilian pass system was not yet changed. I spent a full morning every two weeks getting a new temporary pass. The darn things always expired just when I had a ride to Santa Fe.

Finally, one morning after a previous day's hassle in the pass office, I said, "I'm going to find myself a cozy nook in Santa Fe if something isn't done about that faucet. I'm not going to carry any more water."

Eric emerged from his metallurgical fog with an unhappy face.

"They yap, yap, yap, REPORT LEAKY FAUCETS IMMEDIATELY!" I continued. "I turned ours off so it wouldn't leak, and what happened? Nothing!"

Eric's face cleared. "I have an idea. I'll call repair service and tell them I'm going to open the faucet with a wrench and let it run until they get here!"

The plumber was in the apartment before we sat down to lunch at noon. He couldn't understand why he received the repair order, dated six weeks previously, only that morning.

In the evenings the Hill dwellers gathered in groups. Dick Feynman's private war with the censors provided much-needed comic relief from the tensions generated by the Tech Area. Dick was married to his childhood sweetheart, and she was in a sanitarium in Albuquerque, a victim of tuberculosis.

The censorship rule that prohibited the use of codes, ciphers, and such provided Dick with a fertile field of operation. He and his young wife corresponded in code. Their method of communication entertained and distracted her, but it almost drove our censors crazy. Dick was on the carpet at regular intervals. He always gave his inquisitors the key to the current Feynman code. The Feynmans then waited just long enough for the censors to break it and switched to other systems of cryptography.

We discussed our former lives in the Outer World and our

66

adventures prior to our arrival, or after, while we sipped our rum. The Potratzes, who lived west of us on the north road, arrived from Denver University about two weeks after we did. Their trip to Los Alamos was uneventful, but the afternoon after their arrival was windy. A tall pine tree in front of their house was uprooted; it missed the cars in front of the apartment but landed in the master bedroom. When I heard their story, I wondered if Bill's bed would follow Eric out the window if we had occasion to use our fire rope.

The evening gatherings speculated about the cause of the steam and hot water that spouted from our cold water faucets. We decided that the brochure's innocent remark, "There is ample hot water constantly," was an understatement. We knew that plastic gaskets on the hot water lines melted away, but we never did figure out how the army got the lines hooked up so the hot water came out of the cold water faucets. Hans Staub, wiry and Swiss born, summed up the problem in salty language, with an inimitable accent. "Jesus Christ! Where else in the United States of America can you flush the toilet with live steam?"

For Eric, there were unforgettable evenings of music. His was the only cello in town, and he was in constant demand. The Manleys, Weisskopfs, and some others brought their pianos with them to Los Alamos. The Manleys and Weisskopfs lived in the same apartment house. Kay Manley directed the choral society, and Victor Weisskopf enjoyed chamber music. They tried to plan their musical activities on separate evenings, but there were occasional slip-ups that resulted in interesting tonal effects and frayed tempers.

There was, of course, no professional piano tuner on the Hill. The piano players tuned their own instruments as best they could. The results were not always satisfactory, but they were much better than one might expect. Otto Frisch, of the British Mission, could coax Mozart's heavenly melodies from the most ill-tuned instrument.

Otto performed regularly for the local radio station, which was an offshoot of the town communication system. The absence of telephones in the homes made it necessary for the authorities to devise a means to communicate with the town residents over the radio. The power lines served in place of an antenna and confined the broadcast to our immediate locality.

Otto Frisch in Fuller Lodge playing KRS' first remote broadcast

Devoted volunteers made broadcasts and played records from the collections of the assembled scientists over the communications system. When the announcer said, "Otto will now play Mozart's C Major Sonata" or some other Mozart selection, you knew you were getting a real, live broadcast.

At our evening meetings, we pan-fried the Washington administration and the restrictions on our lives. We agreed that Our General occupied an unenviable position behind a large eight ball. (It had to be large. He was a plump general.) But there was no excuse for the way matters were handled. One man said, "I was on the committee that planned this laboratory. I thought, when we planned it, we should plan for a town of five thousand people. I was almost laughed off the Hill when I suggested it, but I still think we're going to need it."

Every time any one of us went to Santa Fe, we heard a different rumor about what the people down there thought we were doing at Los Alamos. We wondered if we could elude security long enough to start a rumor that we were manufacturing the front ends of horses to be shipped to Washington for completion.

We seized any conversational gambit available to divert the men from the grim atmosphere in the Tech Area and divert everyone from the even grimmer war in the Outer World. I disinterred my great, great Aunt Melinda who lived until I was thirteen and was my favorite ancestor.

Before she died, at a great age, she held Preston and me enthralled with tales of her adventures when she pioneered the West in '49 with her husband, a shadowy character named Mr. Mac. Preston and I never did learn Mr. Mac's first name, although I suppose it was on his headstone. We gathered that Aunt Melinda never quite forgave Mr. Mac when he pushed into the mountains to seek gold instead of staking out a homestead at the confluence of Cherry Creek and the Platte River. When I was a child, the Denver City Hall stood on the site Aunt Melinda wanted to homestead.

My grandfather handled Aunt Melinda's business for her. She was a shrewd woman and caused him much difficulty. When Grandfather knew Aunt Melinda was displeased with him, he placated her with White Owl cigars. Her obituary occupied a full page when she passed away. It concluded, ". . . she was a familiar figure, moving about in her garden smoking her corncob pipe or black cigar."

When my redheaded mother read the obituary, she was fit to be tied, but Aunt Melinda made a wonderful conversation piece.

When I interviewed Eric about his work, years later, he said, "Aunt Melinda and her forty-niner adventures gave us fits. The name plutonium was seldom used in the Tech Area; we always called it *forty-nine*."

Sometimes the evening gatherings had a different complexion. The Haleys and Ayres belonged to a square dance group; they persuaded us to join it. The men took turns and checked the children every half hour. Under Ruth's tutelage, I stitched the necessary squaw dress (an easy blouse and full skirt). I lacked the heavy Indian jewelry to complete the costume, but Ruth lent me her excess pieces until Eric corrected the matter.

The square dance group was catholic in composition. Badge colors and lack of badges were forgotten. Everyone who worked in the Tech Area wore a badge. No one could enter or leave the Tech

Area without his badge, and the color of the badge indicated the extent of his clearance. White badges were fully cleared. Some people deluded themselves with the idea the color of a badge indicated the individual's social standing. The square dancers dismissed the badges as unimportant. We happily do-si-doed and promenaded to George Hillhouse's call.

Eric and I didn't go to any of the dorm dances that winter. They were the offshoots of the "regular dances arranged by the dormitory association," mentioned in the brochure. The dorm dances were not arranged by the dormitory association. The individual dormitories hosted them. Each individual who lived in the dormitory that gave the dance was allowed to invite six to eight guests. The individual host was responsible for the liquor and refreshment of his guests.

We weren't acquainted with any dormitory dwellers, so naturally we weren't invited to the dances. We had plenty of other things to occupy our free time, though. Our borrowing basket was in constant circulation. The newcomers peopled our easy chairs and warmed themselves in front of our fire while they waited for their own things to arrive.

In the afternoons, the women occasionally had tea parties. My closest friends, for the most part, were women in the older age group; most of them were in their thirties. We were the mothers of school children. There were only a handful of women older than we were. A couple of these women came to the Hill to take care of their bachelor sons.

Some of the wives of the scientific staff worked mornings and others taught school. I don't recall that any army wives worked; there seemed to be no pressure on them to do so. Several of my friends quietly quit jobs in the Tech Area after I refused to work. Jean Bacher commented that it was nice to have time to cook for her family. We always had a good time. We visited about our children and discussed our common housekeeping problems. Martha Parsons was generous in offering use of her bathtub if, on occasion, anyone felt she just had to have a good soak.

The Parsons lived at the north end of Bathtub Row, just across the street from Kitty and Robert Oppenhiemer. I didn't meet William Parsons, known as Deak, until later in the spring, but I gathered that he was associate director of the laboratory. Since I was under the illusion that he was an army officer, I was puzzled, because Eric told me, when we were in Croton, that the army had no voice in the work of the laboratory.

Usually I did my housework and washing and gadded around town while Bill was in school. The housework was a cinch after the big house in Croton. Vera Williams, the wife of John Williams, and Anita Martinez presided over the housing office and maid service. Anita was the wife of Popovi Da, son of the illustrious *Maria, The Potter of San Ildefonso* (the famous book by Alice Marriott). They had an excess of maids and saw to it that I got girls fairly regularly to iron the shirts and do the dirty work. There was always a fifty-fifty chance the power would be cut off when a girl came to iron, but, as Helen Allison said later, "One must rise above such things."

There were two community laundries. Each laundry was equipped with four washing machines and wringers, and there were two mangles in the laundry I used. A power failure when you were doing the family washing was a matter of considerable annoyance. If the clothes were in the rinse water, you could take them out and wring the heavy sheets and towels by hand. If they were in the wash

PRICES

WASHERS   30¢ Hour
MANGLES   40¢ Hour
Elec. Irons   30¢ Hour
Patrons must wash tub
after using
DO NOT CROWD
WRINGERS

water you had to stand by to finish the washing when the power was turned on, as it usually was at lunch time. One couldn't just go away and leave a machine full of wash until after lunch. Even at that early date, there were always women waiting for the machines.

My peregrinations around the town disclosed that the Wacs were billeted in a couple of the apartment houses. Another apartment house was given over to a firm of architects for use as drafting rooms. The resident janitorial help and their families were all housed in apartments.

It was late winter. The snow from a blizzard a couple of days before was still on the ground, but the morning was clear and cold. I bundled the family washing into the car and hurried to the laundry to get it finished before the Tech Area got rolling and took all the available power. I finished the wash and hurried home to hang it on the line before the thaw. The morning was uneventful. After lunch, I put on my galoshes and went to take the clothes off the line. With every step I sank deeper into the mire; I plucked the last article from the line and prepared to carry the basket to the steps. The basket, resting on a piece of newspaper, was safe, but I was firmly stuck in the mud. I abandoned the clothes basket, pulled my feet out of my shoes and galoshes, and yanked my footwear out of the mud. I waded to the steps and deposited them before I returned for the basket.

It took an hour to clean the thick adobe mud from my person, wipe up the floor, and extract my shoes from the galoshes without ruining them. My thoughts were black.

"Why couldn't the blasted army lay some slat walks around the apartments and under the clothes lines? It wouldn't cost much."

I sorted the clothes. A pair of my underpants were badly ripped, but I didn't recall even a small rip when I hung them on the line. I examined the rip closely; it was made with a knife blade. The school children had a shortcut between our apartment and the one to the east of us. The boys were forever slashing at any handy object with their penknives. I blasted them mentally and tossed my underpants into my sewing basket in disgust.

A few days later, a young man with a snap-brim hat knocked on my back door. When I opened it, I thought, "Uh-oh, Jean's letter has come home to roost." I mentally consigned myself to Alcatraz or whatever select spot the army sent people who received letters like hers.

The young man flashed his credentials. "May I come in, Ma'am?"

Certainly he could come in; there was no way for me to keep him out. We seated ourselves in the living room. He asked my name and the color of my husband's badge. He noted these matters in his notebook while I wondered why, if he was there about Jean's letter, he didn't know my name.

"Your house overlooks the woodlot, Mrs. Jette. A very disturbing incident occurred out there." He named a date, and I tried to connect it with a day.

"What sort of an incident?"

"A group of pre-school girls were playing in front of the apartment beyond the next house. A man tried to coax a three-year-old into the tool shed in the woodlot, but fortunately, the child balked. One quick-thinking little girl ran to call her mother. The man was gone when the mother reached the scene and no harm was done, but it's unthinkable that such a person should roam free in a restricted community like this one. The children concerned were unable to give a coherent description of the man. I hoped you might have seen something that would furnish us with a clue to his identity."

I thought. The date he named was the day I washed. I had noticed nothing unusual. True, I got stuck in the mud, but— Then I recalled my slashed underpants. I took them out of my sewing basket and handed them to him. We contemplated them with silent horror.

"The school children have a shortcut between this apartment and the next," I explained weakly. "I thought one of the school boys was just slashing at something with his penknife."

He shook his head. "No school boy's penknife mutilated this garment. We've just got to find this creature. Will you put these away unmended? We may need them for evidence."

"Do you suppose it was one of the workmen?" I asked.

"Who knows? The army takes the young men from their homes and puts them into uniforms. They're sent here, where they don't have the normal recreation facilities available in other army camps.

There isn't a chapel or even an army chaplain to whom a troubled lad could turn. The altitude and isolation alone might be enough to push a person with latent psychotic tendencies over the edge. Even the most careful screening doesn't always disclose such tendencies. Whoever it is, we have to find him." He got up to leave.

"Do you think your next door neighbor might have seen anything?" he asked hopefully.

"I'm afraid not. She works mornings, and I took my clothes off the line immediately after lunch."

His eyebrows rose. "That means you're alone up here during the mornings. We've put a stout padlock on the tool shed and given the key to the foreman, who is exceedingly reliable. I suggest that you keep your front door locked."

"We don't want this matter discussed," he added. "Talk about the incident might warn the man that we're hunting for him, or it might cause a panic in town. We'll appreciate it if you'll report anything unusual that you see or hear."

He gave me detailed instructions as to how to contact him at any hour and left.

I sat in my own living room and stared out the window at the beautiful, snow-covered landscape. There was an abandoned log cabin on the potrero to the north. Its vacant window stared back at me. Cold chills ran up and down my spine.

The chills weren't for myself. I wondered what horror might have been perpetrated if the child hadn't balked or the other little girl hadn't run for her mother. The next child might not be so fortunate, but security didn't want the matter discussed.

I resolved to take my revolver out of the storeroom. I had had it stored with the aunties in Denver, but when we came to New Mexico, I dug it out of storage and brought it with me. It was a beautifully balanced side arm. I could buy gun oil to clean it and bullets in Española. What was even more important, I was a very good shot.

Mikey purred comfortingly in my lap while I thought. I picked her up and rubbed my cheek against her silky fur while I whispered to her.

"I suppose the man is right. Maybe they'll find that monster soon. I thought from the way the man talked that they thought he was one of the army boys. Maybe they know more than they led me to believe. A panic would disrupt the Tech Area, and over there they say they're working to end the Pacific War. Your Unkey Preston is still doing business at the old APO number stand, but, like a lot of other women's beloved men, he's got to land someplace. We'd like them to get finished with what they're doing over there in Tech Area before that happens, wouldn't we, little pussycat?"

It was twenty-one hundred miles from Eniwetok to Tokyo. I lowered Mikey gently into my chair when I stood up. It was time to fix lunch.

A few days after my interview with the young man in the snap-brim hat, Gus arrived on one of his consulting trips. I was delighted to see him. He was full of news from the Outer World and had stored up a whole bagful of amusing incidents to entertain me. After dinner, the Smiths, Seybolts, and some other people from the division joined us, and we had a delightful evening.

When the others left, and Gus was preparing to go, he said to Eric, "You're doing a wonderful job here."

"I just hope we're on the right track," Eric replied.

"If your progress is to be gauged by the number of nails you've counted, and the mountains of matches you've consumed, it ought to be phenomenal," I said tartly.

"If we could only tell you about it, Eleanor, you would understand and appreciate the job Eric's doing," Gus said. "And now, my dear, is there anything I can do for you when I go back to New York?"

I replied promptly. "Yes, you can send me a box of Barricini Miniatures. They're my favorite candies."

The miniatures arrived, hard on the heels of Gus's return to New York. I received a box of Barricini Miniatures every six weeks throughout the war years, weather permitting. No candy was ever savored with more appreciation. Gus was right about Eric's work, too. When Eric finally told me about it, it seemed that plutonium must have been "an enigma wrapped in mystery." They knew they wouldn't have enough of it to do a decent experiment for months. It must have been maddening to have to guess at its properties and behavior and experiment only with elements they thought resembled it.

They must have asked themselves constantly, "Will the techniques we're developing with these other elements really be effective with plutonium?"

Spring was in the air when Bill came home one afternoon. He was excited.

"Gee, Ma, there's going to be a PTA meeting tonight. Our teacher wants us all to get our parents to go so we can get the high score for the school."

"A PTA meeting, here?"

Bill assented vigorously. I couldn't imagine anyplace where a PTA could be of less use. The school board was a formality. It had no authority and no money to spend, or at least no money to spend for extracurricular activities. The string of substitute teachers for the fifth and sixth grades marched on. Bill was rapidly forgetting the things he learned in the fourth grade, but there was no use fussing. If I could make him happy by attending the PTA meeting, it was worthwhile.

Eric took a dim view of PTA meetings, so he and Jano Haley stayed home to make sure the children weren't incinerated while Ruth and I attended the meeting.

The turnout for the meeting was surprisingly large. The chairman requested the secretary to read the minutes of the previous meeting. The possible polio epidemic of 1943 was discussed as past business. The departure of the school principal and his wife, Bill's expected teacher, was deplored. The projected spring potluck supper was current business.

Julian Mack, the head of the photographic section, brought up the lack of interest in community activities evidenced by our Spanish American residents.

It was true that only two Spanish American families were represented at the meeting. The men of those families had both worked for the Los Alamos Ranch School, and they had stayed to work on the Hill after the army took possession of the property. The Gonzales and Martinez families were the stalwarts of the Spanish American community at Los Alamos. Bences Gonzales represented his family. He and his wife had three robust sons, one of them in the service, and three diminutive daughters. The Johnny Martinez family had one son, Bobby, who was in the fifth grade.

Julian was appointed to head the potluck supper committee, and he called a meeting to explore ways to promote community relations. Much to our surprise, Ruth and I were both elected to the committee. I think Martha Parsons was responsible. We were to serve with Julian, Bences, and Johnny and Pilar Martinez. There must have been two other people on that committee, too, but I can't for the life of me remember who they were. A date was set for our first meeting.

When Ruth and I got home, Eric and Jano were sipping drinks.

"Well, girls, how did it go?"

"The fifth and sixth grades had a fine turnout," I announced.

"We got put on a committee," Ruth added.

"What kind of a committee?" Eric inquired. He was always apprehensive when I was appointed to a committee.

"Julian Mack thought the Spanish Americans on the Hill needed encouragement to participate in community affairs. Ruth and I, along with Bences, Johnny, and Pilar, are on his potluck supper committee. He's called a meeting to explore ways to promote inter-American relations on the Hill."

"Oh, for God's sake!" Jano clutched his head. "Doesn't Julian know that the Catholic Church has been trying to get the Spanish Americans to accept the Anglos ever since the pioneers came to New Mexico a hundred years ago? Up until these last few years, even the schools were taught in Spanish. Today, New Mexico is the only state in the union with a bilingual ballot. We live at a faster tempo than the Spanish Americans, and they resent Anglo competition. The Spanish Americans and the Indians have feuded ever since the Conquistadors invaded New Mexico—they still do—but today they'll stand together to fight Anglo ideas of progress. Bences and his family and Johnny and Pilar have worked with Anglos and are interested in community affairs, but you'll never get the others to cooperate."

"If you've finished your oration, you can fix us a nightcap," Ruth said. "Eleanor and I will attend to the inter-American relations."

"I'll bet you will," Eric murmured.

On the night of the committee meeting, Ruth and I sallied forth.

Ruth was wearing a broomstick skirt and some of her Indian jewelry, so she could lend the proper atmosphere to the meeting. We were both recipients of much gratuitous husbandly advice. When we arrived at the Mack house, Bences, Johnny, and Pilar were already there.

After a few minutes, the committee was assembled, and Julian called it to order. We pondered ways to persuade the two racial groups to intermingle.

"Let's have a fiesta!" Ruth suggested.

"What a wonderful idea! Everyone will turn out for a fiesta," said Pilar.

"We had a fiesta every year when the school was here," Bences said.

"There are always fiestas in the pueblos on saint's days. Don't we have a patron saint?" I asked.

"San Antonio de Padua is the Los Alamos patron saint; his day is June 13th," Bences said. "We should have our fiesta on our saint's day."

"If we have a fiesta, we'll have to plan some sort of program," Julian warned.

"I'll make sopaipillas. I always made them for the school fiestas," Bences offered.

"Oooh, yummy!"

Ruth came up with another of her red-hot ideas. "Let's have a Gallos!" The Gallos was to New Mexico what the bullfight was to Old Mexico. Spanish American eyes sparkled.

"I began to learn to ride the Gallos when I was ten years old. I just got to the place where I was a good enough horseman to take part, and it was banned," Johnny said.

"It was a shame," said Pilar. "The Humane Society had them banned throughout New Mexico."

"That won't make any difference; we're not part of the state. This is a federal reservation," someone announced.

"Just what is a Gallos?" Julian asked. He sounded a trifle apprehensive.

Ruth began to explain. "You find a level place and bury a chicken up to its neck in sand. There are two teams; each team has four horsemen. The teams line up on opposite sides of the chicken and take turns. They spur their horses into a gallop and try to snatch the chicken from the sand."

"There's plenty of room out in the alfalfa field in front of Fuller Lodge," Bences said.

"It's the same idea as grabbing the ring on a merry-go-round, but the chicken doesn't cooperate. It keeps moving its head back and forth," Ruth said, by way of further clarification.

Johnny chimed in. "Finally, someone on one team or the other gets the chicken and gallops away with it. The others chase him."

"The horsemanship is magnificent!" Ruth exclaimed.

I could close my eyes and see the bright colors worn by the riders. I could almost hear the thunder of the horses' hooves.

"But how do they tell which team wins?" Julian asked.

"Oh, that's easy," Ruth and Johnny chorused. "The team that brings back the biggest piece of chicken wins!"

I stole a covert glance at Julian. He was a delicate shade of green. He hastily adjourned the meeting. Our committee never met again, and henceforth, all business of the potluck supper committee was carried on via the grapevine.

os Alamos was like a giant ant hill. The atom bomb was its queen and the Tech Area was her nest. The queen's demands for nourishment were unceasing, but on Sundays she dozed and the workers fanned out to explore the countryside. They visited the neighboring pueblos and investigated the cliff dwellings which were to be found on the south faces of almost every potrero.

Many men from the pueblos of San Ildefonso, Santa Clara, and Tesuque worked on the Hill. The women worked in our homes as maids, and we visited their homes and met their families. There was abundant evidence of the grinding poverty that had oppressed the pueblos for centuries. I realized that even the meager wages the maids received were riches to most of them.

The pueblos had dances both winter and summer to commemorate special seasons of the year, and they always danced on their saint's day. On the saint's day, we watched the drummers summon our Indian friends from Mass. They carried the image of their patron saint to an evergreen bower to watch over them while they danced the dances that came down to them from their ancestors' antiquity. Drama throbbed, and feet shuffled the pattern of the dance in the four directions.

Eric was fascinated by the rhythm of the dance patterns and tried repeatedly to count the number of drum beats in each dance movement. He was never successful, although on one occasion he counted sequences of steps with something like seven, twelve, and nineteen in each before he lost track. We were warned before we went to any of the religious dances that it was a breach of etiquette to ask any questions about their symbolism. The reserved silence that followed the questions put by tourists emphasized the warning.

To prepare for our Sunday cliff dwelling investigations, we borrowed some books about the archaeology of the region from Alice and Cyril. After we read the books we braved the muddy mountain road to Frijoles Canyon to consult the rangers about our projected outings. By that time, I was a veteran of many mud holes, and a few inches of goo on the road didn't faze me.

Before the snow was off the ground on the Hill, the potreros that jutted out at the base of the Pajarito Plateau were dry, and we set forth on our adventures. The cliff dwellings were, of course, primitive in comparison with those built into the towering cliffs at Mesa Verde, or even the ones in Frijoles Canyon, but they were plenty good enough for amateurs. We competed with our friends for views of plumed serpents.

The team of Jette and Jette suffered under a serious handicap. I was afraid of heights. Reason told me that my fear was nonsense, but it was as real as my breath. I lectured myself mentally.

"Come on now, Ellie, this little cliff is only ten feet high. When you had to fly, you flew and enjoyed it. You'll enjoy climbing, too, but you have to do it first."

Similar self-lectures got me into the caves, but it almost took a blasting charge to get me out of them. We finally worked out a scheme of exploration, but it was applicable only if the cave was accessible from the talus slope. Eric knelt, and I climbed from his knee to his shoulders. I steadied myself against the face of the cliff while he slowly raised himself to his feet. If the cave was at eye level, and there was nothing to be seen, I was lowered by the same method. If there was something to be seen, or if the cave level was above my eye level, I threw my arms across the lip and shimmied into it with Eric boosting me from below. No scheme is foolproof; there were occasional mishaps, such as the one when I was about to heave myself into the upper half of a duplex cave and the floor collapsed.

The caves that were accessible from the slopes didn't bother me too much; the caves we reached from ledges or by toeholds on the cliffs were my undoing. I never screwed up courage for the toeholds, but I'll never forget one of our visits to Tsankawi. There, centuries of moccasined feet wore a deep path in the soft rock that sloped up to the cleft through which one gained access to the top of the potrero. At the entrance to the cleft, a well-preserved pictograph of a warrior reminded us that the ancient inhabitants chose the location because it was eminently defensible.

We wandered about on top of the potrero and examined evidence of the former inhabitants' ceremonial life before we started to explore the caves, which opened off a twenty-inch ledge across the south cliff of the potrero. There was a bend in the face of the cliff, and the ledge followed it. When we reached the bend, I paused with my customary caution and peered around it. The ledge was sheared off and in rubble a hundred feet below. I gasped and clung to the face of the cliff. Eric cautiously edged his way around me to see what reduced me to jelly before he took my wrist and led me to safety.

After those Sundays, it was difficult to remember that men were dying every instant on the far-flung battle fronts of the Outer World. It seemed incredible that the Red Tide was lapping at the foot of the Carpathians and bombs were again falling on London. The battle for Cassino, where the 5th Army and New Zealanders were met with stone wall resistance, was a single scene in a world gone mad. Even the reality of Japanese violence receded, although it was attested to by pictures of exhausted men who fought on Eniwetok and pictures of crosses for those who fell on Tarawa. The Outer World was as remote as another planet.

Even our own closely-guarded world, queened by the atom bomb, which was unknown to all of us except the white badge workers, was less formidable. The Tech Area with its guarded gate, its silences, and its secrecies was less ominous.

Spring brought wind. The wind evaporated the remaining snow and dried the ground to a parched khaki color. It swirled small twisters of dust into the rooms through opened windows, and ears were sensitive to changes in barometric pressures. Housekeeping was a discouraging chore, but there were occasional respites. One quiet morning, I polished the apartment, fixed lunch, and went outdoors to sit on the top step and enjoy the sunshine.

My ears clicked, and I glanced over my shoulder. The tops of the Jemez peaks were wrapped in a rolling brown cloud. I ran into the house and slammed the windows shut. Five minutes later a howling, shrieking dust storm enveloped the town. Windows rattled and houses shook. The storm was over in as many minutes as it took to reach its gritty fingers down from the mountain tops, but we could write on any table top.

I traced some doggerel in the center of the lunch table.

> In spring, great winds blow
> Sacred desert of Navajo
> Over the Mountains,
> And into the room
> Where it lies in peace,
> Till you get the broom!

The nonsense took the curse off lunch, which was full of sand.

Spring awakened the rattlesnakes on the lower potreros and suspended our cave explorations. I was secretly relieved that it was no longer safe to throw my arms across the lip of a cave to hoist myself into it. Such a maneuver now might disturb a rattler who was enjoying a siesta in the spring sunshine.

The lower potreros and the White Rock Canyon of the Rio Grande were alive with rattlesnakes. One Sunday some of the MPs went fishing down in White Rock and met a snake that was six feet long. We knew they weren't telling snake stories because they killed it and hung it outside the east guard gate.

There were two schools of thought as to whether there were rattlesnakes on the Hill. I belonged to the school that believed it was not too high for snakes. The altitude was only 7,200 feet; I'd seen rattlesnakes at 8,500 feet in Colorado. They weren't very peppy, but they could strike. I bought a snake bite kit in Santa Fe—it only cost a dollar, a small price to pay for peace of mind. The container was in a small rubber case that you could drop in your pocket; it contained a razor blade, a vial of potassium permanganate, and a tourniquet. The top of the case was a suction cup.

I breathed easier after I bought the kit. I was positive there were snakes in the woodlot where Bill and the other children in the neighborhood played. They crawled in and out of the town fence through a hole that was hidden by a pile of wood, and rattlesnakes loved woodpiles.

The hole in the fence worried me for another reason. It gave the youngsters access to the steep canyon just north of town, and there was always the danger that one of them might try to climb down the sheer walls, lose his grip, and fall.

I waylaid one of the MPs.

"Why don't you boys mend that hole?" I asked. "My youngster and the boys he plays with use it constantly. One of them might fall into a canyon."

"It wouldn't do to mend the holes, Ma'am. Everyone in town has his favorite hole in the fence, and if we closed them up, they'd either find others or make them. They wouldn't be boys unless they did. We know where the holes are and which boys use them. We keep our eyes on them." He smiled reassuringly.

The MP was right, of course. I resigned myself to Bill's illegal expeditions but made sure he understood the procedure he was to follow if he or any one of his friends was struck by a rattler.

The *Bulletin* with its tag line about leaky faucets broke out in a spring rash of reminders: "Have you had your typhoid shots? Are your typhoid shots up to date?" And so on. I sent Bill up to the hospital for typhoid shots, and he came down with a sore arm and grumpy disposition.

Finally the *Bulletin* announced, "Post resident passes will be issued beginning——. Every post resident over the age of six will be required——." My shins were scarred and battered from my bi-weekly expeditions to the pass office. I hightailed it down to the pass office with Bill and Jana. There were four people ahead of us. We were fingerprinted and photographed, and we identified our scars.

When we claimed our passes, I looked like a gun moll on the FBI most-wanted list. Bill, usually a photogenic child, resembled a juvenile delinquent. To complete the illusion, he wore a horizontally striped tee shirt the morning he was processed. Jana turned out pretty well, but when Ruth saw our passes she said, "These are even worse than the pictures on the Tech Area badges. Do you suppose they get their cameras from Leavenworth?"

The passes were numbered 100,005, 100,006 and 100,007. Eric shook his head when he saw them.

Eric was in the throes of a conversational spell. He eschewed the nails in the home ceiling to converse with me. I was glad to have him talk again, although I thought his loquacity was due to the fact some of his problems in the Tech Area were partially solved. (I was right, too. Some of the techniques for the projected study of plutonium and its reduction to metal were improved. In those early days I learned that Eric's silences punctuated the progress of the work.)

"Do you suppose the numbers on our passes are intended to confuse the enemy?" I asked, while we sipped our pre-dinner drinks.

"I suppose so, although, God knows, there'd be plenty of other things to confuse him if he landed here. How would anyone who doesn't belong here guess that Our General is going to pay us a visit?"

"You tell me."

"They're going to enlarge the Tech Area PX. When I went to work this morning, the provisionals were busily taking up those little evergreens and digging post holes in front of it; they were done at noon. But when I came home tonight, the trees were all neatly replanted and the holes refilled."

"I suppose that means the Tech PX won't be enlarged, though Heaven knows it should be."

"Oh, no, after Our General leaves they'll put on the addition. He won't be back for six or eight weeks, and he won't notice the difference."

Eric smiled and finished his drink. "We'd better have dinner; I've got to go back to the Tech Area tonight."

"Don't you spend enough time in the Tech Area during the day?"

"I'm not going back to work, dear." He squirmed and looked abashed. "Security patrols the buildings in the area at night, but we're supposed to put our papers in our safes and lock them before we leave the office. I forgot to lock my safe the other night. The penalty is a fine of one day's salary to be donated to the Red Cross or a night of security patrol. I took the patrol duty; I didn't think you'd like to have the budget upset."

"You're dern tootin' I wouldn't like the budget upset. I'll go to bed with a good book and think of you walking your lonely rounds. Is there, perchance, a place in the Area where you can get a cup of coffee?"

"Lord, no. How about fixing a thermos for me?"

It was the first evening I fixed a thermos for Eric, but by far not the last. When the men in CM Division finally got enough plutonium for experimentation from the Racetrack at Oak Ridge, the regular security patrol was barred from D Building where CM was housed. The staff members themselves did the security patrol. (Please note that throughout this story I use the jargon of the Tech Area when I refer to the work. Any reader who wishes more detailed information about the metallurgical work during the early years at Los Alamos is referred to Cyril Smith's most readable article—"Metallurgy at Los Alamos, 1943-1945"—in the May 1954 issue of *Metal Progress*.)

On the first evening I fixed a thermos, served dinner, and called my menfolk to the table. Bill seated himself with grimy hands, and every hair on his head stood up for its individual rights.

"For Heaven's sake, go comb your hair and wash your hands!" I commanded. He retired to the bathroom to lave himself, and shortly thereafter commenced to scream.

"MA! MA! MAAA!"

I was thoroughly sick and tired of being thus summoned when there was nothing wrong.

"What is it?" I called wearily.

"MAAAAAH!"

I got up from the table and strolled down the hall. The washbasin was undersized; Bill's head was firmly wedged under the spigot. I stood in the doorway surveying the scene.

"Get me out of here, PLEASE!"

"In a moment, dear, this is too good for your father to miss. Eric, come here."

Eric joined me, and our combined mirth added greatly to Bill's outrage, but finally, even he commenced to laugh at the thought of his predicament. While I manipulated his scalp gently to release him, he voluntarily promised never to shriek MA! again when he misplaced the tube of glue for a plane model.

Warm weather multiplied Bill's problems. His main problem, and one which wasn't solved for many years, was his underlying resentment at the way he was deceived when we moved. Had the security restrictions permitted us to prepare him for the move, there would have been no problem. As it was, he was desperately restless and homesick. Eric was preoccupied with war; all the men on the Hill were preoccupied with war.

The women on the Hill could not be termed temporary war widows like my sister-in-law in Phoenix, whose husband, Preston, was in the South Pacific. We could better be termed camp followers, attendants of the men who made the final assault on Japan. We occupied the sidelines of history, and our role was not easy. It was up to us to see that our men were fed and loved and kept serene, so they could give their full attention to the bomb, the still-winged ant queen who reigned in the Tech Area. We coped with our problems alone.

Bill's problems were mine. To mitigate them, I went to the army stable to examine the horseback riding situation. I met Capt. Bob Thomsett, the veterinarian, and his aides: Charlie Raumiller, Sergeant Dawson, and his third aide, the young man who shod the horses. Time has erased his name, but he was big and proud, a true gentleman from the "Land of the Shining Mountains." I often wondered how many acres he occupied in civilian life.

My previous horseback experience was limited to a nasty little Shetland pony owned by my uncle in Idaho. To initiate me, the Shetland tossed me spread-eagled onto the pavement in front of my uncle's home. Uncle, who was a doctor, poked and prodded to determine there were no broken bones and put me back in the saddle. The pony trampled a neighbor's new lawn while I learned to guide him, but he taught me, during the summer, how to stay "on board." When I left Idaho that summer I had a "seat" that rivaled my paternal grandmother's. Uncle Tom was proud of his product.

On the basis of my experience with the pony, and a graduate course atop a burro named Maude, who had a disconcerting habit of putting her head down to nibble the greenery while we were on a sixty degree downgrade, I hired the army horses for fifty cents an hour while hunting for one that a ten-year-old boy could ride. The army horses were hard-mouthed and intractable. Martha Parsons owned a horse named Diamond and boarded him in the army stable. She joined with Bob and his assistants who urged me to buy a horse. I hesitated. It cost $30 a month to board a horse, and I wasn't sure that Bill and I would use a horse enough to justify the expense.

Brownie, Jana and Mike Haley, and Bill

The matter was settled for me in late April when Alan Ayres returned from a visit to the family ranch. He brought one of his horses with him and had also purchased a small brown beast which purportedly was a marvelous horse for children. His name was Brownie. He was pitifully thin, and his high withers were covered with saddle sores. Alan wanted $50 for him, complete with a broken-down saddle.

Brownie had winning ways with children. When Bill mounted him, he whinnied gaily and took off in a fast sprint. When I mounted him, even though I weighed only a few pounds more than Bill, he sighed with resignation and stumbled off in a slow walk. He definitely was not an ideal purchase but Bill fell in love with him.

"The army has given me permission to use the old school barn down at the west end of town," Alan said. "If you buy Brownie, you can keep him down there; there's lots of room."

After Bill went to bed, Eric and I discussed the proposed purchase.

"You know more about horses than I do," Eric said.

"There's no doubt at all that he's crazy about children, and he handles beautifully even though it's obvious that he considers adults necessary evils. It's just that I hate to pay $50 for a horse and then another $50 to $100 to get him in shape so Bill can ride him. His poor back has to be healed, and he needs flesh on those skinny bones."

"Whoa, boy!" Bill's voice exclaimed.

Eric and I tiptoed down the hall. Bill was fast asleep; he had a beatific smile on his face.

The next day we gave Alan a check for Brownie and received his bill of sale. Bill rode Brownie down to the army stable after school, and $60 later the horse emerged sleek, shining, and full of beans. He adored Bill and tolerated me. He was a show-off; all he needed to go into his act was an audience of children, preferably accompanied by an adult with a camera. He had a low opinion of other horses and would back up on a trail to kick the horse behind him. I don't know how many women and small children Brownie taught to ride. I can still hear Dot Seybolt caution him when he went into reverse.

"Do-o-n't do it, Brownie, do-o-o-n't do it!"

The riding I did as a girl was most informal. I rode in anything I happened to wear. As an adult who rode regularly, I needed clothing which gave me more protection than flannel slacks and loafers. Martha Parsons, who was the nucleus of the feminine horseback riders, had regular riding breeches and boots. Gurney Ashbridge, Ione Davis, and Hazel Kline wore blue jeans when they rode.

"You need some saddle pants and boots," Eric said while he watched me plaster band-aids over my scuffed skin.

"I know it, but Moore's won't have any saddle pants until autumn, and I want to ride now."

"How about buying yourself some blue jeans, Miss High and Mighty?"

We laughed together as we recalled my declaration on blue jeans. Croton was a thousand light years away, another life in another world. When we were in Santa Fe a few days later, we bought two pairs of blue jeans, two blue denim shirts, and a pair of cowboy boots. The jeans were available only because they were a small size and zipped on the right side. They were, in a sense, my diploma.

Shortly after, Peg Bainbridge approached me.

"Eleanor, something has to be done about the children in this town; there are no recreational facilities. Some of us are trying to reactivate the Boy Scout troop that was here when the school was in existence. Some of the men have Scouting experience, but we desperately need den mothers. I've volunteered, and I know you're just as concerned about your Bill as I am about Martin. Will you serve as a den mother?"

"Gladly." There were twenty boys, including our own, between the ages of nine and twelve, which meant they were eligible to be Cub Scouts. We couldn't operate in the best Scouting tradition because we couldn't recruit any more den mothers; a den of ten boys was unheard of in real Scouting.

We didn't have too much trouble; the boys, with the exception of Bill, were enthusiastic. I had two stalwart lieutenants, in the persons of Norman Foley and E. R. Bowen. They shepherded my charges when we went on hikes and enforced discipline, a necessary evil when we explored the cliff ruins at Frijoles and Puye. I seldom had an afternoon alone; the lads whose mothers worked came to practice for achievement tests and play with Bill. Sometimes the poor lambs just sat on my kitchen stool while I peeled potatoes and talked about their lives in the Outer World.

The achievement tests caused real heartache. The army insisted that we play its number game with our little Scouts, and the Albuquerque Boy Scout office never caught on that Cub Scout Number 13 was to receive an award at the next court of honor. The boys were bitterly disappointed when their honors failed to materialize.

The Cub Scouts were only one facet of an increasingly busy life. Spring brought a myriad of little birds. Sparrows, grosbeaks, goldfinches, tanagers, orioles, indigo buntings, and cerulean warblers vied for space in the plantings along Bathtub Row. Consultants came and went, and down at Otowi, Miss Warner could have served every night. She was in great demand.

It was fun to have dinner at Fuller Lodge, where the company was fresh from the Outer World and unexpected. Uncle Nick and Jimmy were frequent visitors. I. I. Rabi was a great favorite; he always had a fund of good yarns and was a virtuoso on a comb covered with tissue paper. Gus came and went, and George Kistiakowsky established his residence in the old ranch school pump house.

Additional members of the British Mission arrived with the first birds. Jim Tuck came with his red dancing slippers and pipes. The pipes were marvelous contraptions; I urged Eric to discard his conventional puffing pieces, but he declined. Passage for Jim's wife, Elsie, was cancelled the night before they were due to leave England because her space was needed for high priority personnel. Every available ship was commandeered for the coming invasion of Europe.

The Chadwicks arrived; Sir James and his Lady lost their titles on the Hill. Sir James was a quiet, gentle man. I don't think he cared about his title, and he spent most of his time in Washington. His Lady took a dim view of the proceedings. The army swept out the last of the old faculty houses and did the Chadwicks up in, what was for those days, regal style, but she was unreconciled. They had seventeen-year-old twin daughters, and Mrs. Chadwick did not think that the Hill was a proper social atmosphere.

Lady Chadwick was entirely correct, of course, but her efforts to "tone up" the young wives of the British Mission met with scant response. Philosophy changed fast in our cloistered world, and the British wives agreed with the American wives that if you were in the soup, it was best to swim and not worry too much about the social amenities.

The lack of social amenities worried the cultural arts section of the Women's Club, an organization to which I didn't belong. I'd had enough of women's organizations in the Outer World to last me for a while; I kept abreast of the Women's Club activities at tea parties and through Marge Schreiber. The club was divided into sections: the cultural arts section, the book section, and so on. The cultural arts section was by far the largest—almost the entire membership belonged to it—and it eventually became the club.

The cultural arts section decided that something should be done about the incoming wives. The vegetable counter at the commissary was becoming distinctly crowded, and anyhow, it was not a "toney" place for a woman freshly-arrived from the Outer World to make her debut.

The club agreed to have some newcomer teas. The idea was a good one because the newcomers arrived so fast it was impossible to concentrate on the individual. Those teas had a slightly frenzied flavor. Mrs. Chadwick offered her house to the club for one of them. When the great day arrived, the two senior ladies, Mrs. Chadwick and Mrs. Hirschfelder (who was the mother of physicist Joe Hirschfelder and who always wore a hat), spent their time in the kitchen brewing tea and toasting crumpets while the young women greeted the newcomers and played hostess in the living room. The tea was in the best tradition of the early days.

When the cultural arts section took over the club, they proposed to call it the Cultural Arts Club. They wanted Marge Schrieber to be president of the new organization, but the picture evoked in her mind by the thought of becoming president of a Cultural Arts Club was too vivid. She said she would serve if they changed the club's name. In a spirited meeting, the membership dropped Marge's suggested title of "Hill Biddies" like a lead brick, and it emerged as the Mesa Club.

The spring wasn't very far along when I had the opportunity to examine the medical facilities first hand. The illness that offered the opportunity was brief but violent. I woke in the early morning hours convulsed with pain. I shook Eric.

"Get a doctor," I whispered through clenched teeth.

A fresh paroxysm of pain seized me. Eric was panic-stricken. He hastily pulled his trousers over his pajamas and ran to get Ruth Haley. When he reappeared with Ruth, he asked, "Where's the nearest fire phone? I'll go call for a doctor."

"Oh, Lord, don't try to get a doctor by phone. You'll never waken the operator from her dreams. You can't even waken those girls in the daytime. Go up to the hospital," Ruth commanded.

Eric added a coat to his attire and set out at a dead run. I clung to Ruth's hand while she talked reassuringly. I don't know how long Eric was gone; in my semi-comatose condition it didn't seem very long. Ruth said later, "He was gone for years, Chiquita."

Dr. Jim Nolan arrived, disheveled. He poked, prodded, and asked questions while Eric and Ruth clung to each other in the living room. When the doctor finished, he said, "This could be serious. If it is, I think we've got it in time. I'll send the ambulance. I want you in the hospital where I can make you comfortable and do a proper examination. Don't worry."

He gave me an encouraging smile and vanished into the living room to scare the remaining podwads out of Ruth and Eric. My memory of the short ambulance trip was vague. The ambulance was an army field type, and when the orderlies tried to slide my stretcher out of it they couldn't move it; my fingers were clamped around a metal rod. They persuaded me to loosen my grip and deposited me in the only spot available for women patients, the maternity ward.

Nurses crowded around, and gradually, as morning brightened, my pain lessened. My surroundings came into focus, and I appraised them. The room was about thirty by thirty and contained several beds. The only other occupant was there for the proper reason, and her baby was a few days old.

"How do you feel?" she asked anxiously. "Your poor husband was almost frightened to death."

An orderly came in to sweep. He surveyed me with surprise.

"Well, you certainly made it snappy. We don't get many fast workers around here. Was it a girl or boy?"

I chuckled. Bill would certainly have a nervous breakdown if he knew where I was at the moment. He slept through the entire fracas.

Early in the afternoon, I was wheeled into the examination room. It was about the size of a walk-in closet. A nurse bustled around preparing for the doctors. I made conversation with her.

"These are cramped quarters, aren't they?"

"This is supposed to be the original operating room."

"Did they put the patient's feet out the windows?"

"No, they say they used to push the operating table up so the patient's head was in the hall, where Dr. Louis Hemplemann was stationed to give the anaesthetic. When the patient was anaesthetized, Dr. Hemplemann was supposed to call, 'All quiet, slice away, Jim!' Do you believe that story?"

If the room I occupied really was the original operating room, I believed it. When Drs. Nolan and Paul Hageman entered, the nurse left. There wasn't room for all three of them. The doctors poked, prodded, and squeezed for a miserable twenty minutes. Then they departed to consult. An hour or so later a beaming Dr. Nolan arrived in the maternity ward. "You lucky girl, this is a mechanical thing. A piece of your female plumbing slipped its moorings and was being pinched by an attack of acute indigestion. It's a wonder more people don't get their innards knocked loose on the rough roads in the valley. Exercises will take care of the slipped plumbing, but what did you have for dinner last night?"

"Steak. I've been saving ration coupons for weeks. Gee, it was good!"

Jim assumed an expression of mock horror. "My heart isn't in good enough condition after the scare you gave me last night. Don't eat any more steak. Meat rationing shrinks the stomach. You can't digest rich things like steak. For my sake, please stick to hamburger!"

He was a grand guy. They were all grand guys: Jim Nolan, Paul Hageman, Louis Hemplemann, Henry Barnett, and Jack Brooks, who joined them later. Louis was the only one who wasn't in the army; he headed the health group for the Tech Area. Our medical men did wonders with the facilities they had. Their only trouble was that each of them should have been triplets.

The field in front of Fuller Lodge turned green with young alfalfa.

"There's nothing prettier than an alfalfa field in the springtime," I told myself.

"Except the lilies-of-the-valley under the weeping willow and your peonies. Your rock garden must be a spring dream," my alter ego whispered.

"Go away, you. Don't you know that the battle of the Pacific has just started? It isn't possible for us to assault Japan now, and thousands of men are going to die before we do. Preston may be one of them. Do you want that to happen? Don't you know that even though England is about to sink under the weight of men and supplies for the invasion, the Italian front is dug in? Men are fighting from trenches. They're supposed to end the Pacific war in the Tech Area. Are you chicken or game cock?"

To placate my alter ego, I turned my attention to the meatballs I intended to take to the potluck supper at the school that evening. The whole town was agog about the potluck supper. It was to be the social event of the season.

"You will make lots of meatballs, won't you, Ma?" Bill asked anxiously.

My Swedish meatballs were my *piece de resistance*. They bore as much resemblance to the original Swedish meatballs as Swedes bore to Hottentots, but they were always a hit. Every child, of course, wanted his mother and his room to dazzle the competitors. Scrubbed and polished, the Jette family set out for the potluck supper. Eric led, proudly bearing the meatballs. We paused in the cloak room to leave our wraps. Even in warm spring we needed coats after the sun went down. I stopped and stared at the hat rack in astonishment. There was a naval officer's hat, liberally decorated with gold braid.

"Now, I've seen everything. Who belongs to that?" I asked.

"Deak Parsons, of course," Eric said. "I'm glad he's here tonight; you'll like him as well as you do Martha."

"Why didn't you tell me that the associate director of the laboratory was a captain in the navy?"

"I thought you knew. Let's get rid of this casserole and go find them."

I did like Deak as well as I did Martha. He was brilliant, capable, and endowed with an elegant sense of humor. He enjoyed the paradox of being a navy captain in an army camp. When I speculated about the relative elegance of the school building in comparison with the other facilities, Deak said, "I insisted on an up-to-date school plant. Both our girls are in this school. After the building was finished, I took Our General to see it. He harumphed all over the place, and said, 'I'll hold you personally responsible for this, Parsons.'"

Deak smiled happily. "I guess he forgot that I was in the navy."

he alfalfa in the field in front of Fuller Lodge was a few inches high when there was a stir of construction activity at the southeast end of the field behind the PX. The construction workers' huts from the east end of town were dismantled and relocated. The huts had floor areas of about three hundred square feet, and each was equipped with a sink and water tap. Central community latrines, one for each ten or so huts, were built.

Alice, Muriel, and I inspected them. Alice the Teacher served on the Town Council. Muriel the Doctor was interested in community health. Eleanor the Dubious recalled Eric's fine words, uttered while still in the Outer World, about the academic atmosphere that prevailed at Los Alamos. The hutments wouldn't add a thing to an academic atmosphere.

"The number of latrines meets army specifications," Muriel said.

"Who are the unfortunates condemned to live in these hovels?" I asked.

"The laborers and janitorial help who are presently housed in apartments," Alice answered. She made a helpless gesture with her hands.

"We are out of housing, and Our General doesn't want to build any more. There aren't enough apartments left to take care of the scientific commitments. The administration says that the Spanish-American laborers in the apartments live with their families in only one or two rooms and don't understand modern sanitary facilities. *They* say that this type of housing will be adequate for them. *They* say that the fact that this group of people pays the minimum rent of $19 a month has nothing to do with this move."

"But most of those people have six or eight children," Muriel protested.

"I know, but what can we do? The civilian population in this town is without a franchise unless they have permanent residences

Quonset Huts used for housing during the Manhattan project

elsewhere in New Mexico. The council is helpless. It's only a
sounding board. We don't have any money, and we serve in a purely
advisory capacity. *What can we do?*"

There was no answer to Alice's desperate question. The Town
Council was elected by representative groups on the Hill, but the
only funds at their disposal were the proceeds from traffic fines.
Even those were spotty. The MPs handed out traffic tickets freely, but
the military court had no jurisdiction over civilians. The few traffic
offenders who deigned to appear before the council came voluntarily,
and such fines as were collected were turned over anonymously
to the Red Cross. The devoted representatives of the housewives,
dormitory dwellers, and others were only empowered to advise the
town administration, and the town administration took its orders
from Our General in distant Washington.

The Spanish-Americans were, to a man, ardent politicians.
They all owned bits of land in New Mexico, deeded to them by
their fathers and forefathers. The Hill was their temporary home,
and they took a dark view of the huts. They didn't object to the
outdoor plumbing, they had that at home, but the huts were too small
to accommodate their large families. They raised their voices and
screamed blue bloody murder.

I spoke to Bences Gonzales about the proposed mass move,

but neither his family nor the Martinez family were involved. Both families occupied the same houses they occupied in ranch school days, and some army underling had snuck modern plumbing into them in the early days, probably listed as plumbing of the apartments.

"Don't fret, Señora" Bences said. "They will write to their congressmen if they don't like the housing provided for them."

"What a joyous thought!" I exclaimed. If there was anything that our absentee landlord and his security boys didn't want, it was a congressional investigation. When I made my intelligence report to Eric, he clutched his head.

"All we need at this stage of the game is a congressional investigation. The army had better do something and do it quick."

The army did do something. They delayed the Spanish-American moving day until they moved huts together to make individual dwellings of two, three, and four rooms. After that, our Spanish-American families moved, if not willingly, with good grace.

Barracks were under construction in the west end of town, and immediately after the huts were occupied, construction began in the north end of the alfalfa field. Ruth and I were enjoying a daily visit.

"What on earth are they going to do now?" Ruth asked.

"Eric says they're going to build seventy-five duplexes. He says they need a lot more machinists in the Tech Area, but they can't hire them until they have housing for them."

"I hope they have central heating and indoor plumbing."

"Eric says they will. We're going to look at them just as soon as they're finished. This apartment living is getting us down; it's so noisy we can't hear ourselves think. We like Alan and Virginia, but their ideas of child rearing are different from ours. Bill, aged ten and a half, goes to bed at 8:30. Little Betty is allowed to stay up till the witching hours. We can hear her exercising the sofa at all hours."

"I know what you mean, Chiquita. Let's take a look at the duplexes."

"Do you have any news that's repeatable?" I asked. Ruth had a keen eye for the ridiculous.

"Not much. The MPs are riding the beard growers again. One of the boys in our group has been cultivating a fine stand of brush.

When he showed his badge this morning, the MP told him he'd better shave it off or get a new badge."

"I wish they'd get after that little guy with the black bush on his face. He's positively revolting. Your Jano has the only decent-looking beard on the Hill."

"That little chap will lose his beard next week when he's inducted into the army. Our soldier boys can't wait to get their hands on it. I think Jano looks pretty sharp with his beard, myself, but I sometimes wish he'd shave it off. I'm always combing the girls out of it at the dorm dances."

"I think we must cultivate some dorm dwellers. I'd like to go to one of those dorm dances."

"They're really magnificent safety valves, and the darndest things happen. Last fall one of the young army officers was expounding the sturdy construction of all buildings raised by the army engineers. One of the girls gave him a shove; he hit the wall and went right through it. Was his face red!"

"Last Saturday night, a burro wandered into the dance. Where it came from, nobody knows, but Haley got on and rode it out into the night. After the dances are over, Dick Feynman always does a drum solo, and Willy Higinbotham plays his accordion. Nick Metropolis and Dick have a regular act, and if Rabi is around, he performs on his comb. By the way, last Saturday, one of the girls had a striking necklace. She got it in Jemez. Violet Kissee was simply fascinated by it, and I've got to have one. The girl who had it said it was made of rattlesnake vertebrae strung with coral and turquoise. It was a stunning thing."

"How on earth would you get the rattlesnake vertebrae?"

"The girl who had it said the Indians killed the snakes and boiled them until the bones came to pieces. Keep your eyes skinned for a rattlesnake, and we'll each have a necklace."

Eric and I were watching Bill and Brownie cavort around the combination golf course/cow pasture.

"You know, that looks like fun," Eric said. "I think maybe we'd better get a horse that's big enough for me to ride; goodness knows I need exercise."

"I think you'd enjoy it," I agreed. "We really need two horses, anyhow. I don't know what was wrong with my brain when we bought Brownie. It isn't safe for a ten-year-old to ride alone in this country."

Later in the evening, we paid a call on the Alan and explained our problem.

"I think I've got the horse you want," he said. "I bred him myself. His dam was American Saddle Bred, and his sire was a quarter horse. He's only three years old, but he's big, strong, and has five natural gaits. He's only green-broke, but it shouldn't take very long to get him in shape so Eric can ride him. The man who has him now saddled and rode him a couple of times last fall. He's never been allowed to buck, and he's hackamore broke. Never had a bit in his mouth."

"Where can we see this animal?" I asked. A green-broke horse wasn't exactly the thing I had in mind for Eric, who had never been in a saddle.

"I have to go down to the ranch next weekend. I'm going to bring up some horses for other people. I'll bring him along."

Eric was almost as excited over the prospect of owning a horse as Bill was when we bought Brownie. That week he left his problems in the Tech Area where they belonged when he came home in the evenings. We swallowed hasty dinners before we departed through the west gate where Eric was taught to mount and neck rein a horse named Buttons. Buttons was young and sturdy, but he really wasn't tall enough for Eric. Buttons was high-schooled and would kneel for a rider to mount. He endured Eric's efforts with resignation. He'd much rather have knelt for him. The grapevine carried the word that the Jettes were going to buy a second horse, and Eric always had a good audience. He took the ribald advice with good spirit. I shut my eyes whenever I thought he was going to miss the saddle completely and land on Buttons' starboard side.

It was good for all of us. We could forget, momentarily, that thousands of ships, planes, airmen, and paratroopers had launched their weight against the enemy on the Normandy front. We could forget the losses of personnel from the landing crafts and the numbers of dead that were lapped by the waves on the beachhead or

Eric at the stables

were piled in ditches or hung from the trees in their parachutes. We could forget the price of a scarcely-scarred Rome and that our new secret B-29s rained bombs on Tokyo from an airbase at Saipan. Eric and his colleagues could forget that if the Pacific war did not end before the queen bomb shed her wings, they would be forced to end it with an ultimate horror.

By the end of the week, Eric was quite proficient. When Alan came upstairs late Sunday night to tell us our proposed purchase was safely tethered outside of the west gate, we could hardly wait until Monday noon. The three of us swallowed a hasty lunch and accompanied Alan out the gate.

"If you have any carrots, take them along," Alan instructed. "We grew carrots the year he was foaled; he's crazy about them."

"Isn't he handsome!" Eric exclaimed when we met the future member of our equine family.

He certainly was handsome. He stood about sixteen hands and was beautifully coupled. His pure white coat was decorated with

102

puffs of Maltese. His only fault was that his feet were slightly too big. I suspected he got those feet from his sire, since his dam was a purebred. Anyhow, they didn't matter, we weren't looking for a show horse. He accepted the proffered carrots graciously, without slobbering.

"He's a true pinto," Alan said. He parted his hair so we could see that the skin under the Maltese spots was black.

"What shall we call him?" Eric asked.

"His name is written on him," I replied.

"Smokey!" Bill exclaimed.

"I'll finish breaking him for you," Alan said.

"I'd better lay in a supply of carrots and get busy with the curry comb. That'll be the best way to gentle him," I said.

"I suppose so, but for Heaven's sake be careful, he's a lot of horse," Alan warned.

A couple of weeks passed. I worked on Smokey daily, and he loved it. The rest of his education was not progressing as rapidly as I wished. Alan couldn't spare time to ride him enough.

"I'm going to ride that horse," I announced.

"He's never had a woman on his back," Alan warned. "And he doesn't like the bit."

We bought featherweight aluminum bits for our horses, but a colt who never had a bit in his mouth couldn't be expected to like it.

"He's going to have a woman on his back tomorrow, and he'll like his bit, too, I've no intention of fighting it into his mouth. Do you boys want to come down and see me safely aboard?"

I outlined my strategy to Eric that night.

"If you're going to ride this summer, we must get Smokey used to the saddle and gaited. He's intelligent, and it shouldn't take long. I've never broken or gaited a horse, but he and I can learn together."

The horseback riders' grapevine carried the news that "La Jette" was going to ride the family's new horse, and there was quite an assemblage when I approached Smokey the following noon. I was smothered with gratuitous advice. Jim Allen was present with Mary. He owned a hard-mouthed mare named Dulcey, and Mary was afraid of her. (Mary had reason to be afraid of her; she was a villain.) He wanted to show her that horses should not be feared. Jim and Eric were probably the only onlookers who didn't expect to see me land on my boom tararum.

I approached Smokey and confidently extended his bit. There was a carrot under it. He opened his mouth and took both eagerly. He munched his carrot calmly while I adjusted the saddle and tightened the girth. Eric cupped his hands, I put my feet into them, and swung into the saddle.

There was a faint sigh from the onlookers when I touched him with my heels and started to work him. Later in the afternoon we went along the patrol road around town to the veterinary hospital so Smokey could have an encephalitis shot. We had a little trouble at the town dump; Smokey was afraid the shiny cans would attack him.

Half an hour of patient conversation convinced him that the cans weren't his enemies, and we found a hole in the town fence that was big enough to accommodate both of us. It cut three miles off the trip to the veterinary hospital, where we created a considerable stir. Smokey took his shot without fussing, although I think Bob feared he might explode, and I made an appointment with the smithy for shoes.

While Smokey began his education, other things happened.

George and Kay Kehl arrived. George also taught in the School of Mines at Columbia University. They were assigned to one of the luxury duplexes for married people without children, and miracle of miracles, their furniture arrived three days before they did.

Dorothy McKibbin phoned Eric from Santa Fe to report the Kehls' impending arrival, and he took time off so we could meet them at the east gate. The wind was blowing. I wore a skirt for the occasion and had trouble holding it down. When the Kehls drew up in front of the guard gate, George mopped his brow.

"Boy, am I glad to be here. That damned dog has breathed down my neck for two thousand miles." He indicated a cosmopolitan collie on the back seat. The collie's name was Trouble, and he was. In my private opinion, he was missing some of his marbles.

The duplex buildings in the north end of the alfalfa field were finished, and the townspeople flocked to look at them. We dubbed them Morganville in honor of the contractor who erected them. They were little horrors: the rooms were tiny, and the design was atrocious. The Black Beauties in our apartment kitchens were luxury items compared to the kerosene-fed cooking facilities in Morganville.

"We couldn't get our bed into the master bedroom," Eric said.

"There isn't enough room for our living room furniture," I supplemented.

The Bachers were also looking. We walked home with them.

"What we need right now is a vigorous building program," Bob said.

"Every batch of housing they build is lower standard than the previous one. The second group of apartments isn't as well-built as the first, and they built efficiency apartments instead of duplexes for people without children. These duplexes are pretty bad." Jean shook her head.

"Do you have any idea what the tariff will be on these houses?" Eric asked.

"I suppose it will be based on salary as it is in the apartments," Bob answered.

The rent scale was set forth in the brochure. We paid the highest rent, $69 a month, for our apartment. The Haley and Ayres families occupied identical apartments for less, but the fourth family in the apartment, where the man was a machinist, paid the lowest or next to lowest rent because his rental was based on his pay for an eight-hour day and a forty-hour week. With the overtime he worked, his income probably exceeded that of either Jano or Alan. The inequities of the system were obvious, and it was a constant source of aggravation to the rent payers in other brackets, who had plenty of other matters to exasperate them.

The town was bursting at its seams. The commissary was always jammed, and numbers were distributed at the meat counter, just as they were in the Outer World. The lines at the check-out counter grew longer, and the Wacs who presided over the counters developed the perverse habit of slamming the cash registers shut and departing for lunch just as one was about to deposit her heavy basket for check-out. Grapevine said that the commissary was to be enlarged!

"When?" the women asked.

(Just to put it in the record, the commissary was enlarged not once but ten different times!)

The community laundries sagged under the weight of soiled clothing, and the electricity failed with monotonous regularity. Even if there was current, the women and the SEDs, who also used the laundries, stood only a sporting chance of survival when they washed. The floors were constantly covered with water. There were wooden lattices so we didn't have to wade, but the washing machines shorted, and more than one of us got jolted. I thought the only reason we weren't electrocuted by the dozen was that we were too tough to kill.

One morning I stood in a commissary line behind Mrs. Chadwick. I was returning from tending the horses, and my blue denim outfit was delicately scented with Fumme de Cheval. Her nostrils quivered when I took my place in line, but she masked the quiver manfully when she discovered I was the culprit. We chatted about a lovely alligator purse she carried, and she placed her basket on the counter for check-out. The Wac slammed her cash register shut, and said, "You'll have to get into another line."

We re-aligned ourselves, and she indicated her basket.

"You know, it's wonderful to be able to buy all these things, but my husband spends all his time in Washington. I can't think of a single reason why I should stay here."

"If my husband was in Washington, I wouldn't stay here for a moment." I was tired of orders from girls and boys in khaki.

"But you seem so well adjusted to all this; you have your own horse and work with the Cub Scouts."

"I could part with both, particularly the Cub Scouts."

She smiled with sympathy. Our paths had crossed at the east gate on the occasion I took my Cubs for a hike to Camp Hamilton, a relic of the ranch school. At the time, she had leaned out of her car and whispered, "I see that you're going to have a perfectly hideous day."

We finally checked out and parted to make lunch for our respective families. Eric met me at the door.

"I made some sandwiches and fed Bill. Come in and sit down; I've got bad news." He handed me the following paper:

July 5, 1944

To: Mr. and Mrs. Eric Jette
From: J. R. Oppenheimer

There is a very grave housing shortage at the present time, particularly in the larger size apartments, and it will be some months before new housing can be built. The policy of the project has always been to assign two-bedroom apartments to families with one child and three-bedroom apartments to families with two or more children, except in a few extraordinary cases where medical circumstances required a different assignment. In a number of cases in the past, this policy was not adhered to because of a lack of smaller apartments at the time. When you were assigned your present apartment you were told that such assignment was temporary and that you might be required to move to a smaller apartment at some time in the future.

This time has unfortunately arrived, and it is now necessary to move a number of persons from three-bedroom apartments to two-bedroom apartments. Since we do not wish to move families unless their present apartments are needed for larger families, it has been necessary to establish a priority list for moving. This list was drawn by lot from all of such families, and your name was number 14 out of 14. Number 1 will be moved first, number 2 second, and so on. All moving will be handled by the post through the Housing Office.

I looked at Eric with tears in my eyes. There weren't any four-room apartments available. It meant Morganville.

"Oppie really has no choice in this matter, darling. We've got to have machinists. Morganville was built to house them. The lab recruited the machinists in Dallas, and they sent their union representatives to look at the housing. They don't like Morganville. They want to live in apartments."

"And I suppose when Our General heard that piece of information, he said, 'You've got those duplexes. If the machinists don't like them, move your precious scientists into them and let the machinists have the apartments,'" I retorted.

"I suppose it was something like that," Eric said bitterly.

"You tell Oppie we'll move, but it will be back to Croton-on-the-Hudson. He can get someone else to work on his new-fangled super bomb."

"Oh, my God! Where did you get that idea?"

"I'm not an imbecile. It's a weapon, I'm sure. There've been rumors about German installations for unorthodox weapons, possibly rockets. Some expert pooh-poohed the idea as propaganda for credulous civilians, but who knows? He said rockets only had a range of ninety miles. We've got those new B-29 bombers and an air base within fifteen hundred miles of Japan. Furthermore—"

I didn't get a chance to tell him I thought the bomb would spray radioactive materials all over the landscape. He interrupted.

"Don't tell me! Please, don't tell me any more! Don't tell anyone anything!"

"All right, so I won't tell anyone anything! Right now, I'm saying I won't live in Morganville and pay $69 a month rent while a $19-a-month machinist lives in this apartment and enjoys my linoleum!"

Eric gestured helplessly. Six months of heartbreaking frustration were almost at an end. His group had a gram of plutonium to work with and more was on its way. Naturally, I didn't know about plutonium. My knowledge of the periodic table extended only to uranium and the fact there were transuranium elements. The most recent work was top secret, but the crisis in Eric's personal life transcended even top secret matters. He was as upset as I was.

The grapevine spread the news of the lottery like wildfire. The town and Tech Area were in an uproar. We were one of three families in our building who occupied oversized apartments, and the only ones whose names were in the lottery. Our situation was universal. I met Alice in the commissary.

"What can we do to help you?" she asked. "Cyril says he can't let Eric leave."

"Nothing except give us your moral support."

Ruth came home from the Tech Area breathing fire. "What a way to end a war! Nobody got a darn thing done this morning. If they do something like this to the fourteen of you, what will happen to the rest of us?"

The embattled fourteen called a meeting, and a recording was made of it. I wish I owned the record; it was priceless. We first moved to call ourselves The Fourteen Furious Fighting Families; then everyone talked at once.

"I called on Oppie and Hughes. I told them I'd quit, and they said, 'Go ahead,' so we went to Santa Fe, and I got myself another job. It pays a thousand a year more than I'm getting here, and—" The speaker was a young designer-draftsman. Good designers were scarce in those days.

"And *he* said he'd come to look at *his* apartment. We didn't even get the notice of the lottery till the next day."

"Just wait until you hear what they told me."

"We've got it in writing that we don't have to move." The Holloways passed around their meaningless sheet of paper.

The meeting went on and on.

"Let's do this in an orderly fashion and take it to the Town Council," Dave Hawkins suggested.

"What good will that do? We need to write to a good, fat congressman," Eric said belligerently. "Has anybody got one?"

"The council is our only recourse to the administration. What we do will affect every member of the scientific staff," Dave said soberly.

We finally appointed a committee to investigate the apartment situation and another to draft our reply to the administration. We knew the Wacs and architects occupied apartment space, and Housing Office records were always askew.

Our petition was presented to the Town Council at their next meeting. It was verbose, and the grammar was questionable, but it conveyed the idea.

July 10, 1944

Wednesday of last week fourteen families received notices that it would be necessary for them to move. They were told a lottery had been conducted and that each had been assigned a moving order number. The reasons given for the proposed shift was that each family is occupying an apartment larger than necessary and that their present quarters are needed by new arrivals.

We are bringing this matter to the attention of the Town Council because the obvious mishandling of this situation is a matter of public concern.

The letter stated that we had been informed our housing was temporary. This is a false statement for twelve of the fourteen families. We were arbitrarily placed in our present apartments, because no others were available. Families who requested four-room apartments were refused because there were none.

The families scheduled to move immediately were offered no adequate quarters. We strongly object to our names being placed in lottery without our being called together for previous discussion. The only intelligent manner in which to handle such a situation is by open discussion among those concerned and presentation of all pertinent facts.

We have been told that commitments have been made to the newcomers that cancel all commitments previously made to us. Continual injustices and inconsistencies caused by improper personnel handling are damaging to group morale. The personal turmoil caused by such mismanagement is endangering the rapid successful conclusion of this project.

Therefore, we recommend the following considerations.

1. All moving should be immediately suspended until the situation has been reviewed. Persons who have signed housing contracts under duress should be released immediately, and all future moving should be done within thirty-day notice.

2. When it is necessary to move people, adequate quarters in good condition should be provided. A list of all housing should be available, and the list should include

    a.   all empty apartments, assigned or not;

    b.   apartments to be vacated in the near future; and

    c.   apartments not completely utilized.

This will give families requested to move the greatest possible freedom of choice.

3.   In cases where families are moved from larger quarters, surplus furniture should be given satisfactory storage or, at the option of the owner, furniture should be transported to a point designated by the owner at the project's expense.

4.   The apparent present policy of making commitments that invalidate commitments made to present residents should be discontinued.

5.   Temporary quarters should be arranged to house newcomers until permanent quarters can be provided for them as was done for many people now at the project. Steps should be taken immediately to provide such accommodations.

6.   A change should be made in the policies of the Personnel and Housing offices so that

    a.   much closer cooperation between the two will be in effect,

    b.   distribution of authority will be such as to enable the housing to be handled in a reasonable and competent way, and

    c.   a written statement of future housing policy be made.

The council meeting went down in history as the Battle of the Fourteen Furious Fighting Families. Army representatives were present, and the laboratory's personnel man Hughes attended (he was really a physicist, probably theoretical). Representatives of the incoming machinists were there, and the dining room in Fuller Lodge overflowed with representatives of the Fighting Fourteen, their friends, and sympathizers.

The rafters of the big dining room rang with impassioned oratory. Our foreign-born scientists leaped up and down waving the Constitution and Bill of Rights. (They had powerful ammunition in those documents; after the meeting I went home and became a student of early American history.) The sound and fury were impressive. We didn't need the marines; the administration recognized a first-class insurrection. The first casualty, the designer, would be followed by many more if the moving order was enforced.

"Nobody will move unless they want to move. This is all a most unfortunate misunderstanding." Representatives of the army and the civilian administration pleaded, "Please, please, go back to work, and forget the whole thing!"

"HA!"

7

rs. Chadwick tucked her twins under her wings and departed for Washington.

"Who will have the Chadwick house?" people asked.

"The Fermi's are coming; it's reserved for them," the housing office answered.

Enrico Fermi arrived on the local scene with the family car. Laura and the children followed by train. They looked at the house.

"We'd rather have an apartment, if you don't mind," they said.

There were two vacant apartments in the house just west of ours; they chose the second floor apartment. The ground floor apartment was reserved for Rudy and Genia Peierls; he was the incoming head of the British Mission. The Chadwick house was assigned to Bob and Jean Bacher, much to the joy of their friends.

The architects were evicted from the building diagonally opposite ours, and the Wacs were assigned to newly-completed barracks at the west end of town. The barracks building program in that area was accelerated. Additional dormitories were constructed at both ends of town. The new dormitories bore no resemblance to the original dormitories, which were laid out in two-room suites with the baths between the rooms. The new dormitories had sixteen nine-by-twelve rooms and a community bath on each floor.

A hundred prefabricated houses were raised adjacent to Morganville; we named them McKeeville. The houses were small, but they were individual homes and quite livable; they also had modern plumbing. Utilities for a trailer camp were run into a small area near the hutments. Machinists and skilled workmen arrived by the dozen; many of them were assigned to Morganville. Some of the skilled craftsmen came in trailers, which were set up in the new trailer camp. The view from the dining room in Fuller Lodge was distinctly cluttered.

Ditches were dug around the commissary for the foundations of the first enlargement, and women wrestled with heavy grocery sacks as they jumped over them. The mid-day sun blazed, and the wind continued to blow. The *Bulletin* added hints on "How to Save Water" to its tag line. The grass around the houses on Bathtub Row dried up.

Kitty Oppenheimer was a botanist; she worked hard on her flowers, but without water, her efforts were to no avail.

"I'll grow flowers yet," she promised.

"We'll ride out and look at the wild ones," her horseback-riding friends declared. The fields on the potreros to the north were blue with wild lupine, and the Indian paintbrush was scarlet.

I rode Smokey daily. He was shod, and his education had advanced to the stage where Eric could ride him. On Sundays, I requisitioned Brownie to ride with him and had to wrangle with Bill every time we rode. He put up the same argument every time.

Bill, about an hour before we were ready to start for our ride, would fire the first round. "Well, I guess I'll go for a ride this afternoon."

Ma, holding herself firmly in check to keep from assaulting him, would say, "Dear, I told you that you were to ride Brownie on weekdays and Saturdays. Sunday is Dad's day."

Bill, with an aggrieved air: "Okay, but this week I had a deal with Brant. I didn't have time to ride."

Ma, her blood pressure rising: "You didn't have time to clean his stall, feed, or groom him either."

Bill: " Okay, okay, so what? I was going to ride him today."

Ma: "Bill, we've been over this argument a dozen times. Sunday is Dad's only free day, and he likes me to ride with him. You certainly can occupy yourself for a couple of hours."

The arguments went on interminably. Bill was always liberal with the red herrings he dragged into them. He never failed to touch on the fact that we would not allow him to ride Smokey, and he was not above threatening to persuade some GI to take him out in one of the canoes on Ashley Pond. He knew that the canoes were a real source of worry to me.

The canoes were left over from the ranch school. Muriel Cuykendall and I spotted them one day when we walked home from the commissary. We were discussing the pond at the time.

"I wish they'd hire a lifeguard so the youngsters could swim," I said.

"They can't swim in the pond, it's polluted," Muriel said.

"The ranch school boys used to swim there. There's a picture in the Big—"

Muriel laid her hand on my arm and silenced me.

"What do you see over there?" she asked.

"Oh, dear Heaven! There are two canoes in the old boat house!"

"Can Bill swim?"

"He swims like a fish, but what about these dry land children we have here?"

"Mary and Robert swim, too, but what about the GIs? They're not much more than children themselves."

We looked at each other with mutual consternation.

I attended Town Council meetings regularly after the Battle of the Fighting Fourteen. My suspicions were thoroughly aroused by that episode, and I was determined to keep abreast of events as they transpired. I raised the question of the canoes at the next council meeting; the GIs and town youngsters were standing in line for them.

"Canoes are treacherous crafts," I contended.

"The GIs don't have enough recreational facilities."

"Let the army buy a couple of flat bottom boats."

"They won't do it; they say the pond is shallow."

I polled my Cub Scouts at our next meeting.

"How many of you boys can swim? Only three of you? E. R., where were you born?"

"Raton. I wasn't old enough to take swimming lessons when we left there."

And so it went.

"Promise me, please promise me, that none of you non-swimming boys will go out in those canoes."

"Oh, Mrs. Jette, we won't go out in the canoes."

To know the mind of a boy is to saddle the wind, and what is to be, will be. A few days later I joined a frantic group behind the commissary. Ginny Brooks shivered as the hot sun dried her. Her shoes were kicked askew where she shed them before diving in.

"He hung on to the side of the canoe until I reached him." She indicated the GI who sat with his head cradled in his arms.

"It took her forty minutes to find E. R. He must have been hit on the head with something," Eddie Brooks murmured.

The army removed the canoes and fenced the pond.

Bill was capricious, and I didn't know what to do about him. He suffered from headaches, and I was positive he needed glasses. I was sure that something was wrong with his eyes even before we disappeared from the Outer World, but four opthamologists denied it. I took him to a man in Santa Fe, and again the verdict was negative. He vacillated about everything. In Croton, he couldn't wait until we bought him a bicycle, but he refused to ride it at Los Alamos and spent his odd moments taking it to pieces.

One fine, hot noontime, he managed to take the front wheel off of the bicycle and couldn't put it on again. He came upstairs to wash his hands before he went back to school.

"Ma, will you put the wheel on my bike? I want to ride it down to the barn when I feed the horses this afternoon."

"Why did you take it off if you want to ride it this afternoon?"

"Oh, I don't know."

I sighed. He followed a usual pattern; he'd fret if I didn't have the bicycle in usable condition, and if I did, he'd decide to walk. He left for school.

I dug the family wrecking bar out of the store room and went out in the midday sun to operate on the bicycle. The fork was stiff, even with the bar, and I couldn't pry it open far enough to slide the wheel into place. I struggled on, dripping with perspiration. Behind me, a stentorian voice with a Russian accent said, "What are you doing there?"

I dropped the bar with a start and swung around to face the speaker. She was a sturdily constructed woman of about my own height. She had an empty knapsack on her back, and her hair was cut in a Dutch-boy bob. By no stretch of the imagination could she lay any claim to beauty, but she radiated vitality, with the 14-karat gold lining of her plain exterior shining through it.

"I am Genia Peierls. We just got here, and I am going to the commissary to stock up. What happened to the bicycle?"

"I'm Eleanor Jette," I said and explained what happened to the bicycle.

"Ah! These boys of ours! It's lucky I came along. I am very strong. Here, let me help you."

She brushed me aside, put her foot on the down arm of the fork, and yanked it open with her hand. She shoved the wheel into place, flipped the bicycle over, and repeated the process.

"There," she dusted her hands. "You are just not in good form today." She adjusted her knapsack. "Do you like to hike?"

"Heavens, no, I don't use two legs when I have four to carry me."

"You have a horse? I must get one."

"We have two horses. Bill's little horse wouldn't get nearly enough exercise if my friends didn't ride him. Martha Parsons and I ride every day. Why don't you join us tomorrow morning?"

"It is a date." She departed to the commissary, and I went upstairs to lie down for an hour and recoup my strength for the rest of my off-form day. Note: Bill decided to walk to the stable!

It was the beginning of a wonderful friendship with the Peierls. Both Rudy and Genia were blessed with a boundless enthusiasm for life and a fund of good sense. Rudy was German born but English educated, and he got out of Germany early. Genia, as her accent said, was Russian born. They were both good, solid British citizens. When invasion threatened England after Dunkirk, they sent their children, Gwen and Ronny, to Canada, and their arrival at Los Alamos marked their reunion with the youngsters after a four-year separation.

Genia and I were, in the language of the New Mexicans, simpatico. The word conveys more than mere friendship; it implies a rare understanding between two people. The only enthusiasm we didn't share was hiking. Genia loved to tramp over the hills with about fifty pounds of groceries on her back. Her addiction to hiking held no allure whatever for me, but even so, she swore that I was the only woman in town who could wear her to exhaustion.

The arrival of the Peierls marked the final assembly of the British Mission, except for Elsie Tuck who was to arrive when shipping space was available for her. They were fine people, every one of them, with the glaring exception of Klaus Fuchs, and we accepted him without the slightest doubt of his integrity. British Intelligence guaranteed him; what our own intelligence people were doing when he met his contact at the bridge on the Alameda, I never guessed.

Fuchs was a cipher to me, a faceless nonentity despite all the occasions we were in his company. When the light of day was turned on his treachery, I realized he was perfect in his role. Some years before I had discussed secret service work with a woman who was retired from it; I remarked that I always had a yen for it. She appraised me critically and shook her head.

"You would never do, my dear. Your eyes are too blue, and your hair has too much red in it. Secret service work requires the operator to fade into the background."

I didn't recall her words the day Marge Schreiber and I specifically discussed Fuchs.

"That guy baffles me," I said. "I can't remember what he looks like until the next time I see him."

Marge shivered slightly. "He gives me the creeps. He sits in the corners at parties and never says a word. I've never heard him laugh. He has a high-pitched giggle, and it gives me chills."

Unfortunately, Fuchs didn't baffle or chill the intelligence people, who were so busy with the forest they didn't see the trees. David Greenglass, whose acquaintance I was spared, was shacked up in the west barracks area, but Joan Hinton, who defected to Red China after the war, was very much on the scene. She played either fiddle or viola. Whichever it was, she played well and joined the music lovers. She was a congenital twitcher, human fly type. The night she first played at our apartment, she wore a skirt and did everything but climb the walls when she wasn't fiddling. When the musicians left, I asked, "Does that girl ever sit still? Does she behave that way at work?"

"When you're talking with her, she's just as likely to end up on the back of a chair with her feet on the seat as not," Eric admitted.

"She's a smart cookie, but she had a progressive education. "

"Too progressive, if you ask me. I hope she wears slacks to work."

"Not always; it gets pretty embarrassing."

On the battle fronts of the Outer World, the Russians pushed toward the Baltic, and there was hard fighting for every mile in northern Italy. Buzz bombs rained on Britain, and the Allies struggled to break out of Normandy. Our positions on Saipan were consolidated, and the marines drove on to take the rest of the island in the bloodiest battle of the Pacific War. As heavy as American casualties were, eyewitness accounts placed the Japanese casualties at several times the figure of our own. The accounts described mass suicides and suicidal charges of Japanese that swelled the numbers of their casualties.

The rainy season was late in 1944. The wind blew, and fire sirens howled constantly. They signaled fire in the town or outlying experimental sites to the south. I watched Eric's hands clench while he counted the blasts until I wondered if I would ever again hear a fire siren without the icy fingers of fear clutching my heart.

When the thunderheads finally gathered over the mountaintops, they dueled with lightning and thunder instead of dropping their precious burden of rain. The forest at the head of Guaje Canyon was struck and set ablaze. Ruth, Jano, Eric, and I watched the fire's progress from our front porch.

For a few nights we saw only a glow in the sky, then the fire reached the ridge. Flames leaped and trees exploded with showers of sparks.

"My God, there goes our watershed," Jano said softly.

"How long before it reaches the town?" Eric whispered grimly.

"About seven miles, it depends on the wind."

"Let's each of us ask Mr. God to change the direction of his wind," Ruth suggested.

The wind finally did change. The fire blew back on the burn and died. Battered troops, who were hauled to the end of the water line road and dumped off to make their way to the fire line on foot, straggled back to town, scratched and weary. Many of them never reached the fire line; there were no trails or wagon tracks to follow. The young medical captain who directed the firefighters reported that the fire was extinguished with the assistance of a thousand GIs and a young lady physicist. The clouds stopped dueling and released some moisture for us.

We acquired slickers and rode despite the weather. Eric wasn't ready for the trails then, and our rides were confined to the portreros north of town where there were primitive roads. The horses loved those rides; they were allowed to gallop to their hearts' content. Old Brownie was five-gaited. He undoubtedly taught himself his gaits, and he taught Smokey even more than I did. Brownie was a quarter horse and had the fastest sprint on the Hill. After he beat Smokey to the quarter mile, he always paused to give instructions to the colt before he went into his rack. Smokey worked hard to imitate him, and it made smooth riding for Eric and me.

The potreros were inhabited before the army took possession of them. We dismounted, dropped our reins, and let the horses graze while we went through abandoned log houses and speculated about remodeling them. At one place the remnants of a woman's garden bloomed despite encroaching wild grasses. The house was papered with newspaper, and the first time we went into it, Eric picked a folder off a rickety table and looked at it.

"See what I found." He spread the folder open so I could see it.

It was an old map of the area; all the trails were clearly marked. There was a trail over to Guaje Canyon; one didn't have to follow the water line road, which was fenced. Quemazon Trail threaded its way through the Jemez Mountains and led to the northern end of the Baca Location (a magnificent summer grazing area in a volcanic caldera and forbidden to Hill people). The Baca Location was known as the Valle Grande, but the map showed it was divided into a number of valleys, each with a separate name. Quemazon Trail eventually led to the Rio de los Indios in the Valle San Antonio.

Eric's discovery was an open sesame to the tops of the mountains; the trails to the tops of Caballo and Tschicoma were clear. All north-central New Mexico was accessible to horseback riders and hikers. Eric's find was a sensation; Cyril, who represented the hikers, was enthralled. He, Genia, Rudy, Eric, Martha, and I argued the relative merits of two feet versus four feet at our evening get-togethers while assorted spouses and innocent bystanders dodged the brickbats. The hikers were determined to go every place the riders did. Martha and I laughed at them; Genia was torn.

"I will ride and hike, also. That way we can tell who makes the better time and has most fun!" she declared.

"Let's ride over to Guaje and take a look at the dams," Martha suggested. "John said that he went over there with Our General when they were finished, and they didn't look adequate for even a small community when he saw them. He said he told the general so, and His Nibs puffed up and announced, 'If there's anything the army engineers do know how to do, it's to keep water flowing to a community.'"

I didn't think to ask which John she meant; it really didn't matter anyway. His was a lone voice in the wilderness.

"It will be an all-day trip," I protested.

"Take a picnic lunch and stop worrying. I can open a can of soup and make sandwiches as well as you can," Eric rebutted.

"Eric and Bill can eat with us if you don't get home in time for dinner," Ruth volunteered. "I'll bet Virginia Ayres would like to go, too. I'll feed Alan and Betty along with your boys."

Thus the all-day riding club was organized. Its charter members were Martha, Genia, Ione (whose husband was a banker in civilian life but was currently a captain in the army), Hazel Kline (whose husband was a craftsman), Virginia, and me. We were a cosmopolitan group, but none of us gave it a thought. It was the way things were done inside Box 1663 in pioneer days.

The Allens, Mary on Brownie and Jim on Dulcey, joined us occasionally. Muriel and Trevor Cuykendall enjoyed infrequent expeditions. Trevor's hobby was photography, and he took some wonderful pictures. Brownie was in constant demand. Rudy and Genia acquired a small buckskin horse named The Pill. Oppie, Dr. Louis Hemplemann, and George Kistiakowsky all owned horses and sometimes escaped from the pressure of the Tech Area on horseback. All kinds and ranks of people rode—scientists, GIs, technicians, and machinists.

When the all-day riding club made its first trip to Guaje, only the charter members were present. We gloried in the country and inhaled the pure air of the highlands. Wild iris was still in bloom and wild anemones nodded. Jeep tracks led west, up the floor of the canyon; we followed them. The stream was approximately five feet wide.

"See, there's the pumping station!" Martha cried.

The pipeline was above the ground from the pumping station to

~ *The aboveground pipeline*

the rim of the canyon, and its insulation was mutilated.

"What do you suppose happened to it?" someone asked.

"I suppose it was the bears; it looks to me as though they liked the flavor of the adhesive. What they didn't eat, they probably pulled off through sheer devilment." The bare pipe looked to have an outside diameter of about seven inches.

"Where are the dams?"

We looked ahead but saw no dams. We turned our horses into the stream. The water was good for their hooves, and we couldn't miss the dams if we rode in it. Water from a small pool cascaded merrily over the top of a grassy embankment that blocked the stream. Smokey stepped over the obstruction and paused to drink. I looked down idly; the end of the pipeline opened into the pool. The embankment was just high enough to back the water into the pipeline.

"Great jumping Jupiter! Come here and look!"

The other five gathered around and conversation was general.

"My Heavens, is this the town water supply?"

"All I can say is that I hope this stream keeps running."

"It must freeze in the winter."

"There's quite a drop here, and if there's a sufficient flow of water it wouldn't freeze solid."

"We'd better get our horses out of the drinking water."

We picnicked downstream from the dam. The horses grazed peacefully while we assessed the situation further. There were several obstructions above the one that filled the pipeline.

"I suppose those are stilling pools." Martha said.

"I suppose so," I replied, "but I don't like the look of this at all. This source might have had adequate water for the original installation, but with Morganville, McKeeville, the huts, the trailer area, and new dormitories and barracks, we're going to be out of water before we know it."

"Mr. Armstead, who's in charge of the water supply, said they're going to develop a secondary water source for the town at Water Canyon. It's south of S Site. The site gets its water supply from the upper canyon, but there are springs in the lower canyon, also."

"Does the pipeline empty into the storage reservoir?"

"Yes. It's chlorinated before it's pumped into the water tower."

We were a thoughtful group of women when we rode home.

"Let's go for a picnic," Bill urged. The day was Sunday.

"Let's go down to Water Canyon and take a look at the springs you heard about," Eric suggested.

"The Kehls haven't seen much of the countryside; maybe they'd like to come with us. I'll run over and ask them," I said.

So the five of us went for a picnic in lower Water Canyon just before it was fenced off for development of the springs. There were several springs, but they were sluggish. There wasn't much of a flow.

"I hope they give more water than that when they're dug out," Eric said.

"What are those things floating around in there?" George pointed. "They look like horsehairs."

Bill, Kay, and I joined the men.

"They look as though they're alive," Kay said.

"They are. They look like snakes," Bill guessed.

"Ugh, I hope they filter the water when they pump it out of the storage dam!" Kay exclaimed.

I'm sure there was some kind of a filter, but it wasn't fine enough to keep hair snakes out of the water lines. When our shower head was clogged, Eric took it off to clean it and found a defunct snake. Bob Dunlop poured himself a glass of water and a lively hair snake was in it; fortunately, the light was on and he saw it before he drank it. An eighteen-inch hair snake came out of the tap at the horses' trough; it was a fine specimen.

The grapevine hummed constantly. The non-working wives were only human; they speculated on the activity in the Tech Area, and took some wild guesses. After Eric's warning outburst at the time of the Battle of the Fighting Fourteen, I kept my mouth shut and my ears open. To distract myself, I carried on a voluminous correspondence. I wrote to my friends, to my father, to the aunties, and to all other relatives. I wrote volumes to Preston, who languished in the South Pacific, and was much freer in my documented conversation with him than I was with the others.

My brother was my only family contemporary, and I worried more and more as the Pacific War advanced.

"Maybe his medical unit will move up when they assault the Philippines," I thought.

"Don't be silly," the sixth sense said. "Preston's unit is being held for the final assault on the Japanese homeland. It will be a slaughter. The second wave will climb over the hills of the dead. It will be far worse than the slaughter at Saipan."

One evening at a party, I discussed my worry with Dr. Nolan.

"It's a wicked waste of talent," I said. "I had a letter today; an army nurse was flown in for a hysterectomy and he wrote that he did an extra special fine job for her. He said he was like an old fire horse smelling smoke."

"I could use his kind of help around here; if he'll put in for a transfer, I'll do the rest. Are you sure he doesn't want to die for his country or do something noble?"

"I'm not sure about anything these days, and I'm not sure I could ask such a question with the mail censored."

I couched the question with many words in my next letter. My brother missed it, but so did two sets of censors. I probably should have asked it in plain words; the censors might have passed it.

I never had trouble with the boys and girls in uniform who read the mail. They acquired a nice understanding of family situations. The mail to the South Pacific was cleared posthaste. The censors developed a sympathetic interest in all our doings. They congratulated the Hill folk when babies were born and rebuked them for failing to enclose promised checks or other things in letters.

The censors were extremely handy when the mail-order houses sent the wrong merchandise, a common occurrence. They wrapped clumsy packages and saw that all essential papers were in the envelopes attached to the outgoing packages. On occasions their exasperation with the mail-order houses exceeded our own. One time the censor felt my protest wasn't strong enough. I followed the suggestion he made and got results.

"Well, Violet got her rattlesnake; she brought it into the Tech Area this morning to boil it. She says she already has the coral and turquoise," Ruth reported one Monday when she came home for lunch.

We were finished with our lunch when the fire sirens shrieked. Fire in the Tech Area! Eric put down his napkin and hurried out. Bill and I trailed him to the door, but he was already out of sight. We joined the Haleys on the back porch. We couldn't see any smoke. "You girls stay here. I'll walk over to the fence and see if I can see anything," Jano said.

Ruth and I waited apprehensively for his return.

"I couldn't see a darn thing," he reported. "Apparently it was a small fire and they got it under control immediately, so there's nothing to worry about."

He left us and went back to work. That evening when Eric came home, I asked, "Did you find where the fire was?"

"No, it wasn't in D Building, thank God." (D Building housed CM Division.)

The next noontime Ruth came up the steps laughing.

"I found out about the fire. Violet left the snake to simmer in her lab while she went to lunch. It boiled dry and began to smoke. There's a sign on her cubby hole that reads:

DANGER!
Do not enter except
by express permission

"She rushed back to the Tech Area when she heard the fire siren and found the firemen clustered around her door looking at the sign while smoke from her scorching reptile filled the corridor."

"Poor Violet. She'll have to find another snake."

"Yes, but I'll bet a dollar they don't let her boil it in the Tech Area. The CO has to report all fires officially."

The official explanation must have been a bit awkward.

8

"That will teach them!" Muriel exclaimed darkly. She was on her way home from the hospital, and I was on my way to the PX.

"What will teach who?"

"A carpenter working on the floor of the new barracks dropped his hammer this morning. He reached through an opening in the floor to get it and was struck by a rattlesnake. His friends put a tourniquet on his arm and hauled him up to the hospital. What do you suppose they told him in emergency?"

"They probably said he was having DTs."

"They laughed themselves silly and said," Don't you know rattlesnakes aren't found at this altitude?" Fortunately his friends had killed the snake and taken it to the hospital with him. They changed their tune in a hurry when they saw the snake and they actually had one—just one—dose of anti-venom."

"Probably left over from ranch school days. I could lend them my snake bite kit."

"They're sending some more serum up from Santa Fe this afternoon. I told them if anybody else got struck before Don arrived with the serum, you had a kit."

"They learn the hard way around here. I haven't seen you since a bunch of us rode over to Guaje the other day. The so-called dams are nothing but stilling pools, and the pool that drains into the pipeline is just high enough to back the water into the pipe. The line lies above ground most of the way into town. We went over the trail but came home along the road. Somehow, Martha got a key to the gate."

"Eleanor, what will happen to us?"

"We'll live and learn, I hope!"

Croton-on-Hudson was a place that existed in the dim past of the Outer World.

Eric, who disappeared into the Tech Area morning and noon and emerged distraught for lunch or on the shank of the evening, bore only faint resemblance to the Eric who taught at the School of Mines. From his classes Eric had come home relaxed to sip his drink in front of the fire or under the willow tree until our Reba whispered, "Dinner is served."

Bill, who crawled in and out of the town fence at will and rode Brownie without saddle or bridle, guiding him with a handful of mane, was not the Bill who swam in the pools of the Croton River or the one who played contentedly with the Harris youngsters.

Mikey, small tiger cat, brought home half-eaten chipmunks and occasional live ones instead of small dead mice that she spurned as food. She turned tail and ran when the Haley tiger tomcat made lecherous advances, instead of standing her ground and swatting him firmly as she did with her brother Johno.

Eleanor, who roamed the beautiful country on her big pinto horse and worried about her family, her brother, the war, the expanding community, and what the hell they were doing in the Tech Area, was only faintly similar to the professor's wife, the woman who was once a very active member of the League of Women Voters and gave the hometown politicians fits. The new Eleanor transferred her political interests to the army via the Town Council.

Alice's description of the council was true—a public sounding board without any real authority—but the university personnel office was always officially represented at the meetings and so was the army administration. When I first attended the meetings, the army representative was a tall, dark major built like a football player. I can't remember his name, so I'll call him Major Spade.

The grapevine said Major Spade was one of Our General's stooges, i.e. a member of the general's Washington staff temporarily stationed on the Hill to check up on our local army administration. Stooge or not, I liked the major. He had a good sense of humor, and we almost always found our mutual chuckle at each meeting. Things to chuckle about were few and far between. We also tilted publicly on the floor.

The public eating facilities, the hospital, the community laundries, and the commissary were constantly on the council's agenda.

The public eating facilities were Fuller Lodge, the Tech Area PX, and two mess halls. Most of the dormitory dwellers ate in the mess halls. The food was unspeakable, but Archie the Cockroach and all his progeny thrived on it. The eating places served meals only at regular hours with the exception of the Tech PX, and it closed at ten o'clock. There was no place for the unmarried to eat when they worked the swing shifts.

"When will we have acceptable eating facilities?" asked the dormitory dwellers.

The hospital was too small and inadequately staffed. People who needed immediate medical attention waited for hours in the crowded reception room.

"When are we going to have a proper medical installation?" demanded the town's people.

"The hospital has been enlarged."

"Enlarge it again."

The enlarged commissary was already outgrown.

"When will we be able to shop without being killed in the crush? Why doesn't someone requisition grocery carts for us?" questioned the outraged housewives.

The washing machines in the community laundries broke down regularly. The wringers were temperamental when sheets and towels were fed to them. They slipped their moorings and whirled like dervishes, whipping the heavy, wet articles around and around.

"Those eight machines are worn out. We're tired of playing squat tag with the wringers. We need new machines and a lot more of them," the women chorused.

At one typical meeting, a dormitory dweller complained of the consistency of the gravy in the mess halls. The food, according to him, was fine, but the gravy was not like the gravy Mom made.

The major snorted, "I went to the west mess the other night to see just how bad it was," he whispered.

"Well?"

"It's not bad—it's God-awful—and I almost bit down on a cockroach."

"I understand some of the aborigines consider them to be great delicacies—crunchy, you know."

"I belong to the wrong tribe."

Our whispered asides always drew dirty looks from the chairman. Later, when the laundries were under attack, the major rose to his feet and announced, "The women abuse the machines."

I almost knocked him down when I rose to the bait.

"Have you ever done the family washing, major? No? I thought not. Well, I'd like to inform you that those eight machines get more wear in two or three weeks than most washing machines get in a year."

The power failures in the town were discussed. There were complaints about the amount of disinfectant used in the water and the exotic flavor of the milk. I knew the answers to the latter two complaints. Every time I thought about the water supply, I had the silent, screaming meemies, but I refrained from saying so in a public meeting.

As for the milk, veterinarian Bob Thompsett worked indefatigably to make sure that all the animals in the milk shed were healthy, but he had no control over their food. As the population swelled, the milk shed expanded, other flavors clashed with that of sagebrush.

On one occasion, the major walked me home, and we argued Washington policy.

"I don't see why that man in Washington is so darned tight-fisted," I said.

"You have no idea of the extent of this project. It's costing hundreds of millions of dollars. He's acting under presidential directive, and he'll be accountable to Congress at the end of the war."

"I have a better idea of the extent of this project than you think. I know the laboratories at Chicago, Ames, and Berkeley are mixed up in it and that Oak Ridge and Hanford are part of it. In spite of that, I understand this laboratory will give the final answers to the project's success or failure. If the work here is a success, Congress is going to be too pleased to criticize. If it's a flop, will Congress land on his neck any harder if he spends $605 million or $606 million?"

"A million dollars is still a lot of money. Men have no right to subject their wives to life on this Hill. You're an educated woman with an academic background. What are you doing here?"

"A million dollars is peanuts, and you know it. We pay taxes, too. My man is doing a job over there in the Tech Area, and I'm here to take care of him."

The major gave up.

Time moved on. The children were released from school. I attended graduation exercises for the first graduating class from the Los Alamos High School. Hazel Kline's only daughter and Sally Flanders' elder daughter were sweet in their white dresses, and their mothers were proud of them. Both mothers knew they would part with their daughters until the end of the war when the girls left for college in September. Security was adamant; if you lived on the Hill and left to live elsewhere, for any reason whatsoever, you could not return to it.

The PTA organized a summer playground for children of working mothers. Bill picked up some loose change by taking Brownie to the playground and giving rides for 25¢ apiece. The east end of town was jammed, and the trailers spilled out of their assigned area. Harassed provisionals ran current to them; the power lines snaked along the ground. The latrines were crowded.

Bradley's army erupted from Normandy, cut off Brittany, penetrated Brest, and aimed an arm of its thrust at Paris. Planes fanned out from Chungking, Saipan, and New Guinea to drop bombs on Japanese positions as far north and east as Tokyo.

The tensions generated from the Tech Area increased, and a new warning blossomed in the Bulletin:

HIKERS AND RIDERS ATTENTION
Bears are wild animals;
do not try to get close to them. It is especially dangerous
to come between a mother bear and her cub!

Ruth and I laughed over the headline.

"We're always scared to death of meeting a bear on the trails," I said. "Last week we were up on the ridge, and Virginia and I were about fifty feet behind the others. We passed a thicket and heard a formidable growl. Fortunately, we were downwind from the bear so the horses didn't bolt."

Ruth shivered. "What would you do if they did?"

"Hang on to the reins, grab leather, and indulge in fervent prayer. I understand the chances of survival are better if you let your horse run as long as he wants to run."

"One of the boys in our group had a close call on Sunday. He took a couple of the girls out for a fish fry. He was going to catch the fish, and the girls were going to cook them. They hiked down the trail in upper Frijoles Canyon, and the girls decided to go for a walk while he fished.

"He was so busy trying to catch the fish for lunch that he didn't look around when he heard them come back. He came to and thought it was odd they didn't say anything. He looked over his shoulder, and there stood mama bear on her hind feet. She was about ten feet from him. Baby bear was about fifty feet downstream.

"Our boy said he was paralyzed with fright. He couldn't have moved to save his life. Fortunately, baby bear decided to climb a tree, and his mama dropped down on her four legs and rumbled off to slap him down. Our boy dropped his rod and took off at a dead run to find the girls and get the hell out of there."

"It's lucky he was paralyzed. She'd probably have attacked if he had made a move."

"I'd be scared to death to ride out on those broken-down trails the way you do. What if you met a bear on the Quemazon Trail?"

Ruth's question posed some nice points. The Quemazon Trail was about two feet wide and ran up the side of a mountain that sloped at a seventy-degree angle down to a canyon one thousand feet below. Before the Hill came into existence, the forest service kept it in good condition. After the government took control of the property, the trail was cluttered with windfalls at several points.

Most of the windfalls presented no problem, but at the steepest point on the trail a tree fully two feet thick blocked it. The first time the all-day riders rode the trail, they decided to lead their horses down the mountain around the root of the tree and back up to the trail. Martha and I made up our minds then and there that it was more dangerous to keep out of the way of our lunging horses on the way back to the trail than it was to stay on their backs while they slid down the mountainside on their rumps and lunged up again. Henceforth, we stayed put, but a bear on the Quemazon would cause real trouble.

"It's worth the risk," I said. "The views are magnificent, and the wildflowers are simply divine. When you drop down into the Valle San Antonio and look back, the boughs of the spruce on the sides of the mountains intertwine into waving lines. Eric says the spruce in the Black Forest grow like that. I won't let Smokey eat while I'm on his back, but in Valle San Antonio he doesn't have to put his head down, he just opens his mouth and nibbles as he goes along."

"It sounds heavenly."

"It is, and I can forget all my problems."

I wasn't the only one who needed to forget problems. The men who theorized, experimented, and finally fabricated and assembled the components of the bomb were under tremendous pressure. They communicated the pressure to their wives and to the Tech Area workers who did not have access to classified information. The pioneers of the new and frightening era escaped their tasks with hard play whenever opportunity offered itself, which was every Saturday night and Sunday.

The Hill dwellers were amateur everything: hikers, riders, photographers, ethnographers, mineralogists, musicians, and artist-craftsmen in assorted fields. Saturday nights they partied and square danced. Sundays they fished or exploited their hobbies. The parties were diversified.

Sometimes there were dorm parties; sometimes groups gathered spontaneously to indulge in all sorts of silliness; sometimes small parties were planned.

Some of the gatherings were homogeneous—all from one division or group. CM Division had a lusty crew. I have fond memories of Cyril puffing at the fires to coax them into flame and of the Kolodneys, Morris and Edith, acting out their version of spectators at a City College football game: "City Collitch! City Collitch! Ve Vin! Ve Vin! Ve Vin! VOT? Ve LOST?! Ve vas ROBBED!!"

~~~~~ *British Mission Party in Fuller Lodge*

How Joe Kennedy loved a party! His eyes sparkled, and his engaging grin was always in evidence. CMers had good times together.

Some of the parties were heterogeneous—they cut across division lines. At the British Mission parties we frequently sipped mulled wine while Otto Frisch recited limericks learned from years of riding the London Tube or sketched our pictures in caricature. When Frisch finished a caricature of you, you wanted to cut off your head.

It would take an entire volume to list the pioneers and their hidden talents, which were sharpened by altitude and isolation.

Occasionally individuals or groups of individuals gave big parties, cocktail parties, or dances in the dining room of Fuller Lodge or at the Big House. The dances were always spiced with skits. We were able to laugh at ourselves and lampoon our gripes: Our General, security, and the eternal priorities that governed our lives. We hauled them out and roughed them up periodically. Nothing was sacred, and woe betide a stuffed shirt! Visiting consultants were always welcomed to the parties, large or small.

Scientists of the British Mission performing a skit at their party

The one-month school vacation was almost over. It was fiesta time in Santa Fe. The Hill dwellers piled their children into the cars and went to watch the burning of Zozobra (Old Man Gloom) and the re-entry of the conquistadores on Friday evening. The British Mission, almost to a man, took Saturday off and returned to town to participate in the nonsense.

On Sunday morning Genia hammered on our door.

"Come and see our car. We have named it Conquistador in honor of the occasion!"

The neighbors gathered. Conquistador's hood was up. Rudy and Enrico were in conference over its engine. The Kolodneys, who lived across the street from us, joined Conquistador's admirers. Norris Bradbury, who arrived on the Hill in July and with his family occupied an apartment in the house recently vacated by the architects, put in an appearance. Norris was then a lieutenant commander in the navy, and I knew Deak Parsons was happy to have him aboard.

"It's a rattletrap, but it will get us about," Genia proclaimed jubilantly, while the men examined the engine.

Conquistador was, indeed, a rattletrap. It rattled, trapped, coughed, and died at regular intervals, but as Genia said, it got them about. It joined Timoshenko, Brownie, Aunt Melinda, Dick Feynman, and other town characters as a conversation piece.

The children were safely tucked away in school. The incoming principal, Miss Alice Hamilton, was a sound, sensible administrator. She announced that the school year 1944–45 would follow the patterns of the school years in the Outer World. Every thoughtful mother in town wanted to kiss her.

"Furthermore," said Miss Hamilton, "I will serve at Los Alamos only if I can hire professional teachers for the grades that need them."

La Jette gave a loud cheer and the Washington administration capitulated. I don't know what methods of persuasion were used on Our General. It was probably the "We wanna go home, Papa" type.

The dual occupancy of schoolrooms was abolished; the sixth grade had a room to itself. Bill liked his teacher and she liked him. Ma leaned back with a sigh. At least one problem was temporarily licked.

"Let's make the most of this heavenly weather," Martha urged, eager for a ride.

"Let's take the trail map to the commissary and go over it with Bences. He knows this country like the palm of his hand. He'll know where the springs are," I suggested.

Bences examined the map.

"Ah, Señoras, I would love to go with you and guide you, but unfortunately, I cannot. There are three pine trees just here," he put a dot on the map. "The spring is about thirty feet this way." He made a small sketch. "At Camp May, a spring gushes. The ranch school boys loved Camp May," he smiled reminiscently and described the landmarks for other springs in the Camp May vicinity.

"Darn it, I just found out I am going to have a baby next spring," Virginia said when she learned what we were planning.

"I have to get Jean ready for college," Hazel added.

"I have a ride to Santa Fe," Genia whined, not wanting to miss out on either event.

"I have a long-standing commitment. Can't you change the date?" Ione protested.

"No, we'll go anyhow. If it's nice we'll go again."

On the morning of our first expedition to Camp May, Martha loafed in her saddle while I adjusted the saddle bags, cinched Smokey's girth, and maneuvered him into a hollow to mount. My legs weren't long enough to reach the stirrup if I was on level ground, and he knew it.

"Have you got everything we need?" Martha asked.

"I've got the map, gun, and elastic bandage. I didn't think we'd need the fence tool and bailing wire; we won't leave the site today."

The fence that separated the project's property from the Baca Location was a four-strand, barbed-wire affair. Cattle grazing in Valle San Antonio knocked it down from time to time, but occasionally the mounted MPs mended it. When we left the site we went prepared to take the fence down and replace it when we returned.

Needless to say, we were the bane of the mounted MPs' existence. Veterinary Capt. Bob Thompsett always alerted them after we departed on our expeditions. Bob was a peppery guy who viewed the local scene with distaste. He expressed our own sentiments when he said, "Those boys will be our first line of defense in case of enemy invasion. It's a good thing to keep them on their toes."

In a sense, we were part of the mounted troop. We used many trails of whose existence they were ignorant. We were always on the alert for Japanese balloons carrying firebombs. On one occasion we flushed a mysterious character for them.

There were five of us in the party that day. A dog came bursting out of the forest to greet each horse and rider joyously. He was a miniature collie and his coat bespoke loving care. After he greeted us, he turned and ran back into the underbrush.

"Is he trying to tell us that his master's injured?" someone asked.

We called and called, but no human or canine voice answered. We rode on for perhaps fifteen minutes.

"I don't like people lurking in the bushes," Martha said.

"I think we should go back. I'm sure that dog would've come to us if someone hadn't restrained him," I said.

We retraced our steps, and when we burst out into the open in the meadow overlooking the town, we saw a man in a white shirt take shelter under a tree on the opposite side of the meadow. The dog was at his heels. The man stood motionless under the tree watching us, and little cold squiggles ran up and down our spines. No one in our selected company of workers would behave that way.

We returned home post haste and reported the mysterious visitor. The mounted troop beat the bushes, sprained their ankles, and cursed us, but they found no sign of our man in the white shirt or his dog.

The morning Martha and I rode up to Camp May alone, the horses set out briskly. Diamond had a fast trot that matched Smokey's rack for speed. Martha and I visited comfortably when we were on a path wide enough for us to ride abreast. When we reached the foot of the Camp May trail, we reined our horses to give them a breather before they started the steep ascent. The Camp May trail led off the road that went south from the town to the test sites, and the road itself climbed approximately five hundred feet before it reached the foot of the trail. We looked back at the town.

"Do you suppose it will be there when we come home this afternoon?" Martha asked.

"Who knows? *C'est le guerre.*"

The horses climbed with long strides. They knew better than to rush a climb or a descent. The Camp May trail was wide enough for a jeep and the horses vied to stay even.

"I was at the Hemplemanns' last night," Martha said. "Tuck was there, too. His wife is coming, and he asked if she could ride with us." Deak traveled a lot; Martha was alone about half the time. Why so many men wanted their wives to ride with us remains a mystery. It was a miracle that we survived.

"Has she ridden?"

"He said she took riding lessons in England, but he thinks she should review the walk!"

There was a lovely meadow for the horses at Camp May. We unsaddled them and dropped their reins while we explored our

 Preston

immediate surroundings. The ranch school shelter was a big, one-room log cabin with bunks and a fireplace. The spring was clogged with leaves, and water dripped slowly from the discharge pipe.

"This doesn't look much like the gushing spring Bences remembered." Martha observed.

"It would probably help some if it was cleaned out, but it looks as though the water level has fallen."

We dipped our cups into the spring to fill them and drank our fill of the cold, sweet water.

"Umm, isn't this good?"

"No flavor, mama!"

We filled buckets left behind by the ranch school for the horses and stretched out to laze awhile in the warm September sun before we ate our lunch.

The Outer World, in which the noose tightened on Japan, the battle of France was ending, and a whole army of paratroopers had landed behind enemy lines in the low countries, faded into nebulous unreality. My memory picture of Preston, who waited in the South Pacific for fate to touch him on the shoulder, was blurred. The problems of the town were forgotten, and the menace of the Tech Area was reduced to a minor alarm.

We returned to the real world unwillingly and resaddled the horses to look for the other springs Bences described to us. We didn't have any trouble finding his landmarks, but every spring was dry.

"Let's hope the springs on our watershed don't dry up like these did," I said.

"I guess the snow last winter didn't do much good. If we have lots of snow this year it might help," Martha suggested hopefully.

"It might, but from the looks of things the water table is way down."

We paused at the Camp May spring for one last drink before we started our horses toward home.

The delectable September days slipped by one by one. There was great excitement when a Japanese balloon was sighted one dawn. The word of it was flashed to Kirtland Field in Albuquerque, and they sent a squadron of fighter planes to shoot it down, but it was too high for them to reach. It turned out to be the planet Venus!

The new Scout year began, and I had fifteen little boys in my den. I was appalled. How was I going to handle fifteen without help? Norman turned twelve in the summer. He was in the regular Scouts, and E. R. slept, forever ten years old.

The PTA held its first meeting to plan the activities of the coming year, and I finally went to the hospital for typhoid shots. I didn't even try to go in through the reception room. I used the emergency entrance.

The *Bulletin* continued to warn against wasting water, and its pleas to use extreme care with fire became more urgent. One evening Eric came home and said, "I've got good news. Shad Marshall is coming."

I was delighted. Shad was part of a few idyllic months we spent in Middletown, Ohio, when we were first married. He was a bachelor at the time, so I hadn't met his wife, Natalee, but I was sure any girl Shad had married would be extra special. I was anxious to meet Natalee and see their two babies, who were born about a year apart.

"I had the devil's own time prying Shad loose for this job," Eric said. "Al Seybolt and I are particularly anxious for everything to go smoothly. Will you go to the housing office and check their housing assignments?"

I was happy to oblige Eric and hastened to the housing office.

"These are extra special people," I announced to Vera and Anita.

"We haven't assigned housing to them yet. We'll have three vacancies when they arrive: an apartment, a duplex in Morganville, and a place in McKeeville. We thought of assigning them the apartment, but it has only two bedrooms. We thought we'd better wait and let them decide which place they wanted when they arrived."

When I reported the conversation to Eric, he said, "That's queer, the way everybody in the Tech Area is screaming for housing for their incoming personnel. I wouldn't think there'd be three places vacant."

"Neither did I, but Vera showed me the housing list."

The last September day slipped away in a light snowstorm but left the aspens gold. Eric went to the Tech Area one morning in early October, and I was astonished when he returned home almost immediately. His face was like a thundercloud.

"The Marshalls arrived last night. Nobody let us know, and they spent the night in one of the dormitories. There wasn't room for them at Fuller."

"My heavens, where are they now?"

"Shad's in the Tech Area being processed. Natalee and the babies are at the Seybolt's. Will you straighten out this mess?"

He departed. I jumped into the car and headed for the Seybolt's. My thoughts boded ill for someone. Natalee was a lovely girl, and her babes were darlings. They were immaculate. Judy was wrapped in a snowy blanket, and baby Bill's rompers were spotless.

"We weren't even assigned to the same dormitory," Natalee said. "The babies and I were assigned to a women's dormitory and Shad was assigned to the men's dormitory. Shad didn't use his room. He slept on the floor in my room. We made a bed for Judy in a dresser drawer. Bill and I slept in the bed. Judy was the only one of us who got much sleep, and Shad almost scared the podwads out of one of the dormitory girls when he went down to the day room to heat Judy's bottle. I don't know what we'll do if we have to spend another night like that."

"You won't have to spend another night like that if Eleanor has anything to do with it," Dot Seybold assured her. "I'll take care of the babies, and she'll show you the ropes."

"We have an extra bedroom ourselves if the worst comes to the worst, although I don't know what we'd use for a crib," I soothed.

"Oh, you wouldn't have to worry about a crib. We ordered one from Montgomery Ward in Denver and it's at the warehouse." Natalee brightened perceptibly, and we set out for the housing office.

Vera and Anita awaited our arrival with evident trepidation.

"I'm terribly sorry. The personnel office just goes ahead and assigns housing without telling us about it. The Morganville house is all we have left," Vera said.

I sympathized with Vera but was in no mood to express it. I accepted the key to the Morganville house without comment, and we left to look at it. I never saw such filth. Compared to the pigpen we beheld when we opened the door, my apartment was pristine when I first entered it. Poor exhausted Natalee was speechless and heartsick. Her eyes filled with tears. I was speechless, too—with fury.

"You stay in the car," I commanded when we returned to the housing office. I didn't think she was in any condition to listen to me raise verbal blisters on Vera and Anita. I stalked into the office. Vera and Anita cringed.

"When was that house vacated?"

"Last week."

"Have either of you looked at it since it was vacated?"

Of course they hadn't looked at the house. I proceeded to tell them exactly what I thought, and I concluded, "I want that house cleaned, disinfected, and furnished by six o'clock tonight. If that's not done and Shad Marshall leaves the Hill tomorrow, you can explain to the powers that be why the man CM worked so hard to get left immediately after he arrived. And furthermore, I want you to supply a hot plate so the poor lamb won't have to fire up that kerosene monstrosity every time she fixes a bottle for her baby."

"We can't supply a hot plate. There were only a few left after the apartments were furnished, and the army took charge of them. It almost requires an act of God to get one because our power demand is so far in excess of our supply."

"Okay, who's the vice president in charge of acts of God?"

"Major Spade, and he's a tough nut to crack. We tried to get a hot plate for someone last week, and he turned us down cold."

I wasn't in the least worried about Major Spade and set forth to find him. I finally ran him to earth at the hospital where he was conducting an inspection. He took a look at my face, waved his inspection party aside, and forgot to be formal.

"What on earth is the matter, Eleanor?"

I poured out my story. When I finished, he grabbed a sheet of paper from a nearby desk, wrote out a requisition, and thrust it into my hand. Then, rough, tough, blustering guy that he was, bless his heart, he grabbed me by the shoulders and shook me.

"Will you *now, please* explain why men bring their wives to this place? I wouldn't bring my wife here for any amount of money!"

At the moment I couldn't muster a single valid reason. I took Natalee back to the Seybolt's to rest and stopped at the housing office to leave the requisition for the hot plate. Vera greeted me.

"Eleanor, I went to look at that house right after you left. I never dreamed a house tenanted so briefly could be in such dreadful condition. The cleaning crew is there now."

We agreed there were no hard feelings.

I took Natalee back to the house in the late afternoon to supervise the arrangement of the furniture. The house smelled of disinfectant, but it was shining. Natalee hugged me.

"This can't be the same place," she exclaimed.

Shad found his way home from the Tech Area.

"Say! This is kind of cute."

Natalee and I exchanged smiles; she had joined the sisterhood. I ended my busy day helping Shad assemble Judy's new crib.

The golden October days marched by. SEDs and civilian personnel poured onto the Hill. The SEDs were sometimes racked up—ninety men to a barracks intended to hold sixty until additional quarters were provided for them. I didn't know about the civilians unless they were in my province. I guess they were hung from sky hooks. The incidence of power failures increased.

Our pained awareness of the inadequacies of our water system led us to commit strange acts. Eric had a dental appointment in Santa Fe; he emerged from Dee Lord's office laughing. "I'm hopelessly Hill Happy," he declared.

"What happened?"

"You know that little basin where Dee leaves the water trickling all the time? Well, he went out of the room to get something, and I just couldn't stand it any longer. I turned the water off. He thought I was nuts."

I added my agreement. "You know that sign on the nut vending machine in Payless Drugstore—Nuts from All Over the World? I think that's us. None of us would be on the Hill unless we were nutty."

Eric considered my statement momentarily and grinned widely. "You're right. The physicists make impossible demands, and my boys accept them as routine. They do things every day that no sane guy in the Outer World would even attempt." He took my arm. "Come on, let's go over to La Cantina and have lunch. It's early. Maybe we can get one of Lulu's tables."

"We should take another long ride before the mountain trails are clogged by snow," Martha said.

"I'd like to ride up Caballo." Caballo was the third highest peak in the Jemez Range; it was distinguished by a big square meadow just below the summit on the south side.

Martha and I pored over the trail map. The ride up Caballo was not as long as the ride over the ridge to Rio de los Indios in Valle San Antonio, but it was long and Caballo was a stiff climb. The trail up the mountains started at the head of Guaje Canyon.

"I think we can do it in a day," Martha said. "We can take the road over to Guaje. That'll save time. Who shall we ask to go along?"

"We can't take a tenderfoot on this jaunt."

Five seasoned feminine riders left the west barn at seven o'clock on Halloween morning. Smokey kicked his heels and gaily jumped every gully and twig while his rider led an off-key chorus. "Oh, what a beautiful morning—."

It was a beautiful ride. A ponderosa pine marked the beginning of the trail at the head of Guaje Canyon. A forest service sign proclaimed it was 298 feet high. Our way was cushioned with fragrant pine needles. An infant stream gurgled merrily as it threaded its way beside the trail for a while. We paused to rest our horses and let them drink, where the trail to the summit branched from the one that led to Vallecitos de los Caballos. In the "little valley of the horses," grass grew waist-high, bluebells nodded, and the little stream sang.

We wound our way up and up, through lush spruce forest festooned with moss. Aspens and scrub oak clung to their gold and scarlet leaves. Our seasoned trail horses, in their winter coats, were dripping with sweat when we reached the field below the summit. I had a towel and rubbed Smokey down. The others used saddle blankets. I exchanged Smokey's bridle for a halter so he could enjoy the luxuriant wild grass to the utmost.

"Isn't this air sublime?" Martha asked as we inhaled great gulps of it.

Southern New Mexico stretched as far as the eye could see. We could see where the highlands dropped off at La Bajada. The map of Santa Fe was as clear as was our townsite, the Tech Area, and the test sites to the south.

"Distance lends enchantment, doesn't it?" I asked.

We picnicked, sunbathed, and made our way home by the light of the Halloween moon. Women and horses were tired. Martha and I threw our right legs over the pommels to rest them and came home sidesaddle.

When we opened our eyes the next morning, ten inches of snow covered the ground.

9

he first snow of the season was accompanied by bitter cold and gray weather. When I went to feed the horses, I discovered Smokey had a torn leg, and he had some suspicious-looking spots on his back. The horse in the stall next to his had been in a section of the Valle Grande where there were sheep; he had ringworm. I cursed the other occupants of the west barn heartily. Several of them allowed their horses to stand unattended in their own filth, and I'd repeatedly nailed up the board on the corral fence upon which Smokey tore his leg.

In defense of the owner of the horse with ringworm, I consoled myself with the fact that his animals were almost as carefully-tended as mine. I saddled Smokey and rode him straight through town to the veterinary hospital. When we approached the gate to the Tech Area the brakes of an oncoming truck screamed and Smokey, who was frisky from the cold, almost sat down on his rump to avoid trampling Uncle Nick.

Uncle Nick was deep in the throes of some complex problem and looked neither right nor left when he charged out of the Tech Area. The MPs on the Tech Area gate gasped with relief when all traffic, equine and vehicular, ground to a halt. His son, Jimmy, was no place in sight.

"Uncle Nick!" I shrieked, "look where you're going!"

He emerged from his intellectual mists with a start and beamed at me. "What a beautiful animal!"

We were right smack in the middle of the road. Smokey arched his neck and pranced while he was admired. I chided our absent-minded friend.

"You mustn't do things like this. You must stop at the gate and count to ten before you look both ways and cross the street. There's a wild turkey that struts around in Los Alamos Canyon below Omega. I'm trying to teach Smokey it's a dangerous bird and that he should step on its neck in self-defense. I don't want him to practice on you."

He considered my statement solemnly.

"Will you invite us to dinner if he slays the predatory bird?"

"Indeed I will, but you must take care of yourself or you won't live that long."

He crossed the street and entered the Tech PX safely. The onlookers exchanged meaningful glances. I could almost hear them saying, "Both of them are nuts."

(The Tech Area was built on the north rim of Los Alamos Canyon and wastes from the laboratories were washed into it below Omega. Omega was a detached part of the Tech Area. I knew it was the home of the "water boiler," but I didn't yet know it was the code name for a small nuclear reactor. I did know from the remote location and the number of signs on the fence saying Danger—*Peligro*—Keep Out that the water boiler was not an outsized tea kettle!)

The veterinary hospital was east of the town fence. I had to show my pass to reach it, and on my return trip I accomplished a feat never matched in the history of the pass system. I went through both the east and west gates of the town without showing a pass.

It was simple. Bob Thompsett confirmed my fears about Smokey's ailments and sent me away loaded with remedies and advice. I had a large bottle of horse liniment tucked under my right arm in addition to the palliatives in my pockets. The bottle looked like pink calamine lotion; it was labeled, *Massage Thoroughly at Regular Intervals*. When I reached the east gate on my return trip, I couldn't hold the bottle, remove my gloves, control my horse, and dig my pass out of my pocket without outside assistance. Smokey wanted to "go home, Ma."

"If you'll just hold his bridle for a minute, I'll get my pass," I promised the MP.

Smokey gave him a dirty look, and the lad shrank back. I knew most of the MPs, SEDs, and provisionals by that time. The scientists and their wives always picked up as many boys as they could carry when both had mutual days off and went to Santa Fe.

"Oh, no, Mrs. Jette! You had your pass when you went out an hour ago. I'm sure you still have it!" We repeated our performance at the west end of town, and the whole Hill chuckled. It didn't take much to amuse us. The lad on the east gate was a particularly nice boy; he was the one who set my mind at rest over our would-be child rapist. One evening, when we returned from Santa Fe, we picked him up with a couple of his cronies at the 'please give us a ride' spot.

The boys discussed a member of their outfit who was sent to a hospital for psychiatric treatment. I had my mind on the road and half heard their conversation.

"Who was that? I can't place him," I said.

"Surely you remember the shack in the wood lot and your washing. Didn't security let you know they caught him?"

"No, and I do thank you."

"What was that boy talking about?" Eric asked me when we were alone.

"My slashed underpants. If you'll build a small fire in the fireplace, we'll burn the evidence." My underclothing was almost in ribbons, but nothing could have persuaded me to mend and don the desecrated garment in my sewing basket.

In the Outer World, Franklin D. Roosevelt was re-elected for a fourth term. Douglas MacArthur made a surprise landing on Leyte and overran two-thirds of it. The casualty lists were appalling. Almost fifteen thousand Japanese were reported dead. The battle of the Philippine Sea was over. A decisive victory at ghastly cost.

The armies in Northern Italy slugged it out over impassable roads bogged down with wind and rain. The Russians battled for East Prussia, and Budapest fell. The Germans fought like tigers at Antwerp, and V-2 rockets, forty feet long and five feet in diameter, with ranges of two or three hundred miles, were beamed at Southern Britain, killing women and children alike. Vengeance weapons, with a capital V.

Vinegar Joe Stilwell was recalled from the Asiatic theater, and Patton prepared to attack the Saar. The Burma Road was a military must. Ernie Pyle was awarded an honorary degree at the University of New Mexico, and twenty-five thousand Japanese dug in on Leyte, more than when MacArthur first attacked it.

In our world, the atmosphere generated by the Tech Area became more frenzied. The theorists, whom we called "the ten to the tenth boys," gathered in groups at the parties and spouted complex equations which had no meaning to anyone not intimately acquainted with the intricacies of modern physics. Even our horses were so accustomed to the sound of high explosives that they didn't even hear the sounds of the tests on the southern sites.

The men in CM had already discovered to their dismay that plutonium did not resemble uranium and that the deadly element existed in five different phases. They worked frantically on one-gram lots, remelting, reshaping, and repurifying them to develop the chemistry and metallurgy of the material. Some metal was malleable, some was brittle. It's no wonder Eric counted the nails in the ceiling. When I read about the work today, many years later, I can feel the urgency behind the printed words.

We got a new commanding officer, Lt. Col. Gerald Tyler. Colonel Tyler was on the Alaskan Highway before he came to Los Alamos, and although I never heard him say so, it's my guess that he wished he'd stayed in the Klondike after he looked at the Hill.

The town had begun to assume the aspect of a drunken nightmare, and, *as usual*, we were out of housing. We were also out of eating spaces, and our enlisted personnel had nothing in the way of recreational facilities, save the movies, Saturday night dances, and basketball games. There was absolutely no place they could go to get away from their over-crowded barracks. Again, the commissary was "busting its bastings."

Our new CO was a man of action. He put in for housing, for money to build an eating place, enlarge the commissary, and do all the myriad things we needed done for us as a town. The answer came back from Washington loud and clear—NO! If we needed housing, he could get some government trailers and Pacific huts; but anything he did had to be strictly accounted for. As for the eating place, he used what money he had available to start a cafeteria—it wasn't enough—he went to Washington for more, which he got under protest, and it still wasn't enough to finish the building. He incurred Our General's everlasting displeasure when he ordered the building finished anyhow, and he built a recreation hall for our soldiers. He was indeed a brave man.

Of course, all those things weren't built overnight, but they were in the mill as the Christmas season approached. With the onset of the holiday season it was time for the Hill dwellers to make plans for it. They couldn't reach all their drafted personnel and bachelors, both male and female, but collectively they did their best. There were very few homes that didn't have at least one uniform at their festive boards.

Ruth and Jano had taken pity on a couple of the bachelors, and their regular dinnertime family numbered six. Ruth called her dinnertime boarders Toby and Dick, and I didn't learn their real names until after the war. When we discussed our Christmas plans, Ruth said, "I don't envy you, Chiquita, I don't know how you're going to do it."

"I can pray that some of them will have other invitations." George Kehl and Eric Jette had decided that we should ask *all* the single people in both groups for Christmas dinner. Kay and I agreed to do it or die in the attempt. If all of them accepted, our apartment would come apart at the seams.

As it was, there were more than twenty guests, and it was no mean feat to prepare food for that number with our sub-standard cooking facilities. We built out the table from the dinette into the living room, set chairs as close as possible, and for the first time in my life the meal was ready to serve when the first guest arrived at the door.

Kay and I put dinner on the table while the men superintended a round of eggnogs. We demolished two twelve-pound turkeys, seven pies, twenty pounds of mashed potatoes (which George spent the morning peeling—I can still see him perched on the kitchen stool) and various poundages of cranberries, green beans, fruit, nuts, etc. How we ever prepared it I don't know, and where it went is an equal mystery. We finished our meal and put the wreckage in the kitchen before we collapsed over chairs and stretched out on the floor.

We spent a lazy, overstuffed afternoon. There were a pair of inseparable SEDs named Somers and Duffy. Duffy was older than most of the others and a student of all possible means of exits from the army, a real specialist in the field. That afternoon, we built "Duffy's Cliffside Tavern" and furnished a parachute to every departing customer. We selected a large inaccessible cave on a sheer face at the foot of Los Alamos Canyon for the prospective business venture and secured a rope ladder for customers' access to it. When they departed, they would be relaxed, and the parachutes would be safer.

The party began at two in the afternoon, and guests recovered sufficiently to go home at 10:00 that night. Bill, George, and Kay stacked and started dishwashing while Eric and I went to feed the horses, who were exceedingly hungry and annoyed. Eric replaced Bill as a dishwasher, and when I opened his window and kissed him goodnight, he muttered, "Gee, that was fun, Ma."

It was a far way from the tears and the "I want to go home, Ma!" of the previous Christmas. I paused with my fingers on the light switch.

"I'm glad you had fun, darling. Sleep tight, and a happy birthday tomorrow."

I snapped the switch and thought briefly of the men, women, and children for whom there would be no tomorrow, and of Preston who waited in the South Pacific, before I joined the dishwashers.

After we finished the dishes, and before the Kehl's left, Kay handed me a square flat package.

"I wanted to send this to a photographic contest, but Security wouldn't let me. They said it violated the rule about taking pictures of other than the sender's family. I wanted to entitle it *New Mexico Ranch Child*, but they said, 'No! Someone may recognize Eric Jette's son.' So here it is, Merry Christmas!"

Bill Jette

It was a beautiful picture. It embodied to perfection the rough and tumble spirit of a ten-year-old boy. It showed Bill, the light just right on his freckled face, against a dimmed-out background of pasture and mountains. He was dressed in his battered cowboy hat and torn chamois jacket. Even the spatters of mud on his sleeve were just right.

It was a gay holiday season. There was an evening of music, and Theater Two was commandeered for the occasion. Kay Manley directed the Hallelujah Chorus, and the musicians gave a recital. Eric played with the other musicians, and Jano Haley worked with the production staff. Ruth and I took the children and squeezed ourselves together on one of the benches. The theater was jammed.

"Jeepers, these benches are hard. I swore I'd never come to see anything in this place after last spring when I watched Madame Curie stir up her pot full of goop to produce radium. I thought that picture would never end!" I whispered.

"I just counted fourteen hallelujahs. We'll be permanently rump sprung, but we'll be cultured."

Smokey's ringworm was a thing of the past, his leg was healed, and the bottle of liniment was stored under the sink. Martha and I took our children riding on the lower potreros. The mountain trails and the canyons were still clogged by the heavy snow that fell the last of October, but the east end of our own potrero, and those at lower altitudes, were free of snow.

There were parties galore, and several families pooled their resources to give a New Year's Eve party at Fuller Lodge. It was the beginning of a tradition. We laughed, skitted, and danced. We rang out the old year and rang in the new one with the bell that summoned the ranch school boys to meals. We joined hands and sang Auld Lang Syne at 2 A.M. on the morning of January 1, 1945. The very way in which we sang portended momentous events.

Major Spade went home to spend Christmas with his family and didn't return. His place at council meetings was taken by the colonel's adjutant, Capt. Sam Musser, who was fresh from the Burma

Road. I missed the major. I liked Sam, but he didn't enjoy a verbal hassle the way the major did.

A full-time, resident chaplain arrived. He was invalided out of the Pacific Theater. He was red of hair and face, a high church Episcopal; I was neither but called him Padre. He and his red-haired WAC secretary, Sara Hearn, set up office quarters in the Big House. The Padre was indefatigable in his efforts to raise the morale of our troops, Wacs, provisionals, MPs, and SEDs. He visited the overcrowded trailer area and the hutments. Even when he first arrived he was wont to rub the cross on his uniform shoulder, gaze heavenward, and mutter.

"God alone knows there was never another place like this on the face of the earth!"

"You can say that again twice, Padre," Sara prodded. "Once for Eleanor and once for me."

Both Eric and I were exceedingly fond of the Padre. He frequently dropped in on us at about 5:15 to talk about the condition of my nonconformist soul for a few minutes until Eric arrived, when we could all relax with a drink.

The wind blew intermittently, even when 1945 was in its earliest infancy. Great icy blasts parched the earth and swirled dust into the houses. Fire sirens wailed incessantly. The first blast always reduced me to jelly. The all-pervading air of urgency from the Tech Area quickened. The furnace men shoveled coal with a will. Our cooperative fireman of the previous winter left to take care of his sick wife, and a coal-crazy demon replaced him. Apartment temperatures were astronomical despite the outside vents. Physicist Hughes had enough of acting as university personnel man and left, to be replaced by Astronomer Shane.

We were fond of both Shanes. They were parents of two grown sons, and she firmly announced: "All boys should be buried at twelve and not dug up till they're eighteen."

"Could you reduce the age limit?" Eric asked plaintively.

Bill was a case. His disposition rivaled a snapping turtle. I hauled him to the hospital to visit Jack Brooks, the newly arrived eye, ear, and such medic. Jack was fresh from somewhere and waspish.

"Woman, why isn't this child wearing glasses? He's hopelessly nearsighted!"

I counterattacked.

"Half a dozen of your colleagues in the Outer World swore he didn't need glasses during the past four years. How do you explain that one?"

We glared at each other, and Jack finally shrugged.

"Sometimes the symptoms of these conditions appear before the condition shows itself. The onset of adolescence might reveal such a condition as critical."

It was the beginning of an enduring friendship, and Bill's disposition improved noticeably when he had windows with which to see the world.

"What goes on in the Tech Area, Ma?"

"Oh, Roosevelt's bound to be elected for a fifth term. They're making campaign buttons."

I didn't think it would be in good taste to tell an eleven-year-old the one about the front ends of horses, but I was sorely tempted. (The theory caught on that the *front ends of horses* were being made at Los Alamos and shipped to Washington for final assembly!)

Our overworked, water-cooled diesel engines sighed and gave up the ghost with increasing regularity, and a supplementary power line was run from Albuquerque. The line helped during the day, but at night, when lights went on and meals were cooked in both places, the state of our power supply was critical. The supplementary line carried the broadcasts from our radio station to Albuquerque.

Dorothy McKibbin reported the situation to me on one of my visits to her office. (Dorothy always loved her news fresh from the Hill, and I always stopped in her office for a visit when I went to Santa Fe.)

"Some friends from Albuquerque were up last Sunday, and they're simply agog down there. They can't imagine where the broadcasts come from or why none of the entertainers have last names. Children's stories read by Betty, newscasts compiled by Bob, and Mozart's piano sonatas played by Otto have them guessing."

The over-enthusiasm of the coal shovellers caused the brochure's "ample hot water" to pale in insignificance. I never figured out how the apartment plumbing was hooked up so boiling water and live steam gushed through the cold water lines. There were some plastic angle pipes on the lines designed to carry cold water to the water closets, and these led to amusing (in retrospect) incidents.

Marge and Raemer Schreiber and Harriet and Marshall Holloway lived in an apartment a few houses up the road from ours. Their apartments were one above the other. Both families enjoyed music and bridge; they spent a lot of time together. After one quiet, pleasant evening, the two couples separated to retire.

Both men retreated to their respective lavatories. Marshall pressed the toilet handle to flush it; it erupted in a geyser of steam and boiling water that hit the ceiling, hard! He leapt into the shower and pulled the curtain to protect himself from the scalding spray, while Harriet, white-faced, tore up the stairs, calling loudly, "Don't flush the toilet, *don't* flush the toilet!"

Raemer was meditating. Chances were, if he'd tripped the handle, he'd have ridden the column of boiling water right up through the roof! The fire department came, threw the fire out of the furnace, and shut off the water, while Marge and Harriet turned on the cold water spigots to drain the boiling water out of the pipes. Of course, the plastic angle pipe melted completely, so the downstairs apartment was flooded.

When Ruth learned what happened to the Schreibers and Holloways, she shook her head.

"I washed yesterday afternoon. Elsie Tuck and a couple of SEDs were there. Elsie's wringer came loose, and she was playing a fast game of squat tag with it. Both the SEDs watched her with eyes as big as saucers. One of them looked at the other and said, "Gee, it's *dangerous* to be a civilian.""

I laughed. "Of course it's dangerous to be a civilian, but I wouldn't miss a minute of it, would you?"

"Not for myself, but we rub off on our children. Can you guess what Mike said at lunch today?"

I shook my head. Ruth's face was unforgettable with suppressed anguish.

"He started to tell me what he wanted to be, but he said, 'If I grow up—!'"

Altitude, isolation, drought, and the intermittent, howling winds augmented the irritation of the restrictions under which Hill dwellers labored. Even our security people recognized that the restrictions which confined us to an area bounded on the north and south by Taos and Albuquerque, on the east and west by Las Vegas and Cuba, and required us to sever all personal relationships, caused hardship and undermined morale.

Cumbersome handling of personal emergencies bothered everyone. Telegrams announcing serious illnesses or deaths in families were delayed hours or even days due to poor connections with the Outer World and almost complete lack of intra-Hill message delivery facilities. When the people affected received messages, it was frequently too late to respond to them. In many cases, elderly members of the families were not well and complete separation from them was a sore trial.

Those rules were modified early in 1945. We were allowed to travel provided we observed specific and numerous restrictions.

"Why don't you go to Denver for a week? Maybe you can get a new evening dress there," Eric suggested.

The bait he dangled was irresistible. Daytimes, men and women alike went about dressed in bright gingham shirts with slacks or blue jeans. Evenings, they dressed to the teeth with their hoarded business suits, pre-war nylons, and best navy blue silks. Black ties and evening gowns dominated the big parties, and there was soon to be one. I was heartily sick of my often-worn evening dress, but there was nothing in Santa Fe less than size forty. Santa Fe was out of everything; there were no allocations for non-existent Los Alamos.

I protested, but briefly, and took the Night Crawler (San Francisco Limited) to Denver, where I was met by a tearful and repentant family.

My father said, "You're too thin, Bugs."

The senior auntie said, "When I went to Montgomery Ward to buy the doormat for you, I told the clerk to send it to Mrs. Eric R.

Jette, Box 1663, and he wrote Santa Fe, New Mexico. I asked him how he knew the city and state. He said he had a son at the same address. We looked at each other, and he said, 'From the number of doormats we send down there, our youngsters must be in a hell of a hole.'"

The junior auntie, who had a sore arm, said, "When did you last have your hair done, honey?"

I had my hair done and my nails tended, and the junior auntie took time off from her job to be with me. I was grateful, for only with her did I feel completely at ease. We went to the Denver Stock Show and shopped.

"I'm not going to question you, darling. I know you can't answer, but our maintenance men say the country is beautiful."

"The country is magnificent, only man is vile."

Her eyes filled with tears. "It's bad enough to have Preston mixed up in this awful war. I just can't bear to think you're involved, too."

I patted her sore arm gently. "Come on now, kiddo, we're never going to find a dress for me unless we get going." Her arm worried me, although she said it was just a touch of arthritis.

We found the dress; it was an elegant black nylon job, with an eyelet-embroidered bodice over pale pink net. It smashed my budget to smithereens, but as the junior auntie said, "Who cares?"

I had the dress shipped to Box 1663, kissed them all goodbye, and departed with relief. The circumstances of my life were so different from theirs that even if I were free to discuss them, they wouldn't be able to understand them.

Eric met me when I stepped off the train at Lamy, and we took the bus to Santa Fe where the car was garaged for an overhaul. The car had no brakes. We cursed and repaired to La Fonda's cantina while the red-faced garage people worked to remedy the situation.

"I haven't seen you folks for a long time," Lulu said as she brought our drinks.

"I'm just back from the Denver Stock Show, and I bought a dress."

"Lucky you. Those people from up there keep this town

stripped." She tossed her head in the general direction of the Hill.

"How was the stock show?"

"The usual. Not as good as the ones in the pre-war years."

Lulu was a lamb. She was a long-time employee at La Fonda and could persuade Conrad, the chef, to make special dishes for us if we didn't like the ones on the menu. (Which we usually didn't.) When she left us, I asked, "Did anything special happen this week?"

"There was one beauty. The Critchfields came to Santa Fe to shop."

"Oh?" Charlie Critchfield was about six-feet-four, Lincolnesque in appearance, and devoted to a broad-brimmed Stetson hat.

"Yep. He passed a tiny, elderly lady who apparently had a phobia about young men who are not in uniform. She tapped him briskly on the arm, 'Young man, why aren't you in the army?'

"Critch bent his knees so his face was level with hers, put his finger to his lips, looked around furtively, and hissed, 'Shhhhhhhhh, I am a Japanese spy!' The whole Hill's laughing."

I joined them. It was good to be home; hazardous though life was, the people spoke my language.

A few evenings later, the daytime wind abated and a blessed calm prevailed as we sat down to dinner. Our forks, loaded with the first morsels of food, were raised, when the fire siren shrieked. The poised forks clattered to our plates when it screamed FIRE IN THE TECH AREA!

Eric's face was ashen. He slammed on his hat and coat and left. Bill and I could see the orange glow of flames reflected in the night sky. We bundled ourselves into jackets and mittens and followed him. The Haleys were also on their way to the fire. C Shop, our main machine shop, was ablaze. It was just inside the Tech Area fence. Frantic MPs struggled to keep the fence and road clear of the townspeople and their children. The buildings inside the Tech Area had brick firewalls. The fire escape from the administration building opened onto its firewall and overlooked C Shop. The commanding officer, the director of the laboratory, and the Tech board and its alternates, including Eric, watched the firefighters from the fire escape.

The flickering light of the flames illuminated their grim, set faces. The faces reflected fear for the work program and concern lest the fire spread and wipe out the entire town. The white-faced onlookers on the outside of the fence watched flames spread through the roof of the building. Ruth and I huddled together.

"Thank God there's no wind tonight," I whispered.

"All that water doesn't seem to do a particle of good."

Others whispered in the dark.

"Do you suppose it was sabotage?"

"One of the quenching tanks got loose."

"Jesus, let's be thankful it isn't D Building. That place is as hot as $7 million. Every time it gets too hot for them to work, they slap on another coat of paint."

"This will delay the end of the Pacific war for months."

"Where are the SEDs tonight?"

"They're confined to barracks for some goddamn infraction of rules. They'd sure be useful around here tonight."

"God, look at that water going to waste!"

"We've only an hour's supply left in the storage reservoir."

"If they ever turn that pond into the mains, we're sunk."

Ten thousand years passed before the flames finally flickered and died. Silent and chastened, the onlookers dispersed to their homes. I calmed Bill, who, like all small boys, gloried in the excitement, and pushed him into bed.

Eric came home hollow-eyed but didn't take off his coat.

"Go to bed, darling. We're going to have a meeting and plan what we can do to mitigate this disaster."

"There was less than an hour's water supply when the fire went out," I said.

"I know."

His clothing reeked of smoke.

I added, "Someone said it was a good thing it wasn't D Building. It was as hot as $7 million."

"Damn. You mustn't be upset. We're so careful it's fantastic."

He held me tight for an instant and disappeared into the night.

10

fter the C Shop fire the atmosphere tightened
perceptibly. Eric and the other men disappeared into
the Tech Area at strange hours for indefinite periods
of time. It no longer surprised me when he returned home after an
evening of chamber music and whispered in my drowsy ear, "I'm
going back to the Tech Area. I don't know when I'll be home."

The wind blew almost constantly and increased in intensity.
Occasional light snow did nothing for the water table but turned the
ground to goo. For once, Eric came home from the Tech Area with a
report.

"It's in the minutes of the Tech Board now."

"What's in the minutes of the Tech Board?"

"The fact we'll run out of water if we have another winter
without snow or an exceedingly cold winter."

It was true that in the Outer World there was reason for some
optimism. Warsaw was in Russian hands, and Von Rundstedt's bulge
was contained. It seemed as though a giant pincher was about to
close on Germany, with the Russians striking from the north and
east and the Canadians, Americans, and British striking from the
west. But how long it would take the pinchers to close, no one could
guess. There was hard, almost forgotten, fighting in northern Italy.
Even though fifty thousand Japanese were cut off in Manila and the
Chinese and Indians were met on the Burma Road, the battle for
Luzon was far from over. The real battle for Japan could not start
until the battle for the Philippines was won. The islands to the south
of Japan were secured.

Every time I heard from Preston I was filled with the sick
premonition that his medical unit was being held back until Japan
itself was invaded. The grapevine crackled constantly. Not every
husband was as discreet as Eric, and I sometimes came home with
morsels of news that were guaranteed to turn his hair gray.

The women referred to the super bomb, that I believed was being built, as "the gadget."

"What if the gadget is a flop?" the grapevine asked.

What will happen to Preston, and the uncounted hundreds of thousands of others, both American and Japanese, if it's a flop and doesn't end the war? I wondered bleakly. Soothsayers in the Outer World predicted that the Japanese war would last through 1946 and probably into 1947.

Colonel Tyler, who was responsible to Our General for everything that happened in the Tech Area and town, crawled out on a limb repeatedly for both civilians and troops.

The east cafeteria opened. It seated several hundred people at one time, and the food—ooh, la la—was first-class. Cleo Tafoya, the governor of Santa Clara Pueblo, presided behind the best hunk of roast beef I ever put a tooth into, and it cost all of one buck twenty-five cents. Tafoya's braids, woven with bright yarn, glistened, and his spotless chef's cap added more inches to his tall figure. He beamed at Bill as he loaded our bottomless pit's plate.

"Growing boys need lots of good, red meat," he said with a smile.

The GIs were jubilant at the completion of their recreation hall. The Wacs were provided with sufficient barracks space. Even the PX occasionally got a few desirable items, such as pressure cookers and electric ovens. Of course, such items were snapped up before the harried supply officer could uncrate them, but we always hoped there'd be more presently.

A third community laundry, with six washing machines, opened its doors at the east end of town, and long lines formed. The wringers on the eight machines in the original laundries went to pot. The women took turns and carted the workable wringers from machine to machine.

The colonel's personal risk was considerable, and the limb on which he swayed was slender. We bled for him when the grapevine carried the news of Our General's displeasure at so-called extravagances, and his threat to make the colonel personally responsible for the additional buildings. We determined to bail him out if necessary.

The cross on the Padre's uniform acquired an elegant patina from constant fingering when we again ran out of housing and a government trailer lot was built. I believe the trailers were borrowed from Fort Leavenworth. Quonset and barracks-type huts were hauled in and divided in half. Each half had a living room/bedroom and a partially-screened kitchen. The kitchen sinks supplied cold running water. Both trailers and huts were served by community latrines. Families with one or more children occupied those places, and they weren't day laborers, either. They were skilled craftsmen, scientific personnel, and junior army and navy officers.

A machinists' barracks was built, and men who lived in it were paid inducement wages to leave their families at home. A rowdy element raised seventeen different kinds of hell. They disturbed their peace-loving brethren as well as the other people who lived on the Hill and the people of Santa Fe.

Security itself stepped into one flagrant case. The man involved left his pass in a Santa Fe tavern as security for a bottle. G-2 picked up the pass so he couldn't get back on the Hill, gathered up his clothes from the barracks, and shipped them to his home. No one heard, or cared, how the individual involved made his way home.

"Those men are giving the Hill a terrible reputation down here," Dorothy McKibbin said when we discussed the subject.

"I know, but what can we do?"

My question was a poser. When I said earlier in this story that the military courts had no jurisdiction over the civilians and that the Town Council heard traffic cases only if the offenders appeared voluntarily, I touched our legal status very lightly. New Mexico State Laws contained a permissive section which allowed the federal government to accept exclusive jurisdiction over lands within the state which the federal government acquired for military or certain other purposes.

Anyone in authority in the federal government could accept federal jurisdiction; in our case, the secretary of war accepted jurisdiction over the "Los Alamos Demolition Grounds." Only a few families who lived in buildings that were on the small section of national forest land at the northwest corner of town were state citizens. The rest of us lost our state citizenship.

We could not vote, probate wills, get divorces, adopt children, or legally obtain resident hunting and fishing licenses under the laws of the state. (Fortunately, the people who sold hunting and fishing licenses didn't know the state law.) Births inside Box 1663 were registered in the department of commerce, and vital statistics were kept in the hospital.

The only court to which we could appeal was the federal court. Very few people were aware that there was any court to which they could appeal. The possessors of such knowledge wielded a powerful weapon. Even the hint of court action was enough to make Security cringe and retreat.

The winter wore on and the electricity failed with increasing regularity. The warnings on ways to save water grew more and more frantic; army wreckers toured the outlying sites to pull mired cars out of the muck. There were no repair facilities for civilian cars; our pre-war automobiles sighed and died with alarming frequency.

One evening at the Smith's we bemoaned the state of our automobiles.

"We'll probably have to hitch the horses to our car when we leave here," I said.

"Well, your Aunt Melinda made history when she came west in a covered wagon. I don't see why you shouldn't make it when you go east in a horse-drawn automobile," Alice said.

My words, and Alice's quick response to them, were typical of the things that made us and our friends laugh. Humor was a precious commodity in our restricted and precarious lives. We wrung some amusement out of every situation no matter how ghastly it was when it actually occurred.

Elsie Tuck was a born mimic and a magnificent storyteller. We shuddered and chuckled with her when she told tales of her adventures. When Elsie joined Martha and me on our rides, we informed her that Jim thought she should review "the walk," and she hooted, "That man! After what I went through, I don't need to review anything!"

Her experiences when she followed Jim to Los Alamos were without rival.

She was ready to leave England with Jim, and her ration books were turned in to the proper authorities, when her passage was cancelled. She had to replace the ration books without telling why the originals were turned in. When her passage to the United States was finally confirmed, the papers for it were delivered at the very last minute. She traveled to the port of embarkation alone, laden with heavy baggage. She arrived late in the afternoon, and of course there were no porters.

Embarkation time was 4 A.M.; she tried unsuccessfully to find a place to rest. In despair, she went to the police station and begged permission to rest in the jail house. The constabulary was horrified but finally relented with the proviso that she must take a last look for quarters elsewhere.

Elsie went to the canteen, where a woman night worker questioned her presence. She whispered her predicament to the woman, and the canteen worker took pity on her. She gave Elsie the key to her own room. When the bewildered young woman arrived in New York, she was met by a man from the British Embassy. He provided her with American money and a ticket to Lamy, New Mexico. He instructed her to parry all questions about her destination with the statement that her husband had a job in Lamy. Quite obviously, his knowledge of Lamy was foggy.

A pleasant older couple from California befriended her on the last leg of her journey. They asked her destination and were aghast when she announced happily, "Oh, my husband has a perfectly wonderful job in Lamy!"

As the train neared Lamy, Elsie's friends' concern for her safety neared panic. She knew they feared she was a victim of white slavers, and she was certain that if Jim was not on hand to meet her, they'd snatch her back onto the train. She wasn't certain that Jim knew she was in the country.

Fortunately, Jim anticipated her arrival and was very much in evidence. While he stowed her luggage into the car, she noted a .22 rifle lying on the back seat and assumed it was for defense against hostile Indians. She was bewildered when they came to the foot of the Hill road, where it branched to Pojoaque and Española, and Jim stopped the car. He got out and took the rifle.

"What are you going to do?" she quavered.

"Oh, just shoot a few prairie dogs."

During the evenings we joked about the ever-diminishing water supply, the power failures, and the constant, increasing danger of death by cremation. We poked fun at security and censorship and barbecued Our General to a lush, crisp brown at regular intervals. We garnished him with the things we lacked and flamed him with rum before we served him.

One small clique of MPs resented the civilians bitterly and did all they could to make life miserable for them. Those MPs were pulled out of combat units, and their buddies were fighting on the front lines. Their attitude was, "What makes you so goddamn precious that you need to be guarded?"

Tales of individual tilts with them enlivened our evenings. The story of the lad who somehow substituted his pup's picture for his own on his Tech Area badge, and got away with it for two weeks, pleased everyone.

Ruth's account of a girl who clipped her badge on the back pocket of her blue jeans was hilarious. The girl sailed through the gate with her nose in the air.

"Put your badge on your shirt where it belongs!" roared a truculent guard.

"Why?" she asked sweetly. "You never look at my face."

The nonsense was a mask. The laws of self-preservation operated perfectly. Coyotes howled dismal dirges for their prey in the nights. The arid winds were almost animate as they snarled through the trees and around buildings to magnify the mounting tension. There was an epidemic of chicken pox that struck the children and the men, who worked until they were too ill to stand. The Tech Area buzzed with activity day and night; the workers were like creatures possessed. Preston stagnated in the South Pacific.

Eric and I went into the living room one noontime, and a foul odor assailed our nostrils.

"Ugh! What have you got here that makes such a stink?" he asked.

I looked around to determine the source of the vile smell. Mikey was huddled under my chair; she should have been curled up in it. I stooped to look at her more closely. Purulent matter dripped from her jaws.

"Oh, Eric, it's Mikey. Look at her. What have you done to yourself, little pussy?"

I extended my hands to pick her up, and she mewed faintly. Eric restrained me from touching her.

"She might be rabid, be careful."

"She doesn't act rabid; I must get her to the vet immediately."

"Wait until I get a towel and her carrying case."

Capt. Bob Thompsett examined our little pet carefully.

"This is the first case I've seen," he said.

"What is it?"

"Necrosis of the jaw bone. Where does she hunt?"

"I haven't the vaguest idea. Is there any chance to save her?"

"I don't know. She'll undoubtedly lose her teeth."

"Then it would be better to put her out of the way immediately."

"You can always feed her baby food; let's not destroy her yet. Her case is a real challenge; let's wait and see what I can do for her. Anything that I learn from her might benefit humanity."

I reluctantly acquiesced and went home to look up "necrosis" in our dictionary. When I read that it meant the death of a limited portion of tissue and when, at the end of the paragraph, the definition related the causes of the condition to the actions of biological, chemical, and physical agents, I came to the conclusion that Mikey somehow, some way, had gotten a dose of the deadly stuff they used in the Tech Area into her system. Whether it was by hunting in a contaminated area—and there were several of those—or by eating a chipmunk or mouse tainted with the stuff, I neither knew nor cared. I was heartsick. I visited the hospital every day, but Bob wouldn't let me see her.

"It would only upset you," he said.

One day I went to the hospital when he was out, and one of the sergeants, who was terribly upset about Mikey himself, let me see her. She was a pitiful sight. Her tongue was swollen and her hair was patchy. She recognized me but was too weak to move. I wept bitter tears on the sergeant's shoulder and returned to the hospital after he went off duty.

"Mikey's been here for weeks. Does she show any signs of progress?"

"Nothing seems to help. Christ, what a business!"

"Then the kindest thing you can do is put her to sleep. I'd like you to do it this afternoon. If you'll give me her bill now, I'll drop in with a check tomorrow."

"There is no bill, not for Mikey."

During Mikey's illness, momentous events transpired in the Outer World. In Europe, the Battle of the Bulge was history. American, British, and Canadian armies drove into Germany from the west. The American First and Third armies were on the Rhine, and Cologne was in their hands. Miracle of miracles, the Remagen Bridge was taken! Men and supplies poured across it. Dozens of bridgeheads were established. The Russians aimed a spear at Berlin from the northern coast.

In the far east, there was new hope for China, as reinforcements and supplies crowded the Burma Road. The bitter battle for Luzon raged. Manila finally fell. There were few prisoners. The Japanese defenders were either killed or committed suicide. The American flag flew over Iwo Jima where the battle had been a carnage; our men crossed beaches paved with the bodies of their comrades. The first American ship entered Manila Bay, and our fleet bombarded Japan.

Aside from my daily visits to the veterinary hospital, life continued its harried way. More and more people, both soldiers and civilians, piled into our bloated town. The Tech Area's gaping maw was insatiable.

The utilities sagged even lower under their additional burden, and shoppers jousted in the commissary. To ease the situation, the army supply people issued commissary cards to Hill residents. If you didn't have a card, you couldn't even enter the building. The cards eased the shopping situation to some extent, and they certainly simplified the supply people's problems because every morsel we ate had to be hauled up the Hill. The Indian and Spanish-American day workers all had large families. When they were able to shop in the commissary, they brought all their ration books with them and hauled the groceries down the Hill almost as soon as the army hauled them up it.

Construction for a huge, new Tech Area installation was under way at the southeast end of the potrero before it forked like the tip of a reptile's tongue.

"What goes on down there?" I asked Eric.

"It's part of our set-up," he admitted. "D Building isn't big enough and we want to get that part of the work as far from town as possible."

"Amen," I said and recalled the whispers at the C Shop fire. The grapevine said the new installation was to be DP and referred to it as the factory of the future when the ventilation system took shape. I privately nicknamed it "Devil's Productions." The grapevine also said the suspicious activity at the far west end of the pasture was a rifle range—the army was going to make soldiers out of the SEDs.

"The boys are riled up. They don't want to learn to shoot," Ruth reported.

"I wonder what idiot generated that brainwave. The money could better be used to build housing and bolster utilities," I replied.

Alice paid me a very formal call. She was all dolled up.

"Where are your hat and white gloves?" I teased. I was dressed in blue jeans and a gingham shirt.

"I've come to see you about a very serious matter; as you know, Town Council elections are coming up soon. The housewives always make it their business to elect a representative to the council. They elected me, and now we want you on the council."

"Oh, no, please! In the Outer World I Leagued of Wooden Boated, I Red Crossed. Here, I PTAed and Cub Scouted. A couple of weeks ago I had to drop my Cub den. I started with fifteen, and I couldn't handle any more. I beat on every door in the trailer area to get help. The trailer children clamor to join the dens, but there are no den mothers. I almost went down on my knees, but would any of those women help? No! Why don't you run for another term?"

"Nothing doing," Alice said. "Nobody runs for a second term. After you serve one term, it's all you can do to drag yourself home to lick your wounds."

I knew that nothing could scream louder than an outraged scientist unless it was a machinist.

"I couldn't run even if I wanted to," Alice continued. "I have to get away. I can't stand another summer here; when school is out, I'm going to take the children and go back to Michigan for the vacation. You've got to run. We've got to have someone who can beat on trailer doors and who's not afraid to say what she thinks."

"Give me twenty-four hours to think about it."

But of course the answer was yes. My term began the first of April 1945 and lasted six months. The council was already expanded from five to seven members to represent all groups of civilian personnel. When we organized the new council, Hitler's Germany was in its death throes and a great invasion armada of fourteen hundred ships assaulted Okinawa with a hundred thousand troops.

It will do no harm to reiterate that the council had no real authority and no funds other than those collected from traffic fines. As a body it heard and tried to arbitrate matters brought to its attention, among which were many minor matters in addition to grave, major problems. We decided to acquaint ourselves thoroughly with all major problems and organized our council to that end.

We elected Tony Grubmann council chairman and, with funds from the traffic fines, we hired Sam Allison's secretary to record our transactions. We didn't think the Red Cross would mind the deduction from our anonymous gifts, and Dorothy Johnson was glad to have something extra to occupy her time. She lived in one of the dormitories at the west end of town and was frightfully worried about her husband who was somewhere in the Pacific Theater.

Three of the newly-elected council members, men who hadn't been on the Hill very long and didn't have time to study any problems first hand, volunteered to serve on the traffic court. None of us could see any reason why all seven of us should be present to hear traffic cases. We appointed the other members of the council to head committees and study the various problems: housing, trailers, dormitories, and such. The council members selected their committee members from qualified personnel outside the council, and made their reports to the council as a whole. I was appointed chairman of the housing-trailer committee.

Becky Bradford and her male counterpart, who were dormitory representatives to the council, didn't have to appoint committees. Even when the project first began, the dormitories had so many problems peculiarly their own that they formed their own council. The dormitory council kept Becky and Company informed on matters which needed the attention of the Town Council, and there were plenty of them.

I was aware of some of the problems in the town even before I took my seat on the council. I soon learned that morale in the town was even lower than I guessed. Impossible living conditions for a majority of the population, and the tensions engendered by the nature of the work in the Tech Area rubbed nerves raw.

The local army administration, trapped between the terrific pressure to get the job done and the necessity to keep peace with Washington, never seemed to miss an opportunity to pull a boner. Indeed, the unhappy arrangement wherein our ensealed civilian population was dominated by an antagonistic Washington administration, created a situation so delicate and touchy that it seemed about to explode at any moment.

The April days hurried along, and we, the council, faced an audience of aroused citizenry at every meeting. Meanwhile, in the Outer World, events transpired at lightning speed.

The savage fighting on Okinawa continued. A hail of bombs fell on the Japanese homeland. President Roosevelt died, and the world mourned him deeply. President Truman took up the burden, and General Patton's tanks rolled forward with incredible speed. A sniper's bullet killed Ernie Pyle on Ie Shima, and we lost a well-loved correspondent who hated war but never shirked his duty.

Men from the U.S. First Army and the First Ukranian Army shook hands on a battered bridge across the Elbe River. The red flag was raised in Berlin, and Mussolini was caught and killed by Italian partisans. His body was hung head down in Milan like that of a slaughtered hog. Hitler was said to have shot himself in a bunker beneath his battered Chancellery in Berlin. The night in Europe was almost over, and the signing of the surrender was in sight.

April was not a month of total absorption in community affairs or events in the Outer World. Eric and I planned a cocktail party on the tenth. We frequently entertained groups of twelve or fifteen, but we were obligated to a number of people who entertained only in large groups.

The apartment cleaning crew hadn't reached our apartment building yet, and the outsides of the windows were filthy. I wanted them clean for the party, but Eric protested so vigorously when I proposed to do the job myself that I finally promised I wouldn't attempt it. On the day that I went to Santa Fe to buy supplies for the party I stopped at the housing office to visit.

"We have an extra maid tomorrow. Do you want her?" one of the girls asked.

"Oh, dear, I planned to go to Santa Fe, and I have a car full of women who'd be disappointed if I cancelled the trip."

"This woman is really good, and she reads English. Why don't you leave her money and a note on the table? She's scrupulously honest."

I thought it was a fine idea and left a note instructing the woman to clean the windows and do the ironing if there was current. I was really pleased to get a cleaning woman who could read. It was a lovely day, and I was quite successful in my shopping. I bought plenty of 'makings' for daiquiris and martinis. I even found some furniture polish, an item in short supply at the commissary.

When I got home, I panted up the stairs eagerly to look at the view through my clean windows. The note and the money on the table were gone. The view was still obscured with grime and the ironing was unfinished, although it was quite obvious that the house was thoroughly cleaned. The furniture shone, and a strange antiseptic odor permeated the place. I opened the cupboard under the sink.

"What on earth did she use?" I muttered. Then, I knew. She had polished every stick of furniture with Smokey's horse liniment.

The house still smelled of horse liniment when the day of the party dawned; ten inches of snow had fallen during the previous night. It was the only really heavy snowfall since the November snow, but it was too late to do any real good.

"Ugh, there would be snow when we're having forty people for cocktails," I complained.

The partying Haleys

"There is snow on Caballo!" Eric sang in an off-key voice. "Listen, we have no flowers, so Bill and I'll go out and cut a small evergreen. We'll decorate it with the Christmas lights."

It was a fine idea, and our guests got right into the spirit of the occasion. Eric presided over the cocktails in a colorful bar apron while I urged people to partake of the solid refreshments. Eric's apron enchanted Joe Kennedy. When the guests thinned out, Joe pressed me into a chair.

"This was an extra fine party, and you've worked hard. You haven't even had time for a drink yet. You sit down, too, Eric. Give me your apron, and I'll fix some drinks for you."

Eric and I surrendered thankfully, and Joe busied himself in the kitchen. The Haleys were still there; Ruth's sparkle and Jano's gay wit always added immeasurably to such occasions. We rehashed the party, and Joe served our drinks.

"You're almost out of liquor. There was just enough for a couple of drinks for each of you."

We sipped our drinks gratefully. I preferred a martini to a daiquiri but presumed we were out of martinis. I began to feel queer — the daiquiri had an odd flavor. I didn't want to mention it because Joe was so pleased with himself. Finally he said, "How do you like the Kennedy special?"

"Oh, fine. How did you make it?"

"Well, there was just a little of the martini mix left, so I added it to the daiquiri."

It was years before I knew Joe was one of the co-discoverers of plutonium. That cocktail was almost as deadly as the element.

It didn't take long for the snow to melt, but before it was entirely gone the apartment cleaning crew reached our house. Fifteen stalwart men descended on us bright and early one morning. They each clutched a scrub pail and brush in one hand and a lunch pail in the other. They lined the lunch pails up along the kitchen sink. Several of them retreated to the bathroom, where they began a spirited crap game.

Two or three others retired to the master bed to rest for their coming ordeal. A couple of them started to work, and the others settled down in the living room to meditate. It took strong nerves to stay home and watch them operate. Some women worried about crew members napping on their beds, but it didn't bother me as long as I wasn't there to watch it. I tucked the family jewels and snake-bite remedy under my arm and departed to explore the countryside on Smokey's back.

Par for the cleaning of a five-room apartment was two days. Eric, Bill and I spent the night in Fuller Lodge where we were assigned to the Throne Room Suite. The two bedrooms and bathroom were so nicknamed because the toilet in the bathroom perched jauntily on a dais—one climbed steps to reach it. The Throne Room was famous throughout the Manhattan District. One consultant photographed it. It was an honor to be assigned to it.

The next afternoon the apartment was immaculate. The windows gleamed, the Black Beauty glistened—a true miracle. Ruth's turn followed mine, and she cut par in half. She took the day off to play her Mexican dance records while the men worked. The sound of song and laughter mingled with the music, and the foreman said, "I'd save the government a lot of money if they'd buy a couple of Victrolas and sets of records."

When the foreman of the cleaning crew spoke of "them" and "they" he referred to the army administration. I liked most of our local army men, but they took their instructions from Our General, who did not like civilians even though they were the people upon whom his future reputation depended. Col. Gerry Tyler was so far out on his limb that he could go no further. As the chairman of the housing-trailer committee for the Town Council, my position was in sharp conflict with the Washington policies to which the hapless colonel was supposed to adhere.

The apartments, dormitories, pre-fabs, hutments, and government trailers were jammed. The machinists' barracks was packed, and the private trailer lot was loaded to capacity. More workers were needed, particularly skilled craftsmen; ownership of a trailer was a prerequisite of employment. The trailers crawled up the Hill in an endless stream like turtles with their shelters on their backs. The man charged with parking them was desperate. He crowded the incoming trailers around the perimeters of the trailer lots, but there were no water or sewage lines for them, and the power lines tangled on the ground. Sewage dripped from trailer waste pipes, and small children swarmed over the scene like flies. In one instance, sixty private and twenty-three government trailers used a single latrine.

I selected the members of the housing-trailer committee from amongst people who were not deeply involved with work in the Tech Area. Muriel and Jean both served on it; the Padre and Sergeant McCall were ex-officio members.

Muriel, Jean, and I pounded on trailer doors, talked to the occupants, and filled little black books with statistics. We implored the trailer people to appoint a committee to take their really pressing grievances to the Town Council so it could act on their behalf to obtain long-range relief for them.

The Padre and his staff concerned themselves with the juvenile problems which arose from the overcrowding, resulting in slum conditions. Sergeant McCall was in charge of sanitation. There was no permanent Health Officer; our handful of army officers met that requirement for a military installation by rotating the title among themselves monthly, but they had no real interest in the situation at the east end of town. Sergeant McCall couldn't pound the table to brass, but he hoped I would. In the meanwhile, he and his men busied themselves with DDT.

We worked carefully, but with all possible speed, to assemble and verify our facts. The situation was ripe with seeds of great trouble. The danger of epidemic was ever present in our minds, and there was no possibility that our overworked doctors in the overcrowded hospital could control a major epidemic. We refused even to think of the holocaust which would result from a fire.

The immediate problem was to get the children off the streets and ground around the trailers. The Padre got a map of the trailer area, and Sara Hearn and I surveyed it in search of play areas. After we finished our survey the Padre took our plans and other recommendations to the colonel for his approval.

As a result, sandboxes and swings were placed at frequent intervals in relatively safe spots for tiny children who had to be kept under their mothers' eyes. For slightly older children, two open spaces which were somehow overlooked for construction purposes were fenced, and playground equipment was installed. School age youngsters got a youth center—a barracks-type hutment with a ping-pong table and a phonograph—and a youth library where they could study away from their crowded trailer homes. Those people who were active in Boy and Girl Scout movements redoubled their efforts to arrange hikes and picnics. Our combined endeavors helped a little.

Our council frequently did business with a bare quorum. With the single exception of myself, everyone on it was deeply embroiled in the affairs of the Tech Area. Preparations for a test of the work were in full swing. A number of the men shuttled back and forth between Los Alamos and the test site, which had the code name "Trinity." Others, like Sam Allison, had occasion to transact business elsewhere in the Manhattan District. Sam went to Chicago.

"I'll miss the next meeting," he said. "I'm going to drive Dorothy Johnson's car back from Chicago."

"I hope you're going to get some decent liquor while you're back there," I said.

"I hope so, too. I'm sick of rum."

At the end of the next week, Eric said, "Sam Allison had a nasty accident on his way back from Chicago."

"My heavens! Is he badly hurt? What happened?"

"He wasn't hurt at all. He was hit by a rockslide in Taos Canyon about four miles above Embudo. It knocked the car into the river, but fortunately it didn't turn over."

I could hardly wait until Monday night to get the details. Sam arrived at the executive session in high spirits.

"I'm glad to be alive," he said.

It was a miracle he *was* alive. The Rio Grande was about forty feet below the road at the point of the slide.

"What happened?" Tony asked.

"I was bowling merrily along with two cases of whiskey stored in the back of the car when all of a sudden the car sailed out into space and dropped straight down for a four-wheel landing. I'm a strong swimmer, but I didn't have to swim. The river was so low it only came up to my shins. It was night, you know, so there was no traffic on the road. I hiked down to the Embudo Hospital and tried to phone Oppie, but he was in bed with chickenpox. The operator finally got hold of someone who sent a jeepload of GIs, armed with flashlights and rope to my rescue. We went back to look at the car, but there was nothing we could do about it. When the boys turned their flashlights on it, one of them said, 'Gee, sir, you must live clean!'"

We all laughed, and I asked, "What did you do about the car?"

"The boys from S Site sent Brooklyn Betsy to its rescue." Brooklyn Betsy was the queen of the army wreckers—a gargantuan machine capable of handling enormous loads.

"When we got to the scene of the wreck, the New Mexico Highway Department was on the job. Their truck was equipped with a hand winch. They couldn't budge the car, but they were slowly dragging their truck toward the edge of the embankment."

"When they saw Betsy, they were glad to let her do the job. Her operator jockeyed her into position, latched onto the car, and lifted it to let it drain. He let it settle on the road without a bump." Sam picked up the agenda and looked at it.

"What about the whiskey?" I whispered.

"Only a couple of bottles were broken, which was fortunate, because from the looks of this agenda, we'll need it."

he month of May blew into town on a grimy wind. Eric was a man with a nightmare. He studied the ceiling with his teeth clenched hard on the stem of his pipe. Bill brought a clarinet home from school.

"Where did you get that thing?" I asked when he set the case down.

"The PTA raised some money for us to have a school orchestra; I'm gonna play the clarinet."

"Not while I'm in the house."

"But Ma, I have to practice."

"You can practice when I'm not home, or you can practice out in the woods the way the GIs do. I suffered for three and a half years while you butchered the piano and cello. I refuse to listen while you massacre the clarinet. You give one toot on that thing while I'm in the house, and you're 'oot."

"But Ma, that's not fair."

The argument continued. Bill finally stamped off to his room. His parting shot was, "I'll ask Dad if I can't practice at home."

I snorted, but I wasn't sure what Eric might do. He always backed my decisions, but his mind was so preoccupied at the moment that he just might slip. I was distinctly cool when he came home.

"What ails you?" he asked.

"Bill brought a clarinet home from school. I told him that he couldn't practice while I was in the house. I told him if he gave one toot, he was 'oot—come to think about it—maybe you'll both be 'oot."

"Don't worry. Even the thought of a beginning wind instrument makes me shudder."

"Dad, we're gonna have a school orchestra, and Ma says I can't practice the clarinet while she's at home."

"You heard her, son. I'll go one step further—take that

instrument of torture back to school."

Bill's anguished moans could be heard all over the Hill.

"Mrs. Jette, please let Bill keep the clarinet. He might get a terrible complex if you make him return it," his teacher pleaded.

"Bill can practice at my house," a prominent member of the PTA announced.

Dear Bill really stirred up a tempest in our teapot. To hear some of the comments, you'd think I had horns and a tail and carried a trident to poke him at every step.

My partisans were indignant.

"Stick to it, Eleanor," Genia encouraged.

"You can't back down," Martha said.

"I can't think of anything more ghastly than having a clarinet beginner in the house," Ruth hugged me.

"Those busybodies could find something better to occupy their time," Muriel commented.

And Muriel was right.

The highly-strung atmosphere of the Tech Area saturated the town and crept into every phase of life. Even the Indian maids from the nearby pueblos were infected by it. My status as a non-working mother of a school-age child didn't entitle me to household help, but the women in the housing office were aware of my work in the community and assigned regular help to me.

I was horrified when one of my regular girls reported an Indian girl murdered and her body cut up and burned in a furnace. I hurried to the Housing Office to ascertain the facts.

"The bus drivers tease the girls unmercifully; they think it's fun to scare them. No one is missing, but they were all saucer-eyed this morning," the women assured me.

"We don't need heat in this weather. It might quiet the girls if the furnaces were turned off for the summer," I suggested.

"The army regulations say heat must be maintained until the fifteenth of May in this climatic zone. You know army regulations."

I certainly did know army regulations. The army constantly took refuge behind them at the council meetings.

That afternoon the partition between the Manley's downstairs apartment kitchen and the furnace room caught fire. The same partition caught fire again the following morning and the next evening. The furnace was shut down to rip out the partition and move it farther away from the furnace.

I came home from a ride, and Virginia Ayers called to me.

"Eleanor, it's ninety in our apartment. Will you call the fire department?"

Virginia couldn't leave her infant son to call the fire department herself. For the first few months of his life he was in constant danger of strangulation. She didn't dare leave him even for a few moments.

I ran to the fire phone on Tech Road but couldn't rouse the operator. Frantically, I waved down an approaching truck; it belonged to the fire department.

"Quick, it's ninety in the downstairs apartment," I gasped while I climbed into the truck.

The GI driver whipped the truck around the corner, broke down the furnace room door, and smothered the furnace fire.

A few days later a group of us planned an all-day ride. The riders gathered at Hazel Kline's corral. The overheated apartments were very much on our minds, and we discussed them while Hazel put the last touches on her gear.

"My husband took care of the situation in our house," she said.

"I'd like to know how he did it; maybe it would work with our furnace man," I said.

"I don't recommend his method. He has a quick temper, you know. He got home before I did the other afternoon, and the apartment was stifling. The mercury was right at the top of the thermometer, and he heard the furnace man shoveling coal into the fire box. He went downstairs and told the man to stop shoveling because it was a hundred and twenty degrees in our apartment. The man said, 'They pay me shovel coal; I shovel coal!' Papa lost his temper. He went upstairs, got his gun, and returned to the furnace room. He pointed the gun at the man. 'You shovel any more coal, I shoot you.' The man took off like a scared jack rabbit. We haven't seen him since."

"The chances are he's still running," Martha guessed after we controlled our mirth.

We laughed when the danger was over, but any wisp of smoke reduced us to jelly. A few mornings earlier, Natalee, Mary, and I were out on the three "Jette Boys." (We had just acquired a third horse, Don Carlos de Los Alamos, better known as Carley.) When we returned from our ride, we saw a column of black smoke. From our observation point at the west end of the pasture, the smoke appeared to come from the Tech Area. We galloped back to the corral, ripped the saddles off the horses with trembling fingers, and jumped into the car to find the source of it. It wasn't in the Tech Area. Someone was burning oily rags down near the dump, but we didn't know it when we saw the smoke. All three of us were wrecks.

In the Outer World, V-E Day was proclaimed, and the true horrors of Hitler and his butchers were revealed to an appalled world. Six million helpless men, women, and children were gassed, garroted, starved to death, or maimed to satisfy the sadistic appetites of the monster and his henchmen.

The battles for the Philippines and Okinawa still raged; rain added to the misery of the men fighting them.

Nerves tensed and apprehensions increased almost visibly. The blue sky was unwinking. The beautiful New Mexico sunshine mocked us. A whole contingent of mounted MPs disappeared. Certain security people left, and men shuttled back and forth between Los Alamos and Trinity. Deak Parsons was on the go constantly. Martha and I were lucky we could escape from the tensions on horseback if only for an hour or so each day.

Every woman had a different idea of what transpired in the Tech Area. A few of them discussed their ideas freely. Eric's vehement denial of my ideas and his warning to keep my ideas to myself led me to think I was on the scent, so I followed his instructions, except on one occasion when Martha and I were sunbathing in lower Los Alamos Canyon. She mentioned one of our friends.

"She thinks they're making some sort of a weapon that will draw its energy from the sun," she remarked.

"That's about the wildest guess yet. If our gadget is going to be finished and used soon, there won't be any sunshine over Japan. It's their rainy season."

"Deak never tells me a thing. Does Eric tell you anything?"

"No, and every time I come up with a bright idea, he hoots. He hoots so loud it makes me think I may be right."

"What do you think it is?"

"I think it's some kind of a super bomb."

"I think so, too, but Deak says I'm balmy."

"That makes two of us."

"Deak won't even tell me where the test site is located. He says the women around here talk too much."

"How long does it take him to get from the test site to Los Alamos?"

"About six hours. They leave in mid-afternoon, and he generally has dinner in either Albuquerque or Bernalillo."

"Hmmm, it shouldn't be hard to locate it. Have you got a map of New Mexico?"

Martha nodded.

"We can figure that the site is about three hours south of Albuquerque. If the gadget is going to end the war, it must be tremendously powerful. Therefore, the site will be in a remote place."

We dropped the subject, but actually it didn't require much detective work for either of us to realize that the gadget was a bomb. We both knew that a carefully selected group of Air Force personnel were training at a secret air base located near Wendover, Utah, for the dangerous task of delivering the superweapon. The young men appeared at Los Alamos from time to time. Each dreamed of the day his plane might unleash the force to end all war. Young Capt. David Semple was one of the ardent dreamers. (He died when his plane crashed in a thunderstorm at Wendover, and the ship that carried the bomb on Able Day a year later at the Bikini test was named "Dave's Dream.")

"You know, Smokey's markings don't seem to be as distinct as they were," Martha observed when we re-saddled the horses.

"I know. He's not color-fast. If he keeps fading as fast as he did in these last few weeks, I'm going to have a white horse, and I don't understand it because he's a true pinto."

I parted the hair in Smokey's coat, and we studied the skin under the fading spots. It was just as black as ever. We cinched our saddle girths and returned to town. Martha had a Girl Scout meeting, and I had a meeting with the Padre.

When my meeting was over, I went home and looked at our own map of New Mexico. South and east of Albuquerque there was a desolate region designated as Jornada del Muerto, Journey of the Dead. Early Spanish colonists had to cross it on their way northward, and early accounts referred to it as "the dread Jornada." It was a desert region studded with lava beds. It had neither wood nor water holes, and in the early days many people were lost and died of thirst or were beset by hostile Indians. It was the center of violent storms and was alive with rattlesnakes, scorpions, and tarantulas. The entire region covered an area about ninety miles long by forty miles wide, and there was an army proving ground near White Sands at the southeast corner. There was an air base at Alamogordo on the east side of the Jornada. I thought it probable that the air base would use the Jornada. The dread Jornada would be an ideal test site.

The furnaces were shut off for the summer. Work on the "Factory of the Future" progressed rapidly. The rifle range neared completion. The water situation was truly critical. We were without power more frequently. Shoppers tangled with each other in the commissary. Attendance at council meetings swelled.

In addition to the really grave problems that confronted the council, we heard complaints about the flavor of the milk, which grew more virulent with the passage of time. Our constituents demanded that we do something about the GIs who drove the rickety army buses back and forth between Santa Fe and the Hill. The blood of mountain goats apparently flowed in the drivers' veins. There was nothing we could do about such matters. We called on Capt. Thompsett to explain the flavor of the milk and referred the bus driver issue to the army transportation corps. Nothing happened in either case.

The hospital was a regular item on the agenda. Like all the utilities and public services, it was set up for a very small community. Although it was enlarged several times and four more doctors supplemented the original staff, there was no hope that the hospital and its staff could cope with the thousands of troops and civilians that were crowded inside our fences. Broken bones waited for hours before they were tended simply because the overworked doctors had more urgent cases before them. Fortunately, the members of our family didn't need much medical care. When we went to the hospital for shots, we never went in the main entrance. We used the emergency entrance and caught the necessary doctor or nurse in the corridor.

Bitter battles resulted from attempts to further infringe upon the already-abridged personal freedom of the civilian population. The subject of searches and car checks made civilians furious. Expensive and irreplaceable equipment was being stolen from the Tech Area. Obviously, something had to be done to apprehend the guilty persons and recover the missing articles. MPs were sent into dormitories to search the rooms during their occupants' absence, and the council was informed that all cars would be searched at the main gate.

"Why don't the authorities do their checking when people enter and leave the Tech Area like they do at other war plants?" one of the machinists asked.

There was a lot of palaver but no satisfactory answer. The council agreed the pilfering must stop, but the methods used to stop it were wrong.

"The next step will be to search people's houses and trailers in their absence," Sam said.

"I know, but what can we do about it?" Tony asked. "I don't think the council has any power to stop these searches."

"I do." I was boiling.

"How would you do it?"

"Article IV of the Bill of Rights reads: 'The right of the people to be secure in their person, houses, papers, and effects—'" I finished the quotation. "I don't believe that search without warrant is legal. The matter can be tested in the federal court in Santa Fe."

The audience was very much interested, and the army representatives decided the matter needed further study. It remained dead while our council was in office.

Dormitory residents had a rough time. Mature adults, they came to the Hill to do a job and were condemned by their single blessedness to existence in nine-by-twelve rooms. They could probably have made fairly adequate homes in them had there been enough dormitories of the original type—individual bedrooms and bathrooms between every two rooms—but there were only four of those dormitories.

The dormitories were almost as overcrowded as the trailer areas. The condition resulted from double occupancies of the rooms and assignment of dormitory rooms to married couples for whom there was no other housing. Assignment of rooms for double occupancy was arbitrary. Housing people designated roommates without consulting persons concerned and frequently neglected to notify the original occupants that they were to have roommates. It was not uncommon for a person to come home from the office to find half his belongings in the hall or carried off to the warehouse for storage and a total stranger sharing his cubbyhole.

Married couples were assigned space in women's dormitories. When this was done, notices were posted that the building was a married couples' dormitory. The notices requested the men to rise and shave early to be out of the way when the women needed the bathrooms. One woman scientist remarked sadly, "It would not be so bad if only the husbands wouldn't clatter and drop their shoes!"

There was a running skirmish between the dormitory people and the army administration over the former's right to do light cooking in their rooms. Army administration contended the use of electric appliances in the rooms increased the fire hazard and impaired sanitation. Occupants countered that they liked an occasional home-cooked meal, particularly breakfast, and if the administration didn't want them to cook in their rooms, it should furnish cooking facilities in the dayrooms of the dormitories.

As I said, the dormitory dwellers had a rough time, and they told the council. I mean TOLD them all about it. Then, as if we didn't have enough trouble with the overcrowded commissary, hospital, trailers, and dormitories, the rifle range was activated.

It was a super-duper rifle range with movable metal target frames to hold man-sized targets and all the latest improvements. It must have cost a pretty penny. The SEDs were bitter about it. They didn't have a chapel; they didn't have proper recreation facilities (the colonel's effort on their behalf was outgrown almost as soon as it was finished); they didn't even have enough barracks space.

"We do the technical work," they almost shouted. "We and our folks pay taxes. The war in Europe is over. If the work here is successful, the Japanese war will be over. Why the hell spend all this money at this late date to make us into soldiers? Why not spend it on something we need?" Our General was somewhat less popular with the SEDs than he was with the civilians.

I sympathized with the SEDs, but the rifle range was a purely military matter. Or so I thought. I couldn't have been more mistaken.

The Monday the range was activated, Martha and I went for a canter. An MP halted us at the end of the road along the east side of the pasture.

"You can't go any farther, ladies. They're shooting on the rifle range."

"But it's over at the foot of the mountains," Martha protested.

"I know," he said, wincing as a bullet ricocheted through the trees.

"I think we should scram," I said.

"I wish I could scram with you. How those jokers over there can spray lead over a hundred and eighty degrees of the landscape beats me," the MP said.

I was furious. So was Martha. But we were helpless. The horses' ears twitched apprehensively. We turned their heads and cantered back to the corral. Genia met us; she had planned a hike and was halted.

"Eleanor, you must do something!" Genia was so mad she sputtered.

I agreed with her, one hundred percent. The council meeting that night was packed with machinists and craftsmen who worked around the clock. The men who worked the night shifts had no recreation facilities. They hiked, rode, or putted golf balls around the pasture; they were as mad as hornets. The rifle range blocked all the trails, and one couldn't putt a golf ball safely except in the extreme southeast corner of the pasture.

Tony appointed me chairman of a committee to survey the situation, and I appointed four members of the machinist/craftsman group to my committee. The committee members didn't realize that the council had no power to correct the matter until they were appointed to the committee. We outlined a plan of action. We first requested a schedule of shooting hours.

Bill came home with a handful of bullet slugs.

"Where did you get those?" I asked.

"Oh, I went out to the rifle range after school. I'm gonna melt them and make some lead soldiers. "

"They were firing on the rifle range today. Why did you go out there?"

"Oh, all the kids were there. We laid down while they were shooting. We got up and collected the bullets after every round."

"We don't need any lead soldiers around this house. If you go out there again when they're shooting, I'll skin you alive. "

"But Ma—"

Shooting hours were eight to twelve and one to five. It was time to take the second step in our plan.

"I've got the petitions ready," I said. "Get as many signatures as you can." I passed multiple copies of my carefully worded composition around and admonished them, "For God's sake, don't tell anybody I wrote this petition."

They chortled with glee and promised to fill the petitions with signatures immediately.

June days moved slowly onward. The wind howled. The air of breathless expectancy exuded by the Tech Area was suffocating. I scanned the sky hopefully for signs of thunderheads. When the rainy season began, the wind might stop blowing. Eric and the other men were driven by demons.

In the Outer World, victory was in sight on Okinawa, and the campaign in the Philippines drew toward a close. I held my breath every time I got a letter from Preston. American troops in Europe were re-deployed. Some of them were sent to the Philippines, and a few of them landed in Los Alamos.

I went to the mail room to get the laundry one day. A soldier in dress uniform stood at the top of the steps. He opened the door courteously every time a woman approached it. His chest was bright with campaign ribbons, and his purple heart ribbon was bedecked with oak leaf cluster and silver star. His face wore a look that said, "I know I'm dreaming, but please don't wake me."

The next day Genia and I went to Santa Fe. The young man at the mail room door and a pal, also bedecked with battle ribbons, waited for a ride at the pick-up spot.

"I saw you standing by the mail room door yesterday," I said to the lad who opened it for me.

"Yes, Ma'am, we just got here yesterday morning. I thought I was dead and had gone to heaven."

Genia and I laughed. We were glad Los Alamos looked like heaven to someone.

"You boys will love it here. There are marvelous trails, and you can hike to your hearts' content," Genia said.

"OH, NO, MA'AM!" they chorused.

"You were in the infantry?" I asked.

"Yes, Ma'am, we hiked north from Anzio."

No wonder Los Alamos looked so good to them.

The machinists filled the petitions with names and presented them to the council. There were more than five hundred signatures. The army representatives agreed that, in view of the fact the rifle range affected so many people vitally important to the project, some action must be taken.

"I'll go out and look the situation over right after lunch tomorrow," Sam Musser promised.

"Mrs. Jette should go with you. She knows more about the situation out there than any of the rest of us do," Tony said.

"I'll be glad to have Mrs. Jette go with me," Sam agreed.

After the meeting, he said, "I rode horseback when I was on the Burma Road. It would be fun to ride again."

"Why don't we meet at my corral at one o'clock?" I suggested.

We agreed to do so and went our separate ways.

While we ate lunch the next afternoon, the fire sirens howled. We held our breath until we were sure the fire wasn't in the Tech Area, then finished our meal. Eric rushed back to work, and Bill returned to school. I drove down to the corral. The fire was at the rifle range. It was a BEAUTIFUL fire. Flames leaped thirty feet into the air. I leaned on the corral fence and enjoyed it.

The fire department made no effort to extinguish the blaze but was deployed to keep the flames from spreading. Sam joined me.

"Do you think it's worth our while to go over there?" I asked.

"Oh sure, we ought to see what's going on."

We saddled the horses and cantered across the pasture. Eddie Brooks was in charge of the fire department.

"What happened?" Sam asked.

"Who knows?" Eddie gave me a suspicious look.

"I have witnesses," I declared.

"So have I," Sam concurred.

The wreckage was impressive. Two target frames were partially intact; the rest were hopelessly twisted. The oil-soaked timbers in the pits beneath the frames blazed with such intensity there was no chance to salvage anything. The town buzzed with speculation.

"Whoopee!" Martha and Genia embraced me with glee.

"You have an alibi. They were shooting on the range when I got home from work, and you were getting lunch," Ruth chuckled. "The grapevine says La Jette passed the range and gave it a blistering look that made it burst into flames, but I know different."

Even Eric was momentarily diverted from his communications with the ceiling.

"Where, oh, where did the rifle range go?" I sang merrily while I served dinner.

"Out in the pasture, up in smoke!" he soloed from the living room.

At the next council meeting, Tony looked at me in mock surprise when I seated myself for the executive session.

"How did you get out of jail?" he quipped.

"I climbed the wall, brother."

The payoff came at the open meeting when a machinist on the rifle range committee rose to his feet. He said solemnly, "Mr. Chairman, I'd like to know what Mrs. Jette thinks about the fire at the rifle range?"

Tony raised his eyebrows and put the question to me.

"I think it settled a burning issue," I retorted.

And so it did. The truth of the matter was that one of the GIs dropped a lighted cigarette into a pool of oil in a pit just before he left for lunch. I didn't ask his name; I was grateful to him.

The campaign in the Philippines and on Okinawa ended. There were still heavy mopping-up operations, but the big battles were won. MacArthur and Stilwell announced that the assault on Japan would involve maximum commitments and casualties. Bombs alternated with words in the assault on the Japanese homeland. Chiang Kai-shek announced that the Japanese were unlikely to surrender. He predicted their final defeat in 1947.

A mighty armada sailed toward the Philippines. I got the letter I dreaded to read. It began, "Dear Sis, our outfit is due for a change of address—"

Dry electric storms whipped the forests. They shed blazing tails like gigantic chameleons. The grapevine sizzled. The gadget would be tested on the seventh of July.

Conditions in the trailer areas were appalling. The housing committee had its report ready. The trailer dwellers committee had their report ready. All we needed was a report from the temporary Health Officer. Sergeant. McCall was frantic.

"I can't even get him down there to look at conditions," he lamented.

"Maybe I can help. There's a horse owners meeting tonight. Conditions in the big barn are deplorable." My horses had their own separate quarters on the east side of the pasture by that time. "I understand he'll be there."

He was. When there was a recess in the middle of the meeting, I sauntered over to him.

"This is quite a fuss over a few careless people. I think the other horse owners will take care of them, don't you?"

He agreed.

"There's another matter I want to discuss with you. Something must be done about the trailer area. Conditions there are dreadful.

Have you been down there?"

I had the poor man backed into a comer. He had to admit he hadn't.

"I'll inspect the trailer area tomorrow afternoon," he promised.

"Good. What time will you go?"

"I'll leave the hospital at two o'clock."

"I'll meet you at the hospital at two." I could almost hear my victim groan, but I had to have his report.

I strolled to the hospital a trifle before two o'clock. Sergeant McCall was standing beside a staff car. He grabbed me and waltzed me around.

"Mama Mia, how did you do it?"

"I led him into a trap and bullied him. Give us the dollar tour."

The door opened, and our victim emerged.

The sergeant snapped to attention and gave a smart salute.

"Mrs. Jette, this is Sergeant McCall."

"How do you do, Sergeant. "

The tour proceeded. The Health Officer was speechless at what he saw. At one point he managed a small sally, "Oh, look at the chickens!"

"And the goat and the baby all cooped up together," I added.

He really was a nice person, just fearfully overworked.

"I had no idea conditions were as bad as this," he said.

"You will report all this to the colonel immediately, won't you?" I asked.

"I will indeed."

His report was all we needed. The chairman of the council's housing committee and representatives of the trailer dwellers took their reports to Sam Musser, who, as the colonel's adjutant, presented them formally. Surveying teams were at work the next day.

Our General arrived in town. For once he heard the clamor for expanded facilities. The commissary people caught his ear, and he decided to inspect commissary conditions in person on a Saturday morning.

He entered the door, took one horrified look, and beat a hasty retreat. In my opinion, it was a wise decision. To meet death at the hands of a mob of outraged women armed with canned goods and milk bottles would not be to perish in the best military tradition. He sent for the plans of the proposed enlargement and put a hasty O.K. on them.

Eric was wild with anxiety. I shushed Bill and was as unobtrusive as possible. I met Cyril one morning when he was on his way to work.

"Good morning!" I almost sang the words.

"What's good about it?" he growled.

"Nothing, I guess." I slunk off chastened.

Both Eric and Cyril were being inoculated against tropical diseases. When the inoculations started, Eric came home and said, "I'm not supposed to tell you that I'm being immunized against tropical diseases, but I told the security people there were some secrets a man couldn't keep from his wife."

"Dear God, you're not going to the Pacific, too? Isn't it enough to have Preston there?"

"I'm Cyril's alternate. If he can't go, I will."

Cyril developed an infected tooth. Alice didn't worry nearly as much as I did.

My friends and I developed a technique to discover which men were going to the Pacific. When the hapless prospect entered the door, you leaned forward with your right hand outstretched as though to clutch him by the shoulder and whisper a secret in his ear. If he cringed, he told you he was going. The method never failed.

The rains came. They were preceded by pelting hailstorms, which began with monotonous regularity at 11:55 every day, and the stones were big enough to inflict bruises. Excitement was at fever pitch. Eric was frenzied. He confessed that a betting pool was started.

"I'm not going to waste more than a couple of dollars on it," he said pessimistically.

The grapevine said the test was postponed until the sixteenth of July. My circle of friends shook their heads. We looked at each other silently and wondered what was wrong.

"Chiquita, if the gadget is a flop, Congress will be on our necks," Ruth said. The next time you take a long ride, pick out a couple of wee, roomy caves for the Jettes and Haleys."

Eric, Bill, and I had dinner in the cafeteria. Bob and Jean Bacher were there with their two children. They stopped at our table on their way out. Eric rose to confer with Bob. I heard the word "core," and Eric said, "The goddamn physicists can't make up their minds, so I ..."

Unfortunately, Bill was chattering at me about something, and I lost the end of the sentence. There was more low-voiced conversation. Bob's tone was soothing.

"I'd better get back to the Tech Area," Eric said.

"We'd better both get back," Bob added.

On Friday, Eric said, "I'm leaving for an overnight trip Sunday afternoon. I'll need some sandwiches and coffee. There are no eating facilities."

Sunday was the fifteenth of July. Apprehension clutched me.

The momentous day dawned clear but was soon overcast. There was an electric storm of unusual violence. Eric checked with departure headquarters and found that departure time, originally set for mid-afternoon, was advanced to five o'clock. We took a short ride after the storm, then Eric walked to headquarters to check the departure time again. When he returned, he said, "This is it, darling. Meteorologists at Trinity predict the weather will permit the test. Keep your fingers crossed."

We ate a hasty dinner, and I slapped some sandwiches together. I stuffed them and a thermos of coffee into a brown paper bag. Eric departed. His last words were, "You might see something if you stay up all night."

All through the town, people busied themselves with small tasks.

"What's wrong with you, Ma?" Bill asked.

"It's time for you to get to bed, young man."

About midnight, people gathered in groups. I always regretted I wasn't in the one on the south tip of the potrero's tongue. A short wave radio was in operation at south point. The people assembled there could hear the planes assigned to aerial observation of the test, with young pilots from Wendover talking to the ground. Heavy thunderstorms belabored the area, and the pilots feared lightning might strike the tower cradling the fearsome, untried burden destined to end the Pacific war.

The people at south point knew, as the last minutes before the detonation ticked away and another thunderhead bore down on the test area, that only one plane stayed at the test site.

At 5:30 in the morning of July 16, 1945, strained, anxious eyes beheld a sunrise in the south. The sun rose and rose before it disappeared. The work was successful!

The Trinity Test

onday, the sixteenth of July, was a flawless day. The adults who remained in town were jubilant. Women whose husbands were at Trinity shooed their children out of the house if they were of shooable age and toured the town. Other such women, tied at home with tiny children, hung over porch railings or rushed out their doors making the famous Churchill V for Victory sign.

There were tears and laughter. We beat each other on the back, our elation knew no bounds. The long months of loneliness and worry were almost over, the work was a success—the gadget worked! The fact that we didn't know its exact nature didn't dampen our enthusiasm in the least—IT WORKED!

We tried to envision the rejoicing at the observation points at Trinity; we commiserated with each other about the quality of the refreshments we provided for the occasion and agreed among ourselves that the contents of the paper bags we furnished were uninspired.

One woman broke out a treasured bottle of whiskey at 10 A.M. We toasted our men, the men and women of the Manhattan District, and the end of the war. The war would certainly end, we told each other. Japan would surely yield before the tremendous new force unleashed at dawn. I thought of Preston and all the others converging on the Philippines or assaulting Japan.

During the morning, several groups who went unofficially to the Manzano Mountains south of Albuquerque to view the test came home. They, of course, had a much better view of the test and a much better idea of the magnitude of the explosion than those who were at Los Alamos. About noon, men who were at Trinity began to trickle home. Those who made the trip in their own cars arrived first. The grapevine hummed. The test was conducted in Jornada del Muerto. There was now even greater reason than the historic one to call it the dread Jornada.

We heard about the celebration at test headquarters when the gadget was proven successful. We chortled with unholy glee when we heard that Our General cautioned a security officer to keep the result of the test SECRET, particularly from the wives at Los Alamos.

The security officer reportedly said, in a wry aside, "The next thing he'll ask me to do is keep the Mississippi River secret."

We agreed that the poor security officer knew us well and wondered how Our General could expect to keep anything seen over such a wide area secret, most particularly from the wives at Los Alamos.

It was said that the wires which were to carry the detonating impulse to the gadget were laid in open trenches and that some inspired soul commandeered a bulldozer to cover them, but unfortunately the bulldozer ripped the wires apart in the covering process. The scientists in the advance party were pressed into service to dig out the trenches and repair the damage. Dot Seybolt and I heard that Cyril, who was a member of the advance party, labored on the business end of a shovel. We chuckled heartily because Cyril always proclaimed himself allergic to physical labor of that type.

We took everything we heard with salt tablets, but good stories were good stories. We lapped them up that day.

The men who went to the twenty-mile observation line by bus on Sunday afternoon came home. I waited for Eric on the apartment porch. When he saw me, he grinned from ear to ear and raised his fingers in a V sign. I bubbled with curiosity, but he shook with exhaustion. I realized his immediate requirements were hot food and rest.

I heated a pot of soup for him while he showered and put on his pajamas. When he came to the table, he handed me a piece of very dark welder's glass and talked while he sipped his soup.

"We sat with our backs to the test tower. That was why I took the flashlight. I wasn't anxious to sit on a cactus or get chummy with a rattlesnake or scorpion. Sam Allison made the count down. He yelled the last few minutes into the microphone. After Sam shouted minus one, we put our heads between our knees. Nobody really knew what was going to happen. The thing might not work at all, or it might blow us all to smithereens."

"Sam bellowed 'Zero,' and the whole landscape was lit up with a blaze of light. It looked the way you might imagine a moonscape would look—desolation and the brilliance of unfiltered sunlight. We turned around after a few seconds with the glass over our eyes so we wouldn't be blinded. Dick Feynman covered only one of his eyes; he's temporarily blind in the one he didn't cover."

"That man! He *would* do something like that! How do you know he's only temporarily blind?"

"I don't, but I imagine it will be like a youngster staring too long at the sun. Didn't you ever do that?"

"Yes, of course," I was partially reassured. "How did it sound?"

"We were at the twenty-mile line. There was no sound for so long I forgot one was coming. It sounded like a rifle shot; it rumbled back from the mountains. The whole thing was magnificent and horrible. Christ, I hope the Japs surrender before we have to use it. It's not just the enormity of the explosion—"

Bill's arrival interrupted him.

"Hi, Dad, how was your trip?"

"So-so. I'm tired."

Bill wore his "Where's my peanut butter?" look. I could have throttled him cheerfully. It took almost superhuman self-control to appear casual in front of him during the past tense weeks, and to have him appear at the strategic moment when Eric was at last talking to me was almost more than I could bear. I knew that Eric's conversational urge would probably evaporate before I could get rid of Bill. I slapped a peanut butter sandwich together for my young thorn-in-the-side and urged him on his way, but Eric's conversational well ran dry while I did so.

He spooned up the last of his soup. "I'm beat," he said. "The seats on those GI buses are so close together that my knees were tucked under my chin, and we got to the observation point at three o'clock this morning."

I made a last effort. "How did you feel when it worked?"

"Flabbergasted." He grinned sheepishly. "We behaved like a bunch of college freshmen after a football victory. When we finished beating each other on the back, it was daylight. We found safe places to sit while we ate our sandwiches and drank our coffee. Then the security boys stuffed us back on the buses and hauled us home."

"I wish you'd stopped in Albuquerque for papers."

"I don't think the security boys dared let us out of the buses where people might see us. We were so excited we might have given the show away. We thought Feynman was going to float through the roof of the bus." He shivered convulsively. "I've just got to get to bed; I can't sit up another minute."

I was disappointed, but there were other fields to cultivate. After Eric retired, I went next door to discuss them with Ruth. We didn't get very far along with our plans when a chap from the division where Ruth worked arrived. He was tense with excitement, just returned from Trinity, and not in the least sleepy. We brewed him a drink and plied him with questions.

He and one of his friends volunteered for the test group and sweated in the blazing sun to prepare for it in the hope they'd be allowed to view it from headquarters at the ten-mile line. Unfortunately, their plans went astray. They were told to retire to the twenty-mile line at midnight on Sunday.

"We were burned up," he said, "but the brass had arrived, and we had to make way for them. We got our stuff out of the hut and were packing it in the car when a soldier who was perched on the steps of the hut next door got up and came over to us."

"Shuuuush," he said, "the general is trying to get some rest in the hut next door. Please be quiet."

"I hope you honked the horn," Ruth chuckled.

"No, we didn't, but the engine was cold. We had to race it!"

He described the unearthly beauty of the great ball of flame which rose into the heavens like a gargantuan kaleidoscope when it changed the dark dawn to high noon and illuminated the mountains in the background before it disappeared into a great mushroom of roiling, multicolored gases.

He was a gentle lad, the son of a missionary, raised in Japan and loving all things good about it and its people. We blotted the knowledge to which the mighty, unknown force would be put from our minds by concentrating on the beauties and trivialities of the scene.

When we parted at mid-afternoon, it was time for me to meet Martha for our daily ride.

She, too, was exuberant. "Did Eric get home? Deak got back an hour or so before I left."

"Eric got home about one o'clock. He's out cold until tomorrow morning."

"Deak had to go to the Tech Area for a while. I expect he's home in bed now. Isn't it wonderful? What have you heard?"

We swapped yarns, and I told her about the short wave radio at south point.

"They could hear the planes talking to the ground," I said. "They were all afraid lightning would hit the tower, and only one of them stayed on the scene."

"I know," Martha said proudly. "Deak was in it. Paul Tibbets piloted it."

"What does Deak think about this thing?"

"He never tells me much, but he said he was sure it would end this war and there'd never be another one. I said he'd be out of a job, but he said it didn't matter."

At the end of the afternoon I stood in line at the PX to buy a paper. There weren't nearly enough papers to go around, and the limited supply was passed from hand to hand. There was a planted statement that an explosives magazine in a remote section of the Alamogordo air base blew up, but all the regional papers carried eye witness accounts of the explosion.

Among the accounts carried by the *El Paso Herald Post* was one by a Mr. Ed Lane, a Santa Fe railroad engineer, who was at Belen, New Mexico, when the explosion occurred. The paper reported that Mr. Lane said he had "a front seat to the greatest fireworks show he had ever seen." He added that there was "a tremendous white flash. This was followed by a great red glare, and high in the sky were three tremendous smoke rings. The highest was many hundreds of feet high. They swirled and twisted as though being agitated by a great force. The glare lasted about three minutes and then everything was dark again, with the dawn breaking in the east."

The *Albuquerque Tribune* interviewed Mrs. Tom Charles of Alamogordo. She lived ten miles from the base and said that she knew of "no damage there from the explosion."

Ruth and I chuckled over the cryptic statement. We were willing to bet G2 interviewed Mrs. Charles before the *Tribune* did, and she could feel its hot breath on the back of her neck. The article in the *Tribune* was next to the weather report. "That big flash to the southwest this morning wasn't sheet lightning," the writer remarked.

In the evening, while the men who were at the test slept, and their children were tucked into bed, their women gathered at various places to discuss the events of the day.

I was one of the group that converged on the Holloway's apartment.

"You can't stay long, girls. Marshall got home half an hour ago. He was a mess, filthy dirty. He's taking a shower now. He'll want to go right to bed, but come in and have a drink in the meantime," Harriet said.

We trooped in, fifteen or twenty strong, and Harriet passed the glasses. We talked about our lives in the Outer World and what we would do when we returned to them. Peggy Titterton of the British Mission was desperately homesick for the green hills of England. I didn't know what my future held, but the west was part of my bone and sinew.

"I saw Cyril coming down the road when I was getting dinner tonight," Dot Seybolt reported. "I went out on the porch and said, "Hi! I understand you swing a mean shovel. He almost jumped out of his skin. He said security was in a hell-of-a-shape around here and threatened to report me. Do you think he will?"

The rest of us laughed. We thought he was tired, missed Alice, and a good night's sleep would cure his bad humor.

"Our local pokey won't hold more than four people. Besides, security is going to be busy for a long time just picking up the little, bitsy pieces," I said practically.

"I'll say it is," said Marshall. He made a grand entrance, scrubbed and shining, his carefully creased pajama pants showing beneath the bottom of his red bathrobe. He basked in the light of feminine admiration. Harriet put a drink into his cupped hand. He settled on the arm of her chair.

"Doesn't ANYBODY want to ask me any questions?" he said wistfully.

"Oh, no! We know all the news that's fit to print," we chorused. "We want you to go to bed and save your strength!"

~ 13 ~

For every action there is an equal and opposite reaction. That physical maxim was also true in the emotional sense. After the first wild elation, the men were thoroughly chastened by the success of their work, and their depression was contagious.

Careful re-reading of the prepared news releases revealed that they also stated that it might be necessary to evacuate personnel from the outlying vicinity of the explosion. News continued to come in during the balance of the week. It was said that the steel tower upon which the gadget was cradled was vaporized and that a crater twelve hundred feet in diameter was hollowed in the desert floor.

Some members of the test group made a brief excursion to point zero, in a lead-lined army tank, and gathered some samples of the fused sand that lined the floor of the crater with a manipulator that was attached to the tank. The gadget that vaporized a steel tower also melted desert sand and was so "hot" humans had to enter the region in a lead-lined tank was to be used on other human beings. It was a somber thought.

On Friday night the Oppenheimers gave a party for the bombmakers and their wives. We decked ourselves in our best bibs and tuckers to dance and play a little before we faced the desperate reality of what was to come. There were a number of military people at the party whom we had never seen before but who were present at Trinity. Their presence served as a grim reminder that not only we but all humanity had passed the point of no return at dawn on Monday.

Grimness showed through the surface of the gaiety. Cyril and Joe Kennedy stood talking together most of the evening. Neither man looked as though he'd ever smile again. Dot Seybolt and I giggled over a triviality.

'What are you two giggling about?" Joe asked.

"Oh, we can't tell you; it's classified information!" I quipped.

They looked at each other and nodded solemnly.

"It probably is," Cyril said.

The next Monday I got a letter from Preston.

"Dear Sis," he began. "Please note the new APO number.
I probably won't be here very long. My outfit is part of a big
operation—"

I read the letter aloud at the lunch table, and my voice broke.

"They've landed in the Philippines. They're part of the invasion
force," I said.

"Maybe the war will end without an invasion," Eric said.

None of us knew how or where the perfected gadget would be
used or even if its use would be announced. Our sense of isolation
deepened. The Outer World was obscured by the mists of anxiety,
and the tension was again almost unbearable.

The men who nursed sore arms in the early summer disappeared
one by one and left their wives wild with anxiety. Deak Parsons
was among their number, and Martha took his departure like a good
soldier. Eric came home from the Tech Area, and said, "Cyril isn't
going to the Pacific."

I clutched the back of a chair for support, and he added, hastily,
"I'm not going either. The gadget may not end the war. We have
work to do here."

The tense atmosphere affected everyone. MPs patrolled the
Oppenheimer and Parsons homes constantly. One evening Martha
went to a treasure hunt. When she returned home about eleven
o'clock, the MP on duty barked, "Halt and be identified!"

The children were asleep and, as Martha said when she told
me about it, "'Who'd think it was necessary to take your pass to a
treasure hunt?"

Apparently the MP did because he followed her into the house
with his hand on his gun and kept it there until she finally found her
purse with the pass inside it.

Fuchs was away when his dormitory burned. Rudy Peierls, who
was a fire warden in London during the blitz, went into the burning
building to rescue Fuch's liquor and shoes. None of us thought it at
all queer that Rudy should risk his valuable life for such a purpose,

206

and we were all furious when we learned that the MPs, who took charge of the liquor, drank it!

The days were interminable. The Potsdam Ultimatum was issued. It was summarized, elaborated, translated, and broadcast to the Japanese people.

"The people themselves have seen with their own eyes the steadily mounting power and fury of our combined offensive," the broadcaster said. "You have seen our mighty battleships bombard your shores. You have seen the thousands of war planes day after day darken your skies.

"Japan must make a choice, upon the wisdom of which her whole future will depend. In the light of the alternatives presented in the joint proclamation, this choice should not be difficult.

"One alternative is prompt and utter destruction. If the Japanese people are forced by their self-willed militaristic leaders to choose the alternative of ruin, centuries of sweat and toil will be brought to naught in a cataclysmic end of a tragic war.

"The other alternative is the end of war. One simple decision will allow tranquility again to return to the city and the countryside. The guns will cease their fire, the bombs will no longer drop from the skies, your sons and brothers will no longer face agonizing and useless death on the battlefields. The homeland of Japan will be saved to continue a sovereign existence under a peacefully inclined and responsible government."

The Japanese leaders rejected the ultimatum and scoffed at the broadcast. The reference made in the broadcast to the "cataclysmic end of a tragic war" was not lost to us.

A further reminder of the bomb's effect came when some stray cattle found wandering some distance from the test area arrived at the veterinary hospital. There were large white spots on their reddish coats; the spots were the result of radiation burns, although no one admitted it. Both the men at the veterinary hospital and the doctors from the post hospital studied them. I wondered about Smokey; the Maltese spots in his coat were completely faded. He was very handsome in his white coat, but I wondered if the grass he nibbled so eagerly in lower Los Alamos Canyon was good for him.

Eric brought home some samples of *trinitite*—the fused sand from the bomb crater. The trinitite was embedded in lucite, but Eric said it was too "hot" to leave in the house and took it back to the Tech Area.

Everyone left their radios on during those last days. I was no exception. On Monday, August 6, 1945, Col. Paul Tibbets piloted the *Enola Gay* over the target city of Hiroshima. Deak Parsons was a member of the crew.

After I gave the horses their breakfast, I returned home just in time to hear the announcer say, in a voice choked with excitement, "Ladies and gentlemen, today the President of the United States announced that an atomic bomb was dropped—"

I listened numbly.

Bill came home during one of the broadcasts. He was in and out constantly, occupied with an eleven-year-old's business, but he paused and listened.

"What's an atomic bomb?"

"That's us, dear."

"You mean to say that bomb was made here?"

"Yes."

He gave me a scathing look. "You sure have some quaint ideas of campaign buttons." He departed with an air of injured dignity.

I didn't know whether to laugh or cry. A news flash said a Distinguished Service Cross was pinned on Colonel Tibbets when he stepped out of his plane after the Hiroshima mission. Radios and newspapers poured out thousands of words. The press at the *Santa Fe New Mexican* broke down in the midst of the excitement.

Self-anointed "Atomic Scientists" sprang into the news. Our General was catapulted from his position behind the mammoth eight ball and took his bow as the "Atom General." Ruth and I read that it cost $2 billion to develop the bomb.

"A lot of that money probably was spent in the Tech Area, but damn little of it went into this town," I commented bitterly.

"You can say that again, Chiquita."

The current was off at the moment.

The Japanese didn't surrender. Russia declared war on Japan.

"They want to sit at the table when the cake is sliced," Eric said.

The day Russia declared war on Japan, Robert Patterson, the under secretary of war, thanked the men and women of the Manhattan District in the name of a grateful nation. He asked us in very polite and elegant language to keep our mouths shut.

The Nagasaki bomb was dropped on Thursday. We heard the broadcast while we ate breakfast. Eric laid his hands on the table and bowed his head.

"Christ, dear Christ, why don't those fools surrender?!"

The world seemed poised on the brink of peace, but no one could guess what would happen next.

Our local news of the second bomb drop was slow coming through. Conflicting reports confused us. The weather over Japan was atrocious, and there was no word of the plane. If the plane was forced down, anything might happen to the men from Los Alamos who were out there to do the technical work on the bombs. There was no news of the plane or its crew for twenty-four hours.

On Friday, when Eric told me the plane was safe, he handed me the *Bulletin*. It carried a notice on the front page which gave us permission to say we lived at Los Alamos. The following paragraphs appeared on the back page.

ATTENTION ALL RESIDENTS

Conserve water—we are now in the most critical period in the history of our water supply system. The increase in population and the addition of new facilities has placed unprecedented demand on the supply. Recent rains have not helped at all, and sources are decreasing at an alarming rate. Every person on the mesa must become water conscious and conserve water in every way possible to avoid the necessity of drastic restrictions.

Sunday was a suffocating day, unusual in New Mexico. Every hour seemed a year. Fortunately, Bill was impervious to the charged atmosphere. Eric and I were as restless as a pair of caged lions. We were just finished with dinner when the false surrender was broadcast. I grabbed a couple of plates. "I always wanted to throw the dinner dishes away—tonight I will."

Eric and Bill jumped to their feet and began to gather up the rest of the plates. I went out on the porch and sent the first one sailing. Laura and Enrico Fermi were on their way to a movie. They heard the plate crash, turned around, waved, and went home. Ruth rushed out and flung her arms around me, "Oh, my darling, now your brother can come home!"

Eric and Jano stepped out on the porch. Each man gathered his wife in his arms.

"Dearie Darling, the broadcast was a horrible mistake," Eric murmured.

It was a hideous letdown; we were puzzled and apprehensive. The weather changed. A thunderstorm bore down. The Haleys joined us for a nightcap. The atmosphere was ominous.

Above the roll of thunder, we heard the unfamiliar sound of airplane engines in our forbidden sky. The four of us rushed to the front porch. Wisps of conversation drifted to our ears; we knew that our friends and neighbors watched with us. It was a big plane. Its lights winked ominously against the dark sky. We were certain it carried bombs addressed to us and cursed the avalanche of publicity that exposed us during the week. There was no place to hide. The plane circled time and time again before it disappeared in the clouds.

There was an official explanation in Monday's *Bulletin*. The plane was a B-29 from Kirtland Field in Albuquerque, and it was lost in the storm.

I didn't listen to the radio on Monday. Martha, Genia, and I gathered up our children and took them for a ride. In the evening, Eric and I went to the Fermi's for dinner. It was a delightful party. The Oppenheimers were in top form. Rabi was present, proudly waving the roll of bills he won by betting that the gadget would have the power of eighteen thousand tons of TNT. Laura Fermi teased Enrico gently when he said the gadget made no sound. "You were so absorbed, you probably didn't hear it," she said.

Harold Urey, an old friend of Eric's, was on the Hill for the first time. He was horrified and proclaimed that he wanted it known that he had nothing to do with the bomb. The rest of us were too drained to care.

Rabi went home with us after the party. He and Eric talked Columbia University business, and I turned on the radio to get the eleven o'clock news.

"We understand that the Japanese have requested surrender terms through the Swiss Government," the announcer said.

"I'll believe that when it's confirmed in Washington," I retorted.

"So will I," Rabi agreed.

He departed, and we went to bed. About two o'clock, bedlam broke loose; word of the surrender request had reached the barracks. GIs in trucks, jeeps, and on foot assembled in front of Theater Two, and a good part of the civilian population joined them. An impromptu parade started. Willy Higinbotham, playing his accordion, balanced precariously on the radiator of the leading jeep, and lids snatched from garbage cans clashed merrily.

The four of us who lived on the top floor of T-185 roused our children to see the fun. We hung over the porch rail, and the parade stopped to serenade us.

"Come on, Eric, get on the band wagon!" shouted the riders of the leading jeep.

The jeep was all but invisible under its load of humanity. Economy-sized Eric laughed and declined the invitation. The army administration opened Theater Two and assembled a band. One of the dormitories threw an unplanned and eminently successful party. Ruth and I pooled our resources to make sandwiches and hot chocolate for our combined families.

The next morning the surrender request was official, but the Tech Area was open for business as usual. Eric reported at noon that no one was particularly interested. In the afternoon Sergeant McCall paid a visit to the corral before I went for my ride.

"I thought you should know that the first trailer moved into our new area this morning."

"Ooh, Mac, not this morning—not V-J Day!"

The pair of us dissolved with laughter. The strain of furnishing acceptable parking space for incoming trailers was over, but so was the necessity for the parking space. A healthy percentage of our population of more than seven thousand lived in trailers, and we knew that a lot of them would leave immediately.

The armed forces lifted the censorship of the mail. In our ultra-exclusive community, incoming mail was no longer censored, but all outgoing mail was.

We received another letter from Preston.

"Dear Eleanor and Eric," it began. "When we got news of the atomic bomb, I realized why you were in New Mexico. I thank you, Eric, for the part you played. Every man who was scheduled to take part in Operation Olympic is happy to have the operation cancelled—"

He went on to tell the reaction of the Japanese prisoners. He spoke of their relief when they learned that the war was over, and their tears when they understood what happened at Hiroshima. "It must have been a beautiful city," he concluded. I was thankful that he was safe and the operation cancelled.

The British government bestowed the Order of the British Empire on Rudy Peierls for his contribution to the work. Our own government honored Oppie with the United States Medal for Merit. There were others who should have gotten it immediately. Some of them, like Joe Kennedy, got it eventually, and others were completely overlooked. The SEDs were rewarded with shoulder patches—small gold wreaths. The SEDs were understandably bitter about a lot of things; their ribald comments would not stand the light of print. The kindest thing I ever heard the patch called was "The Flying Toilet Seat."

The friends and husbands who went to the Pacific returned to their homes. Deak Parsons came home and then went to Washington to report. All his friends were sure he'd be an admiral when he came back.

When Martha joined me the afternoon after he got home, I said, "Do we have an admiral in our midst?"

Martha made a strangled sound. "We have a commodore!"

"A commodore? I thought that rank was abolished after the War of 1812!"

"So did I," she replied disgustedly. Later in the afternoon she told me they'd leave for Washington at Thanksgiving time.

The stream of departing trailers almost blocked the Hill road.

The craftsmen and machinists who were not needed now that the war had ended began looking for other jobs. The members of the scientific staff, most of whom were on leave from universities, made plans to return to their posts in time for the winter terms.

Oppie was anxious to return to his teaching position. Norris Bradbury was fast-talked into taking the job of acting director of the laboratory.

Eric asked if I'd mind spending another winter in New Mexico.

We've got to keep this place staffed and running until Congress decides what to do with it. They've asked me to stay as the head of CM Division. I think Columbia will be willing to extend my leave until next September. Demobilization won't be very far along when the February term begins. "

I couldn't very well say, "I wanna go home, Pa!" I loved New Mexico with its brilliant colors, towering mountains, and old world charm. Life on the Hill was primitive, but what the heck? I think Aunt Melinda put her mark on me. Eric and I kicked the subject around, and I had the idea that he wasn't going to be very happy if he went back to the university. I made one stipulation. If we stayed, we must have a house.

Some days later, Eric reported that the extension of his leave was arranged and that we would have the Oppenheimer house after they moved out and it was re-painted.

"Rudy is going to the University of Birmingham," Genia said. "We will leave at the end of November. We want to go to Mexico before we leave. We may never have another chance."

She, Martha, and I took our children up Caballo before school opened. We had a beautiful day for the trip, and Genia rhapsodized as we rode up the trail. Warm sunshine trickled through the branches of the trees. She raised her face to it and closed her eyes.

"All my life I will remember this sunshine," she whispered.

Oh, Genia," My heart constricted when I thought of her in Birmingham, England. Then, drought-minded as I was, I asked, "But what will you drink?"

"Water, darling, clear, cold water."

It was so long since I'd seen clear, cold water flow from a tap, I'd forgotten it could happen. The water from the taps on the Hill reeked of chlorine and the acrid scent of leaf mold. It was filled with sediment.

The administration issued a special *Bulletin*. It carried the usual banner line and was headed:

24 September 1945

SUBJECT: Conservation of Water
TO: All Los Alamos Personnel

WATER MUST BE CONSERVED!

The context of the two-page *Bulletin* stated facts:

We used 110,000 gallons of water a day more than our supply furnished. The difference between supply and demand came from the storage reservoir in Los Alamos Canyon, which was less than half full, and there was no relief in sight. It suggested eight ways to save our most precious commodity and hoped everyone would cooperate. One of them urged, "*Don't* take long showers. *Don't* take showers every day. Every minute saves seven gallons."

The *Bulletin* was signed by Col. Gerry Tyler and Norris Bradbury. Of course, Our General, who boasted that the army engineers knew how to keep water supplied, was in Washington.

ᴐᴐ *14* ᴐᴐ

t took more than a special bulletin on the water situation to dampen my spirits that day. My council term expired after the evening meeting. I was no longer responsible for events in the town. I left my worries with the luckless successor for whom I'd campaigned earlier in the month and devoted myself to my friends.

The British Mission gave an official party for their hosts in the Los Alamos Scientific Laboratory. The British government eked out some money for the affair—not much—but enough to buy the basic ingredients of a good party, and the Mission members worked like Trojans.

We received engraved invitations, and the dining room in Fuller Lodge was decorated with the flags of our two nations. When all the guests gathered, we sang "The Star Spangled Banner" and "God Save the King." We laughed and danced our way through the evening, and there was a clever skit. We sang "Auld Lang Syne," and many eyes were damp when we said goodnight.

On another occasion, Trevor Cuykendall wanted some pictures of the aspens in their autumn foliage, so we rode up the Quemazon Trail where some of the aspens on the ridge were fifteen inches in diameter. We ate our sandwiches, and Trevor climbed trees to get many of his shots. Storm clouds rolled out of the west and obscured the sun. Trevor waited in a tree top, his legs wound around the trunk and his camera focused, until the last ray of sunshine broke through the clouds, before he snapped his last picture and climbed down.

Our slickers impeded our movements while we mounted and Trevor stored the precious camera away. The horses needed no urging to keep ahead of the storm; they strode down the trail in record time. They never once broke their gait, but they managed to stay ahead of the rain of golden leaves and icy hailstones that chased them.

A couple of inches of snow marked the metamorphosis of September into October, but it melted immediately and the color of the aspen leaves deepened. The Tech Area buzzed with activity while the men who headed the war work accounted for top secret documents and fissionable materials and handed the reins of the various divisions over to their successors.

Colonel Tyler left to return to civilian life. Eric told me that when Colonel Gerry said goodbye to the Tech Board, he still did not know if he would be held accountable for some of the construction. What I said about that grand guy being left hanging on the hook until the last minute need not be repeated here.

A real, regular army bird colonel, L. I. (Skip) Seeman, replaced Gerry, and another real, regular army bird colonel, A. W. (Cy) Betts, came in as second-in-command. They were both aghast at conditions in the town. We were glad to have them with us in our parched wilderness.

The laboratory received the Army-Navy E Award, and the scene imprinted itself on my mind forever.

It was a bright October day with a matchless blue sky. The mighty Sangre de Cristos towered on the east, and the Jemez Mountains rose from the Pajarito Plateau on the west. The mountainsides were dressed in autumn patchwork of evergreen and shining aspen yellow. The faces of the people on the speakers' stand in front of Fuller Lodge were solemn. Our General was there with the visiting dignitaries. Oppie was there to accept the award on behalf of the laboratory and to turn its directorship over to Norris Bradbury, who looked unfamiliar in a gray business suit. The children rushed about collecting autographs. There was the unprecedented spectacle of a radio crew setting up microphones and equipment to broadcast the speech to the Outer World. Bright colors intermingled with drab. The bright shawls around the shoulders of the Indian women and gay plaid shirts worn by the scientists and their wives contrasted sharply with the army's khaki and the navy's blue. The scene was utterly typical of our contrasts and contradictions.

The aspen leaves fell, and the night air had a sharp edge. In the Outer World, men were demobilized, armies of occupation governed

J. Robert Oppenheimer; Leslie R. Groves; R. G. Sprouls, president of University of California; and William (Deak) Parsons

conquered countries, and the United Nations established itself in temporary quarters. Preston went home to his family. He visited Tokyo before he returned and wrote that he didn't see how anybody survived even the ordinary saturation bombings. He also reported that he flew home and held the plane up all the way across the Pacific.

"It didn't seem as though my luck could last," he wrote.

The Smyth Report appeared in print. Santa Fe stores sold out immediately. Everyone wanted to know what he said about Los Alamos. A mighty "Ugh" arose from the throats of the scientific staff when they were dismissed in one chapter. The staff of CMR Division, as Eric renamed CM Division when he took it over, smarted when Smyth dismissed their essential work with one paragraph. I refer you to Cyril Smith's article in *Metal Progress*, May 1954.

Congress pondered our fate; the May-Johnson Bill was under debate. We liked our local army people. They and their families were in the same kettle of soup we were, and the thought of having our fate controlled from Washington by men in brown suits was too much for everybody. If the May-Johnson Bill passed, Los Alamos could be turned into a rest home for retired Congressmen.

The great debate went on, and electricity was rationed. Our dilapidated diesels were shut down in rotation to cool. Our General testified before a Congressional committee. He said the situation at Los Alamos was desperate. It was an understatement. The ground was bare of snow, and Martha said, "Before we leave, I want to take one last ride to Rio de los Indios and another to the Buckman Crossing at the Rio Grande."

We decided to ride over the Jemez ridge and through the Valle San Antonio to Rio de los Indios alone and take the children to Buckman.

"I think we'd better take some whiskey with us this time," Martha said when we planned our trip to the Jemez. I thought so, too. It was plenty cold. The ridge was at an elevation of 10,500 feet. The elevation in Valle San Antonio, through which we rode to reach Rio de los Indios, was 10,000 feet. We planned the trips for the Friday and Saturday before Martha left, and she volunteered some of Deak's extra special aged bourbon for the jaunt.

We left the Hill on a crisp November morning. We were warmly dressed and laden with extra clothing which we donned as we ascended the Quemazon Trail. The horses wore heavy winter coats and climbed swiftly. They chafed at their bits when we paused to add more layers of insulation for our persons. We topped the ridge and rode to the head of the trail into the Valle San Antonio before we paused. Frost crystals glittered in the sun when the horses exhaled. Martha and I tied scarves over our nostrils and under our chins.

"I think we'd better have a sip of Deak's whiskey right now. Where's the bottle?" I asked. My teeth chattered; so did Martha's.

"A good idea. I didn't bring the bottle. I put the whiskey in a canteen."

She opened her saddle bags, and the effluvium of aged whiskey assailed our nostrils.

Eleanor and Smokey

"Oh, no!" we lamented in unison.

But the answer was, "Oh, yes." Only a teaspoon full of whiskey remained in the canteen; the rest leaked out into the saddle bag and soaked the extra sweater Martha brought with her. We took a cup off a thermos and wrung a few drops from the sweater into it.

"You drink what's in the canteen, and I'll drink this," Martha said, shuddering. "I borrowed these saddle bags from the army stables. What do you suppose they'll say when I take them back?"

Neither of us really cared. The horses made their way eagerly down the trail, and we let them race across the valley until they tired of it. All four of us had a wonderful time.

The excursion to the Buckman Crossing the next day was a contrast to the chilly trip in the high country. We rode down Los Alamos Canyon and shed our jackets before we reached the foot of the canyon. At Buckman we rolled up our shirt sleeves, picnicked, and lazed in the sun.

Rudy and Genia returned from Mexico and gave a party at the Big House before they left for home. It was a wonderful party, but my heart was heavy. Too many of my friends were either gone or preparing to go, and I didn't know who I'd miss the most, Martha or Genia. When we left the Peierl's party, Genia put her arms around me and whispered, "Come to England and kick my fire, Eleanor."

Cyril and others huffed and puffed at the logs in the fireplaces, but I just kicked them and never failed to stir up a blaze.

We planned to move into the house on Bathtub Row on the 15th of December, and in anticipation I sent out invitations for a big cocktail party to honor departing friends. Censorship of the outgoing mail was lifted on December 3rd, and it was a big day in my life when I put a stamp on a letter and dropped it in the mail box myself. The act was strange and unfamiliar after almost two years. I never understood why censorship was in force so long. I wondered at the time if someone was afraid we might write to our ex-Congressmen. There were a lot of flubs hidden behind security's sacred skirts.

When censorship was lifted, we were permitted, provided we followed certain specific instructions, to mingle with people from the Outer World and to invite them to our homes. A written invitation to visit anyone who lived on the Hill looked like an invitation into a maximum security jail.

People in Santa Fe were generous with their invitations, and we accepted them eagerly. Dee and Jeanette Lord gave a dinner party for a group of us. I put on my best, pre-Los Alamos, navy silk dress. Eric and I were as excited as a pair of children going to their first party. Despite the efforts of the Santa Feans, I felt gauche and set apart as though I had dropped in from another planet. We joked about problems incomprehensible to our new friends. We lived in the place where the atomic bombs were built.

"Weren't we afraid of the bombs?" they asked.

"No, we weren't afraid of the bombs. We were afraid the town would catch fire and burn us all to cinders. Water was in short supply," we explained.

Aunt Melinda, my childhood adventures at my uncle's ranch in northwest New Mexico, and my youthful life in Colorado were all useful that evening. Eric squirmed uncomfortably every time he was addressed as Doctor Jette. Our isolated, informal, security-permeated

Square dancers from the Hill enjoying the party at San Ildefonso Pueblo

lives left us ill-equipped for social intercourse with those who did not share any phase of our experiences.

San Ildefonso Pueblo invited the square dancers for an evening of fun. It was arranged by Jano and Popovi Da, son of Maria Martinez and husband of Anita Martinez who worked in the housing office when we arrived. Men and women from the pueblo commuted daily to work on the Hill and were aware of our problems. As I said earlier, we visited them to buy pottery and woven belts and attended their dances. We were always welcomed into their homes and enjoyed their feasts. On the great night, the square dancers took cookies, Coca-Colas, and sandwiches with them. San Ildefonso supplied coffee, tamales, and luscious little dried fruit pies as well as other delicacies. The Hill women bedecked themselves in colorful square dance clothes and every piece of silver or turquoise they owned or could borrow.

The long hall at the pueblo was beautifully decorated with boughs; lovely old rugs with soft, mellow colors hid the windows.

~~ *San Ildefonso dancers*

A food-laden table stretched across the end of the room opposite the entrance door. There were chairs on the other three sides of the room. Older women in spotless leggings with bright shawls, their hair done in chongos, occupied some of the chairs. Younger folk, unfamiliar to us, occupied other chairs. Babies sat bright-eyed and quiet on their mothers' knees. Older children flitted silently about the room, grinning in happy anticipation.

We seated ourselves among our hosts and chatted while we waited for proceedings to begin. Po mounted a small dais on the long side of the room. He gave a short speech in Tewa, the language of the local pueblos. I understood only the last word of Po's speech— "jitterbug." During the first part of the program our group did exhibition square dances. When they finished, the people from the pueblo took the floor. They danced "fun dances," very different from the ritualized religious dances we saw when we visited the pueblo on its feast day.

There was a gay and lively belt dance, and then Po and his cousin, Richard Martinez, took the stage. Their feet seemed to touch

~~~ *San Ildefonso drummers*

the floor scarcely at all while they floated through the intricate dance steps. The drummers, laughing, beat their drums with ever-increasing tempo and kept them at their dance until they were limp and exhausted.

When Po and Richard finished dancing, there was a pause for us to eat and visit. The Indian men showed us the mirrored feathers they wore with their dance costumes. The feathers were mounted spoke-like around a shiny center and could be folded like the feathers in a fan for storage in tissue paper and moth balls when they were not in use.

The drummers summoned us back to the dance floor.

"Listen, it's a waltz," my partner said.

It was a waltz—perfect three-four time. Our hosts intermingled with their guests, and we all danced. I lost my partner when the drumbeat changed tempo and found myself in a conga line with a young Indian wearing a brand new discharge button.

"I never thought I'd live to see anything like this," he muttered.

"What do we do now?" I asked.

Eric, Norris Bradbury, Eleanor, and Lois Bradbury pause to eat and visit.

Pueblo dances last all night, but the guests from the Hill went home at three o'clock. Their feet gave out!

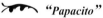 *"Papacito"*   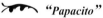 *Jane Wortman, Popovi Da*

 Anita Martinez Da, Jano Haley

"It's easy. Just follow me," he instructed.

The line stomped and swayed and writhed into knots in and out of corners, before we tumbled out of it, breathless. Then everyone square danced. Our Indian friends, with their sense of rhythm, had no trouble with the steps. The older women enjoyed themselves particularly. The sight of "Papacito," his yarn-bound braids flying, swinging a crinoline-clad partner through the steps of the Texas Star or the Virginia Reel, tickled them immensely. The women from Los Alamos enjoyed the sight of their husbands instructing laughing, dark-eyed partners on the intricacies of the steps. I warmed to the sight of Eric, all six feet five inches of him, swinging his tiny partner.

Our friends from the pueblo were a little hurt because our feet gave out. They always danced until sunrise. We went home about three o'clock.

The weather turned bitter cold the week before we moved. The temperature tumbled to zero. No one really minded. The bright, warm sunshine gave the illusion it was warmer. I carted dishes and breakables that I didn't dare trust to the mercies of the moving crew and set them in place. Just then the temperature got tired of sitting on zero and fell through it. It landed at minus twenty; that's cold anywhere!

Eric had very little time to help. He was now responsible not only for the technical work in the newly named CMR Division but also the administrative work. I shuttled between the apartment and the house daily. Ruth announced her intention to help on moving day.

"I certainly hate to see you move, Chiquita, but I'll see that your things are properly handled at this end."

I hated to leave Ruth, but little Jimmy's lung capacity had improved with age. I hugged her.

"You are a real live doll, and I love you." I don't know how I'd have managed without her. I was tired when moving day was over and the dinner dishes stacked. Our bathtub was an antique with tiger feet, but it looked good to me. I hadn't had a soak since my visit to Denver the previous January.

"I'm going to fill the tub and relax," I told Eric.

"I'm looking forward to a good soak, too, but you take your time," he said.

I turned on the taps and adjusted the temperature before undressing. I kicked off my shoes and was about to shimmy out of my blue jeans when there was a knock on the front door. I heard the rumble of masculine voices and swore under my breath. It was almost ten o'clock, a fine hour for someone to come calling. I padded out in my bare feet to see who was there.

Eric and Joe Burke, who was in charge at DP, stood in the middle of the living room and just looked at each other. Eric's face was grim, and Joe's was marked with deep lines of fatigue.

"What on earth is the matter?" I asked.

"We shut down at DP," Joe said.

"But why?"

"No water."

"NO WATER? But I've got the water running in the bathtub right now!"

"You're lucky you had the water running; you're draining your line into the tub."

"I'd better turn off the hot water right now or I'll drain the boiler and we'll blow up," I said grimly.

Eric fixed us some drinks while I attended to the hot water tap.

"The storage reservoir is empty and the line from Guaje is frozen solid—all seven miles of it," Joe announced.

"I just don't see how the line could freeze even with these temperatures when water was being pumped through it," Eric said.

"When we were notified that the line was frozen, someone said an eighteen-foot length of two-by-four was left inside when it was laid and that leaves and debris built up behind it and partially blocked the line. The trouble apparently started there," Joe said.

I could believe it. I could believe anything after two years inside Box 1663.

The next twenty-four hours was a nightmare. The laboratory closed down completely; it had no heat in the bitter weather. Furnaces were shut off; the apartments and houses on Bathtub Row were the only structures with fireplaces so it was fortunate that all the stuff built in the east end of town was heated with kerosene stoves. Bathtub Row homes were heated with closed steam systems, and I thought for a little while we'd have heat and could give some of our friends and their babies shelter. Alas, I heard activity in our furnace room about eight-thirty the next morning. I rushed out and found the fire scattered over the back yard.

"Don't do that, you fool!" I shrieked at the GI who did the scattering. "Don't you know this is a closed steam system?"

"Sure, I know it's a closed system, but THEY don't and orders is orders."

I hurried to the telephone and called Eric. "Our furnace fire was just thrown out—DO something!"

I was dubious about having a telephone in the house before we moved. After my busy life in the Outer World, I had enjoyed our phoneless existence in the apartment, but I found the phone very convenient at that moment. Eric promised to do what he could and said the Tech Board was going to meet with army administration.

I didn't even try to send Bill to school; I knew it would be closed. We dressed ourselves warmly and went to the corral. The water line to the corrals came off the small water line which led from Water Canyon and was buried deep underground. The water line from Water Canyon supplied the sites to the south, the corrals, and a couple of barracks that weren't very far from the corrals. We built a fire around the standpipe to thaw it, then picked up ice already chopped off the water troughs. We put the ice in one of the five-gallon cans we kept in the barn, and I hauled it to a friend with three small children while Bill kept the fire stoked. The ice smelled of horses, but it melted into enough water to flush the toilet.

We were able to carry two five-gallon cans of water at a time in the trunk compartment. We filled the cans as full as we could and distributed their contents among our friends. Of course, some of the precious fluid splashed out of the containers on every trip, and the spare tire froze into its cradle—it remained frozen for the rest of the winter—but that was the least of our worries on that memorable day.

When we went home for lunch, Eric was already there. Fires blazed in both fireplaces, and the other rooms were shut off.

"That was some meeting," he said. "We were all dressed in hats and overcoats, and our mufflers were wrapped around our ears."

"What are they going to do? We're one of the few families in town who don't have small children. These girls can't wash diapers or fix their formulas without water."

"I know. This is a real disaster, and it's going to cost us a lot of the younger personnel we hoped to keep, but the situation isn't completely hopeless. Skip Seeman and Cy Betts saw this coming as soon as they got here, and Cy has been traveling around the Southwest all fall assembling a fleet of tank trucks. The fleet is converging on Los Alamos right now. They expect the first trucks to arrive before evening. Bulldozers scooped out pits down near the Rio Grande, and water is seeping into them already."

"Oh, goody, I've been told the water from the muddy Rio Grande possesses miraculous powers. I can't wait to drink some of it."

"I think the pits are far enough away from the river so the mud, twigs, fish and other solids will be filtered out of it," Eric said cheerfully.

The first tank truck took its station by the hospital before five o'clock that afternoon. It was filled in Española, but the Española village fathers were smart. They knew their water system couldn't carry five thousand extra people for even a short period of time and declined to get mixed up in our drought. The first truck was intended for the hospital, but frantic housewives besieged it. Sergeant McCall's boys dumped extra disinfectant into it and distributed it on a "come and get it" basis. Even in the open air the odor of disinfectant overwhelmed those around the truck. One of the girls splashed water from her bucket onto her stockings. I never understood why she wore stockings that day, and neither did she. The color vanished from the spots where the splashes fell. I was present to get a bucket of water for a friend who couldn't appear in person. I didn't need water; I had a bathtub full of it.

We ate dinner at the Haley's that evening. There was an electric stove at our house; the Black Beauties were superior because they burned wood. We ate by candlelight, and Ruth and I washed the dishes with water I hauled from the corral earlier in the day. We watched the fires of the crews who were out in the wilderness trying to thaw the water line. There wasn't much to laugh about that evening. We drank our whiskey straight and damned the lack of foresight and the parsimony of the Washington echelon.

The exodus began the next day. Every GI who was not

absolutely essential to the maintenance of the town or Tech Area got an unexpected and indefinite furlough. The younger members of our population took their progeny in their arms and left. If the men couldn't get away, they sent their wives and babies home to momma. Other people, who were either childless or had children of school age, took vacations. Some of them went up to Colorado to ski. There was snow in "them thar hills."

The rest of us "made do."

Men who had business at the test sites to the south hauled water from the sites. A number of people hauled their drinking water from Santa Fe in five-gallon containers. We hauled water from the corral and used the bathtub for a reservoir. There was a strong sense of fellowship among those of us who remained, and tattle-tale gray was the high-style color.

We even found things to laugh about. One chap was in the shower and had just worked up a really impressive lather when the water stopped running. He picked soap off himself for days and swore he'd never take another bath. September's suggestion—DON'T take a bath every day—became BATHE ONLY WHEN NECESSARY. "With what?" we asked politely.

"What on earth are you going to do about your party?" a friend asked.

"I've got all my supplies. I'm not going to cancel it."

"But eighty people and no water?"

"I don't expect them to drink water."

Operation Tank Truck was in full swing inside of three or four days. The water was pumped from the trucks into the water tower. A little water was allowed to trickle through the town mains within the week. It had the exotic flavors of gasoline, kerosene, and milk which even the potent disinfectant used by the people responsible for our health failed to mask. It was impossible to stay in the room if you boiled an egg. It couldn't be used internally without some kind of a "stick." Bill and the other children were in seventh heaven when their parents plied them with soft drinks; most adults reeked of rum.

The administration's first task was to restore the utilities. The bitter weather held the town in a firm grip, and we had to have heat.

The minute the furnaces were refueled, the danger of fire increased a thousand fold. We had only the water in Ashley Pond to fight fire. The fire siren called out the commanding officer and laboratory director as well as the fire department. The harried administration issued communiques to reassure the population. The first ones predicted that the water line would be repaired and the crisis would be over in a few days; they predicted that no health problems would arise from the water stoppage. They also advised us to have our typhoid immunizations brought up to date. Of course the water line was not repaired in a few days. Every drop of water used in town and the Tech Area was hauled up in tank trucks until the first of April; half the water supply was hauled until June. As for health problems, no bug could live in the stuff that came out of the taps, and we all had typhoid shots running out of our ears. A few lines in a communique issued early in April caught my eye, but I didn't think they were applicable to the first days of the disaster. The lines said, "While our water supply is not satisfactory for permanent reliability, it is superior in general to that obtained under 'field' conditions: i.e., for troops in rural areas and away from fixed installations—"

It was a gay holiday season. Our party was a smashing success, and there were lots of others. We got away for four days and spent Christmas in Denver, where we washed our dirty selves and our dirty clothes. The senior auntie was much upset by one of Walter Winchell's gems. She read everything he wrote and believed it implicitly.

Mr. Winchell wrote a column about Los Alamos. I wondered where he got his information. The account was so malicious it might easily have been planted to harm the laboratory. He depicted the dorm parties as drunken orgies and hinted that the atom bomb was concocted by scientists lying on couches strewn with rose petals while they plied themselves with fermented grape juice.

"You didn't go to any of those dorm parties, did you?" the senior auntie asked.

"Oh, sweetie, don't be silly!" I didn't like to lie, but there was no use arguing with her. The oracle had spoken.

She sighed with relief. Privately, I said to Eric, "I'd like to take that guy home with us. Maybe some firsthand information would strip the scales off his eyes."

When we arrived home, things were under much better control. Eric said there was some heat in the Tech Area, and the power supply, although it was rationed more stringently than before the disaster, was almost dependable. We were home in plenty of time for the New Year's Eve party, and there was rejoicing throughout the town when the radios announced there was enough water stored so all the townspeople could bathe that evening.

We three Jettes conferred. We weren't very dirty after our trip to Denver, but we thought we'd better bathe again when we had the chance to do so. Our problem was that we didn't dare fill the bathtub three times. We agreed to fill it good and full once and take turns. I climbed in first, Eric followed me, and Bill, voted grimiest member of the family, was last.

An air of optimism prevailed at the party. Everyone was clean, and they were exhilarated by the sensation. The skit was especially funny. It poked fun at the water crisis. It was typical of the spirit that pervaded everything we did.

Then, as the last minutes of 1945 ticked away, I found myself standing alone. I watched the merriment. The bell ringers waited at their post with their eyes on their watches. I thought of the momentous events of the passing year and remembered Oppie's speech when he accepted the War Department scroll on the day of the Army-Navy E Award.

Robert Oppenheimer, with his crew cut and electric blue eyes, was the man who guided the work and wove the threads together. His voice was pregnant with responsibility. That day he was us. He spoke to us, and for us, when he warned that the peoples of this world must unite or they would perish. I realized that the mighty force liberated by the laboratory must be used for mankind's benefit and not for its destruction, lest the name of Los Alamos live in infamy forever.

There, in the place born of war and dedicated to man's most deadly achievement, I closed my eyes and wished for a thousand years of peace.

The bell tolled midnight.

 THE END

Afterword

After the war years, Eric and Eleanor Jette with their son, Bill, remained in Los Alamos, where Eric was CMR Division leader. In 1948 they purchased and spent several years renovating an old adobe home in the Pojoaque Valley in the village of El Rancho, a small, ancient Hispanic community which borders on San Ildefonso Pueblo. At that time it was an isolated community which had just received electricity the preceding year. Only a few Anglo families lived there. Eleanor had started work on the manuscript for *Inside Box 1663* and had completed the first draft by 1949.

In the mid-fifties Eric was offered the position of director of the research institute for Union Carbide Corporation, and the Jettes temporarily left New Mexico for New York, taking residence in Manhattan and later, Tuxedo Park. They returned to New Mexico in the early sixties to enjoy life in the valley.

Eleanor had completed the final draft of *Inside Box 1663* in Tuxedo Park and had also written a science-fiction novel and a number of short stories. These were never published, for Eleanor died in 1964, less than a year after the death of her husband. She is survived by their son, Bill, who returned to New Mexico and is currently an associate with an Albuquerque architectural firm. She is also survived by three grandsons: Eric Rice Jette, Kristian Randolph Jette, and Ramar Norman Jette.

With Eleanor's death, the manuscript lay dormant but not forgotten by her family and friends until the Los Alamos Historical Society suggested publication.

Inside Box 1663 is, in essence, a tribute to the pioneering spirit which permeated a small group of extraordinary people. Uprooted from their former lives, placed together in an isolated situation for one common purpose, they lived and became a unique part of our history.

Margaret Rice Jette
January 1977

Appendix

Part I

THIS IS A RESTRICTED DOCUMENT

Within the meaning of the Espionage Act, the contents of this document are not to be discussed with anyone unless he is known to you to be a member of this project. You may discuss them with your wife if she accepts these limitations in all strictness. We want to keep our work, organization, and future plans from becoming known outside the project for as long as possible in order to reduce the probability of effective espionage.

MEMORANDUM ON THE LOS ALAMOS PROJECT

Introduction

We know you will want to have as clear a picture as possible, before coming to Los Alamos, of the many aspects of life here. We will try in this memorandum to be as concise as possible and yet also give you an accurate picture of the location, housing, community life, and all the other factors that will influence what you bring with you and how it will be when you get here.

Location

Los Alamos, before being taken over for this project, was a small boys' school located in the mountains 35 miles from Santa Fe, New Mexico. It is set in the pines at 7300 feet in very fine country. An hour's drive takes you into Santa Fe for shopping purposes or an occasional dinner in town; a few minutes' walk or ride by horse takes you onto mountain trails in pine, aspen, and spruce country. Winters produce snow and winter sports, but the weather is not too severe for comfort. Spring brings wind, and summer, rain. It can be hot in the daytime, but nights are always comfortable because of the altitude. The country is a mixture of mountain country such as you have met in other parts of the Rockies, and the adobe-housed, picturesque, southwest desert that you have seen in Western movies.

Housing

The army has built the housing, not expecting to produce anything luxurious; but the results are more than adequate and quite comfortable. There are three sizes of houses: couples without children live in three-room apartments (bedroom, living room, kitchen, and bath) which are built eight to a house. Four- and five-room apartments (two and three bedrooms) are built in four-unit, two-story buildings. All apartments are unfurnished; the quartermaster, however, does supply upon request very simple couches, chairs, chests, and single beds.

Since the apartments are fairly small, it is more important that you do not over-furnish than that you bring too little. Heating is done by forced air furnaces, and there is ample hot water constantly. In the kitchen, there is a double sink, half of which is a washtub. (There also is a public laundry equipped with machines and mangles.) There is a fine, new electric refrigerator of good size and a wood-coal stove with an oil burner. One electric hot plate will be furnished. The rooms have hardwood floors that have been oiled and waxed, adequate windows, and closets; in many apartments there is a fireplace in the living room. For single men and women, there are dormitories with individual bedrooms and bathrooms between every two rooms. Each dormitory has a large lounge. Rent for furnished, equipped single rooms including utilities is $13 a month. Room service is $2 extra a month. Rents for unfurnished apartments of all sizes are based on salaries and not on space occupied and are as follows:

Less than $2600	$17 a month
$2600–$3100	$23 a month
$3100–$3400	$29 a month
$3400–$3800	$34 a month
$3800–$4400	$42 a month
$4400–$5200	$50 a month
$5200–$6000	$59 a month
Over $6000	$67 a month

Utilities for the apartments cost $10 to $13 per month, according to the space occupied, and include servicing of furnace, wood, etc. Although it is not possible to have domestic help live with you in your apartment, we have been able to secure a number of San Ildefonso Indian women from a nearby pueblo who come up six days a week to do housework for those desiring it. Since we have expanded and are still growing much beyond our original expectations of personnel at Los Alamos, the housing has not kept up with our growth. There is necessarily, then, a period when people will find themselves in temporary quarters, either on the site or at a nearby lodge. Therefore, come prepared to live out of a suitcase for a period, for even if a house is ready for you, you may have a waiting period until your furniture arrives. If you are coming here before autumn, you should not bring your family unless your wife has a job in the laboratory, too. If you cannot arrange this, please let us know, and we shall try to make arrangements.

Community Life

1. Food

We have a commissary which is set up like any sizeable grocery store and butcher shop. You use your ration books in the usual manner, but if you come from an overcrowded community, you will be pleased with the quantity, variety, quality, and low price of the meats and food in general. We have a cafeteria-style mess hall for the people living in the dormitories and a dining hall for those who wish to take an occasional dinner out in restaurant style.

2. Stores

We have a Post Exchange which is slowly establishing itself as the drug store, soda fountain, beer parlor, dance hall, newspaper stand, etc. It will also have a lunch counter, a beauty parlor, a barber shop, a post office, etc., in a short time.

3. Recreation

We have a large theatre in which movies are shown three nights a week. The hall will also be used for any group activities or meetings. There is a library of general books available to all of us, and there will be hobby rooms. A Women's Club is just getting organized which will have interest groups ranging from Red Cross to bridge and calisthenics. Dances are arranged fairly frequently by the Dormitory Association.

4. Sports

In the winter there is a special pond frozen over for skating and a run for skiing. There are twenty horses available now for riding, and we expect more later. The country is fine for walking. There is a pond for swimming which, although this year may not prove too useful because of the lack of snow this past winter, ordinarily will be a good pond for the children, at least, to swim in.

5. Education

A Nursery School of very fine design has been built and is already functioning under trained personnel. At this time, it is open in the mornings for children from two to five, but the expectation is that it will be an all-day affair for children from three or four months up to school age.

The school system has not yet been established, but Dr. Walter Cook, associate professor of education at the University of Minnesota, is coming to make a survey and recommendations so that it will be set up correctly under adequate and competent personnel.

6. Community Council

A council of five has been elected from our personnel, by all of us here at this time, whose task it is to study the community and make recommendations for improvements. We have a full-time employee whose business it is to see that these recommendations are carried out whenever possible.

7. Hospitalization and Medical Care

We have two resident physicians and three registered nurses, experienced in work with children as well as adults. A well-equipped hospital is on the site, and it is hoped that a dentist will come up at regular intervals from Santa Fe.

8. Laundry

A truck comes up daily from Santa Fe from the largest cleaning and laundry company. We are receiving three- or four-day service.

In other words we are in the process of becoming a small town with all the community comforts and limitations that you might expect. However, we also have near us the larger town of Santa Fe with its stores and restaurants, and also of course, we have the mail order catalogues of Sears Roebuck and Montgomery Ward and the ads in the Sunday *New York Times.*

Security

In addition to the precautions which are customary in all secret war work, and which make it mandatory that no one discuss in public any of the affairs of the laboratory such as type of personnel, etc., there are some measures which are peculiar to our project. These all have to do with preventing the accidental dissemination of information about our work, our personnel, the size of our establishment, the progress of our work, the nature of our problem, and our organization. They are not measures designed primarily against espionage but designed to make espionage more difficult and to enable us more readily to detect it. These measures involve essentially breaking the social relationships between the personnel employed at Los Alamos and people not so employed. If you are employed on the project, you are not permitted to leave Los Alamos and its neighboring communities without special permission. This permission will in general be granted for travel essential to the project or in cases of personal emergency. You should not arrange for visits, either at Los Alamos or in a neighboring community, with friends or relatives. Within these limitations, entry and exit from the Post at Los Alamos is free at all times to employed personnel. You should not give our address, P.O. Box 1663, Santa Fe, to friends, until after your arrival at the site, and you should make arrangements so that scientific journals and the proceedings of scientific societies should not be mailed directly but through a forwarding office. If your own university department does not wish to do this, have the *Physical Review*, etc., etc. sent to you in care of P.O. Box 5370,

Metropolitan Station, Los Angeles 55, California. The reason for this precaution is to reduce the number of lists of personnel at Los Alamos that might fall into enemy hands.

Travel

Automobiles are useful at the site if they are in good condition and you do not mind their being weathered. Worn tires should be recapped, and good chains will be helpful in the winter. Let us know if you would like a letter to enable you to get a supplementary gas ration to bring your car here. If you come by car, you will receive 5 cents a mile plus $6 a day subsistence for the employed individual but not for members of his family. If you travel by rail, all members of the family will be paid the cost of transportation and Pullman (first class, lower berth), but subsistence will only be paid to the employed member of the family. Furniture and household effects may be shipped by rail-freight or motor-van, and the expense of shipping will be borne by the project. Address your goods to 109 East Palace Avenue, Santa Fe, if they are coming by van; if by freight, to P.O. Box 1663, Santa Fe. Please inform us of the date on which you ship. Please save all receipts for packing, shipping, Pullman, train tickets, etc., so that a travel expense bill can be made out and honored upon your arrival here.

Work in the Technical Area

You will receive or have received a questionnaire about your wife's desires and qualifications for working here. May we just note that we still can use many people in a variety of fields and are anxious to use as many of the people that are already here as possible.

Salary Scale

Persons on leave from universities will be paid on the basis of 12/10 of their university salary. Persons now under OSRD contract will be paid the same amount without subsistence allowance. Persons not now holding an academic position but who were in academic work will be paid according to the following schedule:

BS $200
MS or BS plus 1 year education or experience...........$220
MS plus 1 year or BS plus 2 years.............................$240
MS plus 2 years or BS plus 3 years $260
PhD or MS plus 3 years or BS plus 4 years $280
PhD plus 1 year..$305
PhD plus 2 years $330
PhD plus 3 years $355
PhD plus 4 years $380
PhD plus maximum (maximum of this scale) $400

Wherever there may be a conflict between the two scales, the higher amount will be paid. Under a recent ruling of the War Manpower Commission, it is necessary to classify employees according to their duties and to freeze the wage range of each class of employees. The range for our technicians is $185.50 to $300.00 per month.

Useful Odds and Ends of Information

1. Bicycles are nice to have here.
2. It is possible that you may be able to own and stable your own horse.
3. Tennis courts exist.
4. People dress informally—jeans, slacks, khaki pants and shirts, cottons. Bring some good, warm woolens for the winter, too.
5. Electricity is AC, 60 cycle.
6. A pressure cooker is a help at 7000 feet.
7. It is a good idea to pack your van so that cleaning materials can be reached easily.
8. List of things you will find useful here.
    a. Doormats.
    b. Brooms and mops for sweeping outside stairs and porches.
    c. Electrical equipment such as electric coffee or tea pot, waffle iron, sandwich toaster. (One hot plate will be furnished.)
    d. Curtain rods, hooks, thumbtacks.
    e. Closet curtains, all kinds of drapery materials.
    f. Shower curtains.
    g. Tool chest.

h. Shelf paper, all household paper goods.
i. Towel bars, kitchen and bathroom.
j. Clothes pins, clothes line.
k. Ironing boards.
1. Fireplace brush, etc. (Screen and poker furnished.)
9. Pack one box with things you'll want before your van is emptied—cleanser, rags, shelf paper, hammer, thumbtacks, toilet paper, paper towels, soap, scissors. Keep your bedding for first night handy.

Appendix

Part II

RESTRICTED

THIS IS NOT TO BE TAKEN FROM THE SITE

CENSORSHIP REGULATIONS

1. It is deemed necessary in the interests of security to institute censorship over all personal communications to or from any personnel at Site Y. Censorship will accordingly be instituted, effective immediately, over all such communications under provisions of paragraph 3d of War Department Training Circular No. 15 dated 16 February 1943, which provides as follows:

    > When the military authorities deem it necessary in the interest of security, military censorship may be effected over all communications entering, leaving, and within any area, or to or from any personnel, under military jurisdiction within the continental limits of the United States.

2. Censorship will be conducted at a point outside the limits of Site Y and will be done by persons who are not known to you and whom you do not know. All censorship will be conducted by trained censorship officers in strict accordance with army regulations concerning censorship which provide in part as follows:

    > Censorship officers will respect and observe the confidential nature of information which comes into their possession. They will never discuss nor divulge any such matters either in public or private, except when the interest of the public service requires a report to higher authority. Persons revealing information obtained from letters during the course of censorship, other than in the course of official business, will be subject to disciplinary action.

3. Originators of official mail are responsible for seeing that such mail is not used to evade censorship.

4. Personal mail, including all types of letter mail, packages, and parcels will be deposited only in receptacles provided for such purpose on the Post. The use of U.S. Post Office facilities in adjacent towns is specifically denied.

    a. Letters will be mailed in unsealed envelopes. Packages and parcels should be wrapped and tied but not sealed.

    b. Personnel employed in the Technical Area and their families will deposit mail only within the Technical Area or in a separate box which will be reserved for Technical Area personnel in the Trading Post. All other personnel will use Army Postal Service receptacles on the Post but outside of the Technical Area.

    c. All unregistered communications may carry the following return address. In no instance will the name of the sender appear on the outside cover.
Return address: P.O. Box 1663, Santa Fe, New Mexico.

    d. Persons corresponding with project personnel should be instructed to use only the following address: Mr. John Jones. P.O. Box 1663, Santa Fe, New Mexico

    e. Correspondence may be conducted in English, French, German, Italian, and Spanish. Permission to use any other language must first be secured from the Post commander. Codes, ciphers, or any form of secret writing will not be used. Crosses, X's, or other markings of a similar nature are equally objectionable.

    f. Mail received by the censors sealed will be returned to the sender. No outgoing mail will be censored by excision or obliteration, but objectionable letters or letters which contain objectionable passages will be returned to the sender with a notation calling attention to the objectionable features. No censorship stamps or notations will be affixed to outgoing mail. Incoming mail will be opened and resealed after censorship with official censorship stamps and seals.

    g. Every effort will be made to avoid undue delay of the mail.

In no event will any communication be held by the censor longer than 48 hours.

h. If the communication does not contain the full name of the sender, his or her full name will be written on a slip of paper and enclosed in the unsealed envelope. This will be removed before dispatch. Any mail which is particularly urgent will have a slip of paper securely fixed to the outside with the single word "Urgent" on it. This mail will receive first attention by the censors. It is contemplated, however, that except in very unusual circumstances mail received before noon will be censored and dispatched the day it is received.

5. Unofficial telegrams must conform to the letter and spirit of the regulations in paragraph 8. Copies of outgoing telegrams must be filed in the Intelligence Office, Post Headquarters.

6. Use of telephone facilities on the project will be permitted. All restrictions and regulations herein apply equally to the content of telephonic conversations. Use of telephones outside the Post to avoid censorship is prohibited.

7. There are set out below those items which your mail specifically may not contain. They should be read and applied in the light of what censorship is designed to accomplish:

a. To preserve to the greatest extent possible the secrecy of the entire project and its connection with any other installation in the United States;

b. Its size, physical characteristics, the identity and numbers of the scientific personnel working at the project, the extent to which security measures have been taken. These are items of information tending to give the enemy leads for further investigation leading to more important disclosures. Many are items which, standing alone, are of little moment, but which, when continually conveyed to people in other parts of the country, tend to the creation of consistent rumors and reports which inevitably come to the ears of the enemy and focus their attention on this place.

c. To detect and intercept any incoming communications showing undue and unwarranted curiosity about the work going on.

8. Censorship is not interested in and will not report matters bearing upon the internal administration of the Post, violations of law or custom, or any other matters not bearing upon the purposes of censorship set out above. The following should not be discussed in your letters:
   a. Your present location, except that it is in New Mexico as disclosed by your address.
   b. Identifiable names of administrative and scientific personnel. Common first names are permissible, pertaining to family or social affairs.
   c. The professions of personnel employed at the project.
   d. The nature or any details of your work.
   e. The number of people at the project, either military or civilian.
   f. Any information regarding the size or area of the project.
   g. Any information concerning technical and/or maintenance equipment at the project.
   h. The amount and detailed description of housing constructed at the project.
   i. Any estimate of the duration of your job other than the duration of the war.
   j. Any opinions or rumors concerning the project.
   k. Any material which may be in use at the project.
   l. Any information concerning these censorship regulations or any discourse on the subject of censorship.

9. Any and all persons resident on this Post have the privilege of notifying their out-side correspondents of the single fact that censorship is in operation. The method of such notification, however, is confined solely to the procedure described below:

   Persons who consider it necessary to notify a correspondent will secure a printed card, which will be furnished upon personal appearance at the Intelligence Office, Post Headquarters. This card will contain a brief statement concerning censorship and will be enclosed in the outbound letter. Each person must request this card personally, except that one member of a family may appear for any other member of the family.

10 Great care must be exercised in taking photographs, especially as regards subject matter which may appear in the background, such as signs, distinguishing build-ings, or equipment. No photographs will be made of the following subjects:
   a. Any building or installation on the Post, except unidentifiable portions thereof.
   b. Any equipment, material, or signs.
   c. Photographs of personnel other than of the sender's immediate family.
   If film is to be mailed, it will be turned over to the Post commander for developing and censorship prior to mailing.

11. Persons desiring to send registered personal mail may bring it to the Security Office, Post Headquarters, where an officer will receipt for the letter and contents and cause it to be registered in Santa Fe by the examining officer.

12. The rules set out above are intended as minimal requirements. Most of you have better knowledge of what is censorable than anyone else, and the ultimate success of censorship must depend upon your wholehearted cooperation and the exercise by you of judgment and discretion.

INDEX OF NAMES